James Phinney Baxter

The Pioneers of New France in New England

James Phinney Baxter

The Pioneers of New France in New England

ISBN/EAN: 9783744718394

Printed in Europe, USA, Canada, Australia, Japan

Cover: Foto ©ninafisch / pixelio.de

More available books at **www.hansebooks.com**

THE PIONEERS

OF

New France

IN

NEW ENGLAND,

WITH CONTEMPORARY LETTERS AND DOCUMENTS.

BY

JAMES PHINNEY BAXTER, A. M.,

AUTHOR OF GEORGE CLEEVE OF CASCO BAY AND HIS TIMES; THE
BRITISH INVASION FROM THE NORTH; SIR FERDINANDO GORGES
AND HIS PROVINCE OF MAINE; CHRISTOPHER LEVETT, ETC.

ALBANY, N. Y.
JOEL MUNSELL'S SONS, PUBLISHERS.
1894.

PREFACE.

Some time ago, while looking through the New England correspondence in that remarkable depository of historical secrets in Fetter Lane, I came upon a file of papers sent to the Lords of Trade by Governor Dummer, in 1725, entitled: "Thirty-one Papers produced by Mr. Dummer, in Proof of the Right of the Crown of Great Britain to the Lands between New England and Nova Scotia, and of Several Depredations Committed by the French and Indians between 1720 and June, 1725."

A perusal of these papers revealed to me the fact, that, in common with others, I had been misled on several points, with regard to the complicity of the French Jesuits in the depredations committed upon the English frontier settlements by the savages, particularly in the early part of the eighteenth century, and after perusing these papers, which constituted a formidable indictment against the French, and especially against Père Ralé, who was slain at Norridgewock, and who was, perhaps, the best known to our forefathers of all the Jesuits, I concluded to

Preface.

take copies of them, and some while after, returning home, I prepared a brief paper upon the subjects which they involved, and presented it to the Maine Historical Society.

It is not unusual for most of us to form opinions more or less nebulous, upon topics in which we have no especial interest, and having done so, to resent a disturbance of them; hence, when I had concluded my paper, I was not surprised to notice that several of my historical associates were regarding me over their spectacles with mild disapproval; in fact, some went so far as to criticise the acts of our forefathers in connection with the subject of my paper, with considerable asperity.

Finding that entirely erroneous opinions prevailed with regard to some of the acts of these noble men of New England, whose blood was the cement which still holds our social structure together, and whose memory we can never sufficiently revere, I deemed it only a duty to gather all the facts that I could, relating to the subject involved in these documents, and to lay them before their descendants.

My examination of the English accounts made by participants in the events of the period; the correspondence and affidavits of eye witnesses to them, revealed to me that none of them had doubts of the participation of many of the Jesuit missionaries in the cruel attempts of the French to ruin the English settlements in New England.

That careful and conscientious historian, Hutchinson, who was a contemporary of the men who bore the brunt of the conflict, carefully gathered their testimony and recorded it with painstaking fidelity; but his account seems of late to have been lost sight of. The French archives were also open to me, and here I found ample evidence, inaccessible to our early writers, to sustain Hutchinson; in fact, there was no documentary evidence in existence to support any other view of the subject.

How, then, did this strange change of sentiment come about? Evidently through a depicting of the affair at Norridgewock in a style entirely different from the plain and truthful sketch of Hutchinson, which, somewhat later than his sketch, was placed before the public; a masterly piece of delineation, tinged with a pathos which easily enlisted the sympathy of any one, who did not take the trouble to scan it closely.

This bit of attractive workmanship bears the name of the Rev. P. F. X. De Charlevoix, S. J., who is mentioned by Governor Shute as "one Charlevoix, who comes from the Court of France in the quality of an inspector, to make memoirs on Acady and Missisipe and the other countries thereabouts."

This is an exact and truthful statement of the function of Charlevoix, and he fulfilled it well. He gathered together everything that he could collect relating to events which had occurred in New France preceding his arrival; journals, letters, and verbal recitals, and transcribed them often in the precise words in which they came to him, leaving out an occasional *mot*, which might not perhaps be pleasant to those of his school, or heightening the color of one which might be made to serve its interests better.

He never seems to have thought of exercising the critical faculty in arranging his material; to sift evidence, to analyze and compare statements, nor, in fact, to do anything but to gather and arrange chronologically what he could collect. He was "an Inspector to make Memoirs," and he did his work and saved a good deal of valuable material for the use of those coming after him.

He was not then the real author of the story Ralé's death. As it is easy to trace most of his stories to their sources, so this, hardly changed, is found embodied in a letter of the Rev. Peter de la Chasse, S. J., the superior of his order in New France, printed in a collection of letters entitled: "*Lettres Edifiantes et*

Curieuses, ecrites des Missions Étrangères, par quelques Missionaires de la Compaignie de Jesus," in 1726, shortly after the death of Ralé.

But it may be pertinent to ask, how did the author of this letter obtain his account of the transaction? The English, with whom he had no communication, were the only civilized men present on the occasion, and their account differs radically from his. No one can doubt that the story was told him by one of the savages, who fled, panic stricken, almost immediately upon the appearance of the English; possibly the same savage, who told the story, which we find in Vaudreuil's report of the transaction to the government at home. This certainly cannot be reassuring even to a partisan of the French.

That the savages, in common with other Pagan people, were notorious falsifiers, is a proposition which needs no discussion, and that these particular savages were such, appears plainly in the documents of the period, nay, in the words of Ralé himself. An analysis of this romantic story, which our English writers have been so ready to adopt in preference to the more commonplace account of their forefathers, and which will probably be repeated till the end of time by others as careless as themselves, shows it to be false in almost every particular, and it is one of the purposes of this book, not only to make this plain, but to show that our forefathers were not murderers and assassins, as they have frequently been denominated, even by English writers, who should have known better; but, in order to preserve themselves and those dear to them, were driven to the necessity of subduing *vis et armis* their savage neighbors, who were deliberately incited by Ralé, and others of his countrymen, to make warfare upon them, and if in the course of this warfare one of its instigators suffered, he should not be denominated a martyr, nor his opponents by whom he suffered, murderers. My sole purpose in writing the following pages has been to present the exact truth, with regard to all matters connected with the transactions treated therein ; " To naught extenuate, naught set down in malice." It will be observed that several stories, which passed current among the English derogatory to Ralé I have passed by in silence. In my opinion it would be rank injustice to his memory to repeat them, as they are wholly unsupported by proofs, and my intention has been to write nothing which is not so supported. If in these pages I have erred in any particular, no one will be so ready and so glad to correct the fault as myself.

JAMES PHINNEY BAXTER,
61 Deering Street, Portland, Me.

THE

PIONEERS OF NEW FRANCE

IN

NEW ENGLAND.

The spectator, as he reviews the motley company thronging the stage of history, is often struck by some grand figure, or group of figures, appearing in movements of surprising interest, and acting their part with a force and fidelity, which excites his admiration, though the movements in which they are engaged may at times seem to him to run counter to the spendid scheme of the drama before him.

Among these, perhaps, no group of men is more strikingly interesting than the "Blackrobes" of Ignatius Loyola,[1] the zealous, self-sacrificing and

---

[1] Don Iñigo Lopez de Recalde de Loyola was born in 1491, at the castle of Loyola, near the town of Azcoytia, Guipúzcoa, in Spain. The name is said to have been derived from a device on the family escutcheon of two wolves regarding a pot suspended by a chain between them, with the words "*Lobo y olla,*"

8   The Pioneers of New France

heroic Jesuits, in whom strangely commingled the most diverse elements to form a character, at the same time admirable and repellant.

---

or " *The Wolf and Pot,*" inscribed beneath. He was one of a numerous family of children and became, at the age of 14, a page at the luxurious court of Ferdinand and Isabella. He accompanied the king in his Portuguese, French, and Moorish wars, and achieved a high reputation for valor and efficiency. A severe wound in the leg in 1521, at which time he fell into the hands of the French, confined him to a sick bed for a considerable period, during which time his reflections upon religious subjects determined his future career. When he regained health he made a pilgrimage to Montserrat, assuming the garb of a beggar, and dwelling in a solitary cave, during which time he subjected himself to fasting, scourging, and other self-imposed penances, so severe as to often imperil his life. It was at this time that he conceived the idea of a religious organization of a semi-military character, with its headquarters at Jerusalem. It was not, however, until September 27, 1541, that a bull for the establishment of the new order, which he had planned, was issued by Pope Paul the Third. When the organization of the Society of Jesus was effected in the spring of 1541, Loyola was made its general, and he at once established himself at Rome, where he devoted himself to the work of the order which he had founded. He died in Rome, July 31, 1556, and was canonized by Gregory the Fifteenth, in 1622, under the title of Saint Ignatius de Loyola. *Vide* Vie de St. Ignace, Paris, 1679, and Ignatius Loyola and the early Jesuits, London, 1871.

Following closely upon the track of the great voyagers, the Jesuits set up the symbols of their order in the most hopeless places, and undertook, with irrepressible zeal, the sanctification of savage souls, darkened and degraded by ages of besetting superstition and vice, and though the methods which they employed were often pitiably disproportioned to the magnitude of a task, which we now know can be accomplished only through the patient education of head and heart, by processes slow and painful, we do wrong if we fail to concede to them sincerity of purpose, or deny them the merit of having achieved a measure of success.

The Jesuits of the period of which we write, were a fair product of their age; an age of superficial knowledge and chivalrous adventure; of childish superstition and romantic achievement, and in estimating them, as well as their contemporaries, who opposed them, we should keep clearly in view the influences which surrounded both, and helped to shape their characters and qualify their acts. The Jesuit missionaries were pioneers in that great movement, which has already accomplished so much for the uplifting of mankind, and which, with a constantly increasing knowledge of proper methods of work, is slowly but surely transforming the world. When the vancouriers of this movement, Biard[1] and Massé,[2] in the early summer of 1611, knelt on the serene shores of Port Royal, and mingled their voices with the songs

---

[1] Pierre Biard was a native of Grenoble, and was associated with Enemond Massé until the capture of the colony, which they had established at Mount Desert, by Argal in 1613. He died while a chaplain in the French army, at Avignon, November 17, 1622.

[2] Enemond Massé was born at Lyons in 1574, and before leaving his native country was socius to Father Coton. He arrived at Port Royal in company with Biard, June 11, 1611, and with his associate immediately entered upon his missionary labors. Owing to constant discord between the missionaries and the governor of the colony, De Pourtrincourt, they resolved to abandon their mission at Port Royal, and accordingly, in conjunction with the Sieur de la Saussaye, the agent of that great patroness of missions, the Marchioness de Guerchville, the lay brother, Gilbert du Thet and Fathers Quentin and Lalemant, they planned to establish a new mission at Kadesquit, or Kenduskeag, the present site of the city of Bangor. Coasting along the shores of Maine, they were attracted by the enchanting scenery of Mount Desert, and resolved to go no further, but to land and establish their colony there. The place selected for the site of their colony they called St. Saveur, and they went vigorously to work, erecting a small fort and several habitations for the shelter of the colonists, about twenty-five in number. The abandonment of their original design was fatal to the success of their enterprise, for they were hardly settled in their new home when Capt. Samuel Argal,

of the wood birds in thanks for the auspicious ending of their perilous journey, the entire continent was a wilderness, wherein the gospel was unknown to its native inhabitants. These had seen the white-faced European greedy to despoil them of their furry wealth, and had learned to distrust him, hence, they turned instinctively from this new variety of his kind, whose motives in seeking them they were unable to comprehend; but when they saw the blackrobed strangers patiently enduring all the hardships attend-ant upon savage life, and apparently seeking to minister to their welfare, the scornful indifference with which they first listened to their despised visitors, gave place to a vagrant attention, and then to a wondering interest, which often culminated in a par-

---

from the Virginia colony, attacked and broke up their settlement. Gilbert du Thet was killed in the fight, and Biard and Massé, with the others, made prisoners. Massé was transported to France, but returned to Canada in 1625, and was made prisoner by Kirk, and again transported across the ocean; but he returned to Canada in 1633, and died in 1646, while on the way to confess the garrison of Fort Richelieu, to prepare them to celebrate the feast of Candlemas. *Vide* Voyages du Sieur Champlain, Paris, 1632, vol. 1, pp. 98–114. Relations des Jesuites, Quebec, 1858, vol. 1, p. 28 *et passim*. Histoire et Description Generale de la Nouvelle France, à Paris, 1744, Tome, 1, p. 416.

tial subjection of will and purpose to men, whose seeming effeminacy had at first been offensive to them. Biard and Massé were followed by others, and not long after the Puritans, under Winthrop, began to set up the altars of their faith on the sterile New England shores, the Jesuits had already gained the ascendancy in New France, whose southern borders, yet undefined, were soon found to be in dangerous proximity to the rapidly advancing English colonists, to whom everything French was hateful.

Race antagonism, which had existed in the hearts of French and English alike from immemorial time, was quickened as they drew nearer together and regarded the complexion of each other's religious faith; hence conflict was a necessity, a conflict in which the weaker natives were bound to be ground to powder by the opposing forces between which they found themselves. With all the hostility of their race to the English, the French Jesuits, unless we fancy them to have been above the reach of human passions, could hardly be expected to remain indifferent spectators to the encroachment of their enemies upon territory wherein they exercised authority, nor to refrain from arousing against them the jealousy of their savage allies, ever ready, upon the slightest cause, to flash into fury; nor did they do this, but encouraged them, whenever an occasion offered, to repel the advancing English with torch and hatchet; in fact, we may largely ascribe to French machinations the cruel wars, which, in the latter half of the seventeenth and the first half of the eighteenth centuries, at times laid waste some of the fairest portions of New England, and subjected her sons and daughters to suffering and death.

A treaty with the savages at Casco in 1678 afforded encouragement to the poor people, who were laboring patiently and with a fortitude not often equaled, to build their humble homes in the wilderness; but, it was a peace haunted at all times by threatening phantoms, which they felt at any minute might assume substance and form, and destroy all that they cherished at a blow. For ten years of uncertain peace they continued to build and plant, gaining confidence as time passed, when suddenly they were startled by the alarm of war.

In the spring of 1688, Andros, the governor of Massachusetts, visited Pemaquid, and held a conference with the savages there, in which he warned them against French influence. On his way thither he had stopped at the trading post of Baron Castin, which was, as he claimed, on English territory, and seized a quantity of merchandise. This act gave a keener edge to Castin's enmity to the English, and his popularity with the savages caused them to espouse his cause, hence they at once began reprisals.[1]

Wishing to avoid war, Andros issued a conciliatory proclamation, and to show his good will, proceeded to liberate a number of Indian prisoners, hoping that the savages, appreciating his magnanimous example, would release their English captives, and come to an amicable understanding ; but, in this he was disappointed, for disregarding his generous conduct, they not only treated their English prisoners with great cruelty, but killed several of them, which forced him to take the field against them.

This was the condition of affairs when a revolution in England sent James the Second, a staunch Papist, an exile to France, which placed the English colonists, on account of their active sympathy with the movement, to the eyes of his French friends, in the position of rebels, and worse still, of heretical rebels.

With this feeling pervading the French court, Count Frontenac, who, seven years before, had been for good reasons deposed from the governorship of New France, was recalled to court, where one of the

---

[1] *Vide* The Andros Tracts, Boston, 1868, vol. 2, p. 118.

most diabolical plots ever conceived against a people was secretly elaborated. This was to make an attack from Canada on Albany, and having seized that place to proceed down the Hudson to New York, which, with the aid of two French ships, it was believed, would be forced to speedily surrender. This accomplished, the heretics were to be removed root and branch; their homes were to be broken up, their property confiscated, and those who survived were to be driven beyond the limits of French rule. If any possessed means which could be wrung from them for ransom, they were to be imprisoned until they purchased their liberty, while artisans were to be held in captivity, and forced to labor for their French masters. One class of persons only was to be allowed to remain and enjoy their property; namely, Roman Catholics.

New England was also to be invaded, and of course, subjected to a like fate if the saints smiled on the enterprise.[1]

This atrocious plan to destroy an entire people,

---

[1] *Vide* Instruction à Mons. De Frontenac sur l'entreprise contre les Anglois, 7 Juin, 1689, in Collection de Manuscrits, etc., relatifs a la Nouvelle France. Quebec, 1883, vol. 1, p. 455 *et seq.*, and Documentary History of Maine, vol. 5.

said to have numbered over seventeen thousand, happy in the possession of homes hardly won, was carefully elaborated in the luxurious halls of Versailles, and early in 1689, Frontenac sailed from Rochelle to carry it into effect.

It was late in the season when Frontenac, who had met with unexpected delays, reached Quebec, where he found the government under Denonville in a disorganized condition. To get the savages under control so as to use them against the English was his first effort, and in this he was unsuccessful so far as regarded the Iroquois and other tribes west of the English settlements, but with the Eastern tribes, the case was different. The Jesuits had become influential in shaping the affairs of the government, and they exercised a powerful control over these tribes, who were, as we have seen, hostile to the English; indeed, if we may believe Denonville, the predecessor of Frontenac, they had been encouraged by Jesuit influences in their recent outbreak against the frontier settlers. The proof of this appears in a letter of the French governor to the king, dated shortly after Frontenac's arrival at Quebec. In this letter he says: "The good understanding which I have had with these savages by means of the Jesuits, and above all the two fathers, 'the Brothers Bigot,' has made successful all the attacks, which they have made on the English this summer," in which attacks, he concludes. "they have killed more than two hundred men," and this in a time of peace between the two nations.[1]

The Bigot brothers had established on the Chaudière an Abnaki mission, and had extended their influence into Maine, where Father Thury had established himself on the Penobscot, and was exercising a powerful control over the savages of that region; accompanying their war parties against the settlers and thereby identifying himself with them.

It was in this condition of affairs that Frontenac, in the winter of 1690, organized the scheme intrusted to him for exterminating the English "heretics and traitors" from American soil. To accomplish this, three war parties of Frenchmen and savages were set in motion from different points in Canada toward the devoted settlements; one to fall upon Albany, another

---

[1] Pères James and Vincent Bigot, the former born in 1644, died in 1711; the latter born in 1647, died in 1720. *Vide* Histoire et Description Generale de la Nouvelle France, à Paris, 1744, Tome 2, p. 419. Resumè des rapports du Canada avec les notes du ministre, Collection de Manuscrits, etc., vol. 1, p. 474 *et seq.*

upon the settlements in New Hampshire, and yet another upon those of Maine.

The inhuman atrocities perpetrated alike on men, women and children, their utter disregard of pledges given to induce surrender by the two first of these parties, we will not relate. Schuyler said, no pen could write, and no tongue express them. Children were thrown alive into the fire, their heads dashed in pieces against the doorposts, while tortures too dreadful to relate, were inflicted upon their parents.[1] Who can wonder that such cruelties left an ineffacable impression upon the hearts of the English settlers for generations, and convinced them, that self-preservation alone rendered it imperative to reduce the savages to complete subjection whatever might be the cost.

The party sent against Maine set out from Quebec in January, led by Portneuf and Courtemanche. Treading their way through the gloom of trackless forests, and facing the blinding snows, or wallowing waist-deep through the drifts as they emerged on the dreary openings, ever alert for game to add to their scanty stores, the party pushed on, and in May

---

[1] Cf. Belknap, Mather, Charlevoix, De La Potherie, Documentary History of New York and Schuyler's Report, Feb. 15, 1690.

reached the vicinity of Falmouth, where they hovered among the islands and along the shores until ready to attack the settlement. Portneuf had been joined by Castin and Hertel, the latter, the leader of the ruthless band, which had been sent against the New Hampshire settlements, and were now on their return from scenes of carnage, which had sharpened their appetite for the carnival of blood and devastation which they had in anticipation. In the band were the Indians whom Andros had magnanimously released from imprisonment at Fort Loyal, and who, being acquainted with its defenses, were valuable guides to those now seeking its destruction.

The attack on Falmouth began on the 15th day of May, with the slaughter of Lieutenant Clark and thirteen men on Munjoy Hill, and was followed by an attack on Fort Loyal, which resulted, after four days' resistance, in the surrender of Capt. Davis and his garrison, with the women and children, who had sought refuge in the fort. Although the French commander bound himself by oath before the surrender, that the English should have safe conduct to the next town, as soon as he had them in his power he abandoned them to the savages, who murdered men, women and children without pity. They were "heretics and traitors," with whom, in those dismal times, it was not necessary to keep faith.[1] That this war against the English settlers had assumed the lurid hue of a religious crusade cannot be doubted, and the feeling with which they were regarded found frequent expression, as in the case of Père Gay, who, seeing his savage neophytes give way before Schuyler, encouraged them by shouting, "You have at your head the Holy Virgin; what do you fear? We have to do with Infidels, who have only the form of man."[2]

---

[1] *Vide* Magnalia Christi Americana, Hartford, 1853, vol. 2, p. 603 *et seq*. Declaration of Sylvanus Davis, Collections Mass. Hist. Society, 3d series, vol. 1, p. 101. Documentary Hist. of N. Y., vol. 2, p. 259. New York Colonial Documents, vol. IX, p 472. Histoire et Description Generale de la Nouvelle France, à Paris, 1744, Tome, 3, p. 78.

[2] The words are as follows: " DIEU fut servi pendant toute cette Campaigne, comme si c'avait été une Communanté de Religieux. Il nefaut pas que j'oublie la manière avec laquelle M. Gay, Ecclésiastique de la Montagne s'est signalé. Il a agi en Apôtre et en General d'armée. Dans la seconde sortie que l'on fit, il s'aperçut qu'une partie de nos gens lachaient pied, il courut à eux leur criant: 'Vous ne faites donc pas réflexion, que vous avez à votre tête, la Sainte Vierge que nous avons prise pour notre protectrice; que nous avons déja reçu d'elle tant de marques de son assistance, et qu'elle est votre bouclier? Que craignez-vous? Nous avons affaire à des infidèles, qui n'ont que la figure d'homme; et

Naturally, as Denonville wrote from Quebec a few days before the attack on Falmouth, the English regarded all the French missionaries as their most cruel enemies, whom they would not suffer among the savages who were contiguous to them.[1]

While Portneuf and his wild band were stealthily approaching Falmouth, Sir William Phips, adopting the well-known military maxim, that by recalling your enemy to the defense of his own possessions, you can best guarantee the security of your own, was making ready to strike the enemy in his own home, and before the embers of the devoted town had ceased smoking, he had captured Port Royal, and making prisoners of Meneval, the French com-

---

ne vous souvenez-vous pas que vous êtes les sujets du Roi de France, dont le nom fait trembler toute l'Europe ? ' "

Vide L'Héroine Chrétienne du Canada, etc., par L'Abbé Etienne Michel Faillon. Villemarie, Chez les soeurs de la Congregation de Notre Dame, 1860, p. 317.

[1] Alluding to the jealousies existing between the English and French, he speaks of the interests of the Catholic religion, which, he says, they will never permit to make any progress among the savages, "regardant tous nos missionnaires come leurs plus cruels ennemies qu'ils ne veulent pas souffrir avec les Sauvages qui sont à portée d'eulx." *Vide* Collection de Manuscrits, etc., Quebec, 1884, vol. 2, p. 1 *et seq*.

mander, and the garrison under his command, he triumphantly carried them to Boston.[1]

This success seemed an especial mark of divine providence, and Governor Bradstreet issued a proclamation appointing a day of fasting, and admonishing the people to repent of their sins. So well were his wishes complied with, that Mather says: "The churches kept the wheel of prayer in continual motion."[2] A naval expedition to strike at Quebec itself, the center of French power in America, was soon organized, and on the 9th of August, the fleet under the command of Phips sailed from Boston, at the same time a land expedition was making its way from Albany to strike a retaliatory blow at Montreal. The English were not to be rooted out of American soil so easily as the French king in his vain pride imagined they might be. Both expeditions were unsuccessful. Frontenac, the governor of New France, was a man of marked ability, and to his military skill and promptitude, as well as the natural difficulties,

---

[1] *Vide* Prise du Port Royal par les Anglois de Baston. Collection de Manuscrits, etc., vol. 2, p. 6 *et seq.* Lettre de Monsieur de Meneval au Ministre, *Ibid.*, p. 10 *et seq.* A Journal of the Expedition from Boston to Port Royal. Chalmers' papers, Harvard College.

[2] *Vide* Magnalia Christi Americana, vol. 1, p. 192.

which beset Phips and Winthrop, the latter of whom commanded the land expedition, their failure was due.

It is not the purpose of this work to give a particular account of the wars, which culminated in the subjugation of the Eastern tribes by the English, but only to touch upon a few points, which lead toward this event, and particularly to explain the reasons which caused the destruction of Norridgewock, the hotbed of an influence, which imperilled the existence of English civilization in New England. From the failures of the expeditions against Canada by Phips and Winthrop, the war dragged on with varying fortunes to both sides. Both were poor and both bitterly hostile to each other.

While the French king, lulled by his mistresses and sycophants into thoughtlessness of the terrible import of his acts, wrote to Frontenac to excite the savages to continue their murderous warfare against the English settlements, and ordered presents to be made to them for their encouragement, he haggled over the cost of the war, and postponed the undertaking of his scheme against New York, on account of the expense he had already sustained.[1] War parties, however,

---

[1] Memoire du Roi aux Sieurs de Frontenac et de Champigny. Collection de Manuscrits, etc., vol. 2, pp. 51–54; *Ibid.*, p. 82, *et passim*.

of savages and *coureurs de bois,* many of whom were half breeds, if anything more ferocious than the savages themselves, led by Frenchmen, desolated the frontier settlements. The savages, if left to themselves, would soon have made peace ; indeed, not long after the capture of Port Royal by Phips, several of the chiefs entered into an agreement with the English to meet and arrange a treaty, but this they were not permitted to do. Presents were heaped upon them by the French commander, and their avarice was excited by promises of booty, which would be to them "plus d'avantage qu'à la chasse ;" nor was this all ; Father Thury lent his powerful aid, and exhorted them to continue the war upon the English, which the French minister had declared should be made "sans relache."[1]

---

[1] "Comme vostre principal objèt doibt estre de faire la guerre sans relasche aux Anglois, il faut que vostre plus particulière occupation, soyt de détourner de tout aultre employ, les François qui sont avec vous, surtout de faire aulcun commerce que pour leur subsistance, en leur donnant de vostre part un sy bon exemple en cela qu'ils ne soyent animez que du désir de chercher à faire du profit sur les ennemis.

Je n'ay aussy rien à vous recommander plus fortement que de mettre en usage tout ce que vous pouvez de capacité et de prudence, affin que les Canibas ne s'employent qu'a la guerre, et que par l'économie de ce que vous avez à leur fournir ils y puis-

It was in the dead of the winter of 1692, that Thury with one hundred and fifty of his Christian converts left their village on the Penobscot to accomplish their design on the few remaining settlements of Maine. Soon they were joined by a howling band from Father Bigot's mission on the Kennebec, and for a month pursued their difficult way on snowshoes through the pathless wilds, which lay between them and the doomed settlements. On the night of February 4th, while the candles were being lighted in the rude dwellings of York, and the humble cotters were gathering about their firesides unsuspicious of danger, the savages, like wolves, were crouching in the thick woods, which fringed the slopes of Mount Agamenticus, eager to spring upon their prey.

Several of the houses were fortified for defense, and a watch was probably kept, which may have deterred the savages from making a night attack; anyhow, they kept under cover through the long, cold night. As the day dawned, the snow began silently to fall. The door of one of the cabins opened and a boy, with the visions of youth in his brain and the joys of life all untasted before him, came forth with

---

sent trouver leur subsistance et plus d'avantage qu' à la chasse." Lettre du Roy au Sieur de Villebon, Collection de Manuscrits, etc., vol. 2, p. 83.

his axe. Soon he was busy at his task, when suddenly he was seized by rough hands, forced to answer a few fierce questions, and then his head was split open with a hatchet, and he was left dying on the new fallen snow, while the savages, dividing into two parties, rushed upon the village. Men, women and children were alike butchered, even infants in the cradle were not spared, says Villebon, approvingly.[1]

The venerable minister of the town, the Rev. Shubael Dummer, a man eminent for learning and piety, was preparing to mount his horse to visit in the neighborhood, when he was shot dead at his door.[2] We will not follow the harrowing details of this affair farther, nor follow the fortunes of the war.

---

[1] "Nos Sauvages se sont mis en action, le Sieur de Villieu les y a accompagnez et Monsieur de Thury. Ce coup est très advantageux parce qu'il rompt tous les pourparlers de paix et que l'on doibt compter qu'il n'y aura plus de retour entre nos Sauvages et les Anglois, qui sont au désespoir de ce qu'ils ont tué jusques aux enfans au berceau." Resume d'une lettre de Monsieur de Villebon au Ministre. Collection de Manuscrits, etc., vol. 2, p. 158.

[2] The Rev. Shubael Dummer was born at Roxbury, Mass., Feb. 17th, 1636, and graduated at Harvard College in 1656. He was ordained as the first settled minister of York in 1673. He married the daughter of Edward Rishworth, and at the time of the attack on York, Feb. 5th, 1692, had faithfully and

One can be certain that the French missionaries in Maine were active in inciting the savages to war-

zealously performed his ministerial duties for nearly twenty years. When hostilities threatened, it is said that he was urged to leave York, but refused, preferring to share the dangers of those, whom he had "converted and edified by his ministry." He was just about mounting his horse to make a pastoral visit in the neighborhood when he was shot, and his wife and son taken prisoners. Quite contrary to their usual custom, several old women and small children, who were taken prisoners and appeared unable to take the long journey to Canada, were permitted to remain behind alive when the Indians took their departure. Among these was the delicate wife of the dead minister. Her son, however, was a prisoner, and the half frantic widow returned to the Indian camp after her release to beg the savages to release her boy. This was refused, and she was sent away; but motherly affection prompted her to make another attempt, and she again returned to beg for her son's release. Her prayer was refused, and she was told that as she wanted to be a prisoner her wish should be granted. She had, therefore, the satisfaction of accompanying her son; but the hardships of a mid-winter march through the wilderness without shelter and almost without food were too severe for her, and she soon died. Mather thus sings of the slain pastor:

> DUMMER the *shepherd* sacrificed,
> By *wolves* because the *sheep* he priz'd.
> The *orphan's* father, church's *light*,
> The *love* of heav'n, of hell the *spight*."

Vide Magnalia Christi Americana, vol. 2, p. 612 *et*

fare. During the early years of the war, Thury and Bigot were especially conspicuous in this regard. "The savages," wrote Tibierge, "in the river Pentagoet, have great confidence in Monsieur Thury, who has been a missionary among them for eight years. I am persuaded that he is very necessary in that place for the service of the king and the welfare of the nation, and if it was desired to make use of the savages for some important enterprise, nobody could be found who could better persuade them than he to do what was desired."[1]

And for his success in persuading his converts to renew the war against the English, the French minister not only wrote the bishop of Quebec to "increase his pay," but also wrote Thury himself, that he was glad to serve him in an application to the king for reward, "not only for your zeal and your application in your mission, and the progress it has made in the advancement of religion among the savages, but also for your pains

---

seq. Lettre de Monsieur de Champigny, au ministre, Oct. 5, 1692. Collection de Manuscrits, vol. 2, p. 88 *et seq.* Williamson's Maine, vol. 1, p. 672, and Journal of Rev. John Pike.

[1] *Vide* Memoire sur l'Acadie par Monsieur Tibierge. Collection de Manuscrits, etc, vol. 2, p. 185.

in keeping them in the service of his majesty, and for encouraging them in expeditions of war."[1] Proof is abundant to show how completely some of these missionaries identified themselves with their savage converts in their wars against the border settlers. It is a pleasant duty to recall, that even in this hard

---

[1] "Monsieur le Comte de Frontenac nonseulement a rendu tesmoniage de vostre faveur dans vostre mission — mais j'ay encore appris par les lettres de Monsieur de Villebon, commandant pour Sa Majesté à l'Acadie, et par la relation du Sieur du Villieu, l'usage que vous avez faict pour le service de Sa Majesté de la confiance que vous este acquise parmy ces Sauvages pour ayder à ces officiers à les maintenir dans le fidélité du service de sa majesté contre les Anglois. C'est sur ces assurances que Monsieur de Frontenac, ayant faict connoistre à Sa Majesté la conséquence de secourir plus promtement les sauvages du quartier de Pentagouët et ceulx de la rivière Quinibéqui que nous comprenons soubs le nom de Cannibas, et pour leur plus grande commodité, Sa Majesté a donné l'ordre au Sieur de Bonnaventure, commandant le vaisseau *l'Envieux*, d'aller à Pentagouët pour y discharger la partie des munitions et marchandises destinez pour ceulx de Pentagouët et de Quinibéqui, et les marchandises que la compagnie a en ordre d'envoyer aussy pour la traitte avec eulx, affin qui ces présens, vous estans remis, sur vostre recepissé au pied de l'inventoire par le dit Sieur de Bonnaventure, vous leur en faissiez la distribution comme il est accoustumé, que vous vous entendiez avec ledit

age, there were men who realized what conversion really meant; men who knew that such men as

Sieur de Villebon, et que vous luy envoyiez l'estat de la distribution, affin qu'il me le fasse venir. J'espère que vous voudrez bien continuer de messager les sauvages avec la mesme application, et que leur fais ant connoistre l'affection qui Sa Majesté conserve pour eux par les secours qu'Elle leur donne et qu'Elle est dans le dessein de leur continuer plus fortement, vous maintiendrez le progrez des affaires de la religion avec eulx, en empeschant qu'ils ne se communiquent avec les Anglois." Lettre du Ministre à Monsieur de Thury, missionnaire, à Versailles, le 16° Avril, 1695. "Les tesmoignages qu'on a rendus à Sa Majesté de l'affection et du zèle du Sieur de Thury, missionnaire chez les Cannibas, pour son service, et particulièrment pour l'engagement où il a mis les sauvages de recommencer la guerre contre les Anglois avec lesquels ills avoient faict un accodement, m'oblige de vous pryer en conséquence de ce qu'on a mandé en mesme tems de sa pauvreté, de luy faire une plus fort part sur les 1500 l. de gratiffication que Sa Majeste accorde pour les ecclésiastiques de l'Acadie, dont celuy-cy a beaucoup plus de besoing que les aultres qui sont dans les endroits où ils prennent des dixmes qui sont fut considérables, comme aux Mines, quoyqu'elles ne soyent pas dües." Lettre du Ministre a Monsieur l'Evesque de Quebec, a Versailles le 16 Avril, 1695. "Je suis bien ayse de me servir de cette occasion pour vous dire que j'ay esté informé non seulment de vostre zèle et de vostre application pour vostre mission et du progrez qu'elle faict pour l'avancement de nostre religion avec les

Thury[1] and the Bigots were blind leaders of the blind, countenancing, by their presence amid scenes

---

sauvages, mais encore de vos soigns pour les maintenir dans le service de Sa Majesté, *et pour les encourager aux expéditions de guerre auxquelles elle les faict employer.*" Lettre du Ministre à Monsieur Thury, à Versailles, le 23 Avril, 1697. These are but a few selections from the correspondence in French archives relating to Thury. *Vide* Collection de Manuscrits, etc., vol. 2, pp. 174-5, 179, 274, *et passim.*

[1] The Rev. Peter Thury was a native of Bayeux, France, and was ordained a member of the seminary of Quebec, December 21, 1677. He was a friend of Castin, and through his influence was induced to settle at Pentagoet in 1687. He was active in every intrigue to excite the savages of his mission against the English frontier settlers, whom he denounced to them as heretics and robbers. On one occasion he harangued his savage converts in these words: "My children! when shall the rapacity of the unsparing New Englanders cease to afflict you, and how long will you suffer your lands to be violated by the encroaching heretics? By the religion I have taught, by the liberty you love, I exhort you to resist them. It is time for you to open your eyes which have long been shut; to rise from your mats and look to your arms and make them once more bright. This land belonged to your fathers, long before these wicked men came over the great water, and are you ready to leave the bones of your ancestors, that the cattle of the heretics may eat grass on your graves? The Englishmen think and say to themselves: 'We have cannon; we have grown strong, while the redman

of murder and torture, the crimes committed by their converts, and afterward condoning these crimes against humanity by administering to the perpetrators of them, while their hands were still red with the blood of innocent women and children, the sacraments of the church; men who had laid to heart the words, "Except ye turn and become as little children, ye shall in no wise enter into the kingdom of heaven." Two such men are happily recorded as having refused absolution to some individuals engaged in the service against the English. These were Fathers Baudoin and Petit, and the bishop of Quebec was informed by the French minister, in a

---

has slept; while they are lying in their cabins and do not see, we will knock them on the head; we will destroy their women and children, and then shall we possess their land without fear, for there shall be none left to revenge them. My children! God commands you to shake the sleep from your eyes. The hatchet must be cleaned from its rust, to avenge Him of His enemies, and secure to you your rights. Night and day a continual prayer shall ascend to him for your success, an unceasing rosary shall be observed till you return covered with the glory of triumph." He died at Chebuctou on the 3d of June, 1699. *Vide* Travels of Learned Missionaries, pp. 280, 309, Etat Présent, Quebec, pp. 12, 18; Voyage de l'Acadie, pp. 54, 179; Collections Me. Hist. Society, vol. 1, p. 435 *et seq.;* Taschereau's Memoir sur l'Acadie.

letter from Versailles, that the king was very indignant at their refusal of absolution to certain persons because they were engaged in the service against the English.[1]

---

[1] F. Michael Baudoin and Mathurin le Petit. The former afterwards attempted to found a mission among the Choctaws, and the latter became superior of the Jesuits in Louisiana. The letter of the French minister, Ponchartrain, is as follows: "A Versailles, le 8 May, 1694. Je suis obligé de vous dire que Sa Majesté a esté fort indignée de la mauvaise conduitte des Sieurs Beaudoin et Petit, missionnaires de l'Acadie, dans les choses qui ont eu relation à son service, et dans la résistance que Monsieur de Villebon, commandant à l'Acadie, a trouvé en cela de leur part. Elle a aussy apris qu'ils ont refusé l'absolution à des particuliers, à cause qu'ils étoient engagez dans le service contre les Anglois. Sa Majesté auroit donné ses ordres pour les faire retirer, sy elle n'avoit trouvé plus à propos, par considération pour vous, de m'ordonner de vous pryer d'empescher la continuation de ces desordres et que ces ecclésiastiques ne s'ingèrent point des affaires qui concernent le temporel, sy ce n'est pas l'ordre de ceulx auxquels. Sa Majesté a confié son authorité, affin qu'en cela ils soyent soubmis comme ils doyvent l'estre, et que sy vous ne croyiez par pouvoir vous assurer de leur obéissance, vous les retiriez pour en mettre d'aultres à leur place." Two other missionaries are mentioned by Tibierge, who evidently thought more of teaching the gospel to the savages than inciting them to war against their English neighbors, namely Pères Simon and Elizée. Of the

We know that the reason assigned was not the real cause of their refusal. The cause was a deeper one, involving the manner of conducting the "services," and the names of these two missionaries should be held in grateful remembrance. They were bright lights in a season of deepest gloom, and without doubt there were many others whose names are only recorded in the imperishable archives of a world of love and peace.

When Frontenac sailed from Rochelle in the summer of 1689, he was accompanied by a Jesuit priest, who afterward became famous in the annals of New England, Père Sebastian Ralé, a native of Franche Comté; where he was born on January 28, 1657. As this man for more than thirty years played such an important part in the struggle between the savages and the frontier settlers of New England, he will, of necessity, appear prominently in a considerable portion of the following pages, and that no injustice may be done him, everything thus far discovered which he has written will be re-

---

former he says : "C'est un trés honneste homme qui ne se mesle que des affaires de sa mission," and of the latter, that he is, "un homme assez retiré, ne m'a pas paru jusque à présent se meslee que des fonctions de son ministére." *Vide* Collection de Manuscrits, etc., vol. 2, pp. 155 *et seq*. 187.

produced. In his eighteenth year, or according to the register of the society, on September 24, 1675, Ralé entered as a noviciate the Society of Jesus, in the Province of Lyons, and when, during the rule of Denonville, who was a zealous friend of the Jesuits, the call came from the mission of St. Francis for more men, Ralé was an instructor of Greek in the College of Nismes.[1] He was a man of heroic courage, of an earnest and self-sacrificing spirit, possessed indeed of qualities, which, in spite of some of his misconceptions of the real spirit of Christianity, entitle him to a measure of respect and admiration. He left France at the time when the feeling against the English colonists was most bitter at the French court, where the cause of James the Second was considered a holy cause, which was to be advanced by every means attainable, and when the air was laden with denunciations of the heretic colonists, traitors to their anointed king, and rebels against the Almighty.

With prejudices, which he could not have failed to imbibe against these, to him misguided people, active in his heart, he landed in Quebec in mid-autumn, and

---

[1] The dates given are from the ancient catalogue of the Jesuits, and differ somewhat from those given by Père Martin in "Les Jesuit Martyrs de Canada."

at once came under the influence of the Bigots, who were at the head of an Abnaki mission largely composed of Indians, whom they had induced to leave Maine after King Philip's war. It was among these people that he passed, as he says, his missionary apprenticeship, and here he learned the Abnaki tongue. This was no easy task, but he applied himself to it with his usual zeal, and by persistent intercourse with the savages in their smoky wigwams, subjected to their rude gibes and disgusting habits of life, he finally acquired facility in uttering their harsh gutturals, and threading the intricacies of their bewildering idioms.

The bold imagery which the savages used, appealed to his poetic instinct, and moved him to admiration. Perhaps transmuted in his own thought, they assumed a beauty not wholly their own, if we may judge from examples he has given.

Their food was vile, and to Ralé, born in a country where cooking was a fine art, it seemed impossible to overcome his repugnance to it, but when a greasy savage shrewdly applied one of his own sinapisms to his sensitive conscience, reminding him, that the savage had to overcome his repugnance to prayer and it was the duty of a praying father to subdue his prejudice to dogmeat, he gracefully succumbed, and thereafter ate whatever came to the kettle. For two years he lived at the Abnaki mission, learning in summer to traverse with the savages the perilous waters of the St. Lawrence in their birchen canoes, and in winter, the frozen wastes of that desolate region, on their cumbersome snowshoes, which at first he thought it impossible to walk with; then he took up his weary march to the Illinois, where others of his order had worn out their lives in a task seemingly too heavy for human nature to undertake.

It was late in the summer when Ralé set out with his savage guides with their canoes on his long journey; shooting dangerous rapids, paddling across great lakes, on which storms were as common as on the ocean, and traversing pathless forests beset with difficulties. Often he was ready to faint with hunger and was obliged to scrape the juiceless lichens from the rocks to sustain life.

After many hardships, as winter drew near, the worn-out missionary reached Mackinac, about seven hundred miles from Quebec, and somewhat more than half way to his place of destination.

He could go no farther, for winter was creating impassable barriers to farther progress, and he was, therefore, obliged to remain here until spring. Happily he found at Mackinac two brothers of his society, and their companionship afforded him much comfort during the long and dreary winter. He was no sluggard, however, and while here he applied himself to a careful study of the people, their legends and traditions, and to the acquirement of the Algonkin tongue.

With the opening of spring Ralé again turned his face westward, and after a journey of about two months reached the Indian town on the Illinois, the object of his long pilgrimage. Here he was hospitably received by the Indians, who entertained him in their rude fashion, and whose strange customs and modes of life furnished him with ample material for study and reflection. For two years he devoted himself to missionary work among these people, and to the study of their tongue, when he was again called to Quebec.[1] When he reached here, the war, as we have seen, was raging furiously between the French, aided by their savage allies, and the people of New England, and Ralé was at once dispatched to the Abnakis of Norridgewock to assume charge of them. He had come to Quebec at the beginning of the war, but had not been brought directly in contact with it. Now he was to face the detestable English "heretics

---

[1] *Vide* Lettres Edifiantes, et Curieuses, etc., Paris, 1838, Tome Premier, pp. 675–692.

and traitors," and to aid in preventing them from sowing the pernicious seeds of their faith among the innocent natives, and dragging them down to perdition with themselves.

It was a task which he felt was worth any sacrifice and he undertook it with alacrity; on the other hand, the English viewed the settlement of the new missionary within the limits of what they regarded as their own territory, with distrust and alarm, as they assuredly had reason to view it, judging from the misguided efforts of Thury and others.

We should err in supposing Ralé absorbed at this time with schemes of warfare upon the English settlers. Without doubt the uppermost thought in his mind was to build up his church in the midst of the savages. To overcome the material obstacles in his path; to set up a chapel in the wilderness, and get about him the mere accessories of worship, to say nothing of bending the savage mind to a favorable regard of his efforts, was labor enough to occupy him for a considerable time, and he seems to have given himself up to the work with his usual industry and zeal.

In due time he had a chapel erected and furnished with the required appendages of the worship to which he was devoted; indeed, we are told that his chapel was adorned with considerable taste, the result of his own skillful handiwork.

While Ralé was engaged in these labors, and establishing himself in the favor of the savages of Norridgewock, the war between England and France was drawing to a close. Thury, his co-laborer on the Penobscot, was actively employed during the closing scenes of the war in encouraging his neophytes to deeds of blood, and with them, those of Ralé were joined. While no written evidence exists to show his complicity with Thury in exciting the savages against them at this time, the English fully believed that he was equally responsible with his co-laborer, and a bitter feeling of hostility soon prevailed against him.

It was believed in Versailles that Boston might be captured, and a plan of attack was formulated, in which Castin was mentioned as the leader of the savages, as well as the Sieur de Thury, their missionary.[1] In view of this attack, small parties of savages

---

[1] " Les Canadiens s'embarqueront sur les vaisseaux et il sera au choix des Sauvages de s'y embarquer ou de faire ce chemin en canots le long des costes qui de Pentagouët se continuent et se terminent à cette baye. Et comme le Sieur de St. Castin ne manquera pas de se mettre dans son canot à leur teste, comme il a faict à l'enterprise de Pemkuit, aussi bien

BELL OF RALÉ'S CHAPEL AT NORRIDGEWOCK.

Found in 1808 under a decayed hemlock, where
it had been concealed. Now in possession
of the Maine Historical Society.

were sent out, and for sometime prowled in the vicinity of the town. In August, Thury was at Fort St. John and reported to Tibierge, that the savages of his mission and those of the Kennebec had been in several parties about Boston, and killed much people, "beaucoup de monde," and that one party had taken a prisoner and burned him " a la maniere des Iroquois," and that they had resolved to give no quarter to any of the English who fell into their hands.[1] Such was the character of the war waged

---

que le Sieur Thury leur missionnaire." Memoire sur l'enterprise de Baston à Versailles, le 21st Avril, 1697.

[1]AU FORT ST. JEAN.
le 20 Aoust, 1697.
MONSIEUR :

Monsieur Thury est arrivé ce soir au fort venant de Pentagouët. Il dit que les Sauvages de sa mission et ceulx de Quinibiquy ayant esté cet esté en plusieurs parties autour de Boston, y avoient tué beaucoup de monde, et qu'un party, entr'aultres, ayant faict un prisonnier, ils l avoient interrogé pour avoir des nouvelles :—que les Sauvages avoient ensuitte bruslé leur prisonnier à la manière des Iroquois, (c'est le premier qu'ils ayent bruslé). Ils ont résolu de ne donner de quartier à aulcun des Anglois qui leur tomberont entre le mains."

Lettre du Sieur Tibierge a Monsieur le Comte de Frontenac. Collection de Manuscrits, etc., vol. 2, p. 286.

by the French against the English, and which Charlevoix so complacently regards. Fortunately after raging for ten years, a " Decennium Luctuosum " as designated by Mather, it came to a close, a treaty of peace having been concluded between France and England at Ryswick, Sept. 20, 1697, and the New England settlers were again enabled to cultivate the arts of peace for a short season ; but only for a short season. The French were not willing that the English should establish friendly relations with their savage neighbors even after the conclusion of peace, and made efforts to prevent them from so doing.

Villebon was commended by the French minister for writing to the Jesuit fathers of the Maine missions, to notify the chiefs of the savages not to hold any communication with the English governor, nor any one representing him.[1]

In such a condition of affairs, peace could not long continue ; indeed, the French began at once a careful study of the English towns and their means of de-

---

[1] "Vous avez bien fait d'écrire aux Pères Jesuites, qui sont en mission aux Sauvages de Quinibequi, d'avertir les chefs de ces Sauvages d 'n'avoré aucune communication avec Monsieur le Comte de Bellamont, n'y personne de sa part." Lettre du Ministre a Monsieur Villebon. A Versailles, le 9ᵉ Avril, 1700. Collection de Manuscrits, etc., vol. 2, p. 334.

fense, with a view to future war, and careful calculations of the number of savages as well as of their own people, who could be sent against them, were forwarded to the French king. The boundaries between New England and Acadia, which had been ceded to the French, were still in dispute, and this in itself was a sufficient cause for conflict. The attitude of the French in preventing intercourse between them and the savages, was also irritating to the English, and increased their hostility to the French Jesuits, who, they knew, were instrumental in keeping alive the jealousy of the savages against them.

So intense did this feeling become, that the General Court of Massachusetts, in the summer of 1700, passed an act to expel the Jesuits from the province. And Governor Stoughton wrote to the Lords Commissioners: "I crave leave further to observe to yor Lord^{ps}, the present repose and quiet of this his Ma^{tys} Province after the late Alarm of troubles threatened to Arise from the Indians by a fresh Insurrection & breaking forth in open hostility. And how necessary it is in order to ye continuance of this quiet that the French Priests and Missionaries be removed from their residence among them, the Indians taking measures from their evil counsels and Suggestions, and are bigotted in their zeal to their pernicious and damnable principles. But the removal of these Incendiaries is rendered difficult whilst the Claims and pretensions to the Boundaries of Territory and Dominion betwixt the English and French are depending undetermined, or at least the determination not known in the Plantation."[1]

Dudley, who succeeded to the government of Massachusetts in 1702, found sufficient cause for alarm, and at once sought to establish friendly relations with the savages. A conference was accordingly appointed at Casco, and, on June 20, 1703, a large body of savages assembled at the appointed place, led by their chief sagamores, viz.: Moxus and Hopegood from Norridgewock; Wanungunt and Wanadugunbuent from the Penobscot; Bomazeen and Capt. Samuel from the Kennebec. Besides these came Mesambomett and Wexar from the Androscoggin, with a flotilla of sixty-five canoes, con-

---

[1] A still more stringent law was passed by the legislature of New York, namely, to hang every Popish priest who came into the province. Smith, the historian of New York, declares this law to be one which " ought forever to remain in force," being, says Bancroft, "wholly unconscious of the true nature of his remark." *Vide* Bancroft's History of the U. S., ed. 1841, vol. 3, p. 193, also Letter of Wm. Stoughton, Dec. 20th, 1700, in B. T. New England, vol. 11, I. 15, Office of the Public Records, London.

taining two hundred and fifty painted savages, all armed, a formidable array of wild men, which caused some trepidation among the people of the vicinity.

Under a tent, near the fort at New Casco, surrounded by his officers, and the gentlemen who had accompanied him from Boston, Governor Dudley, arrayed in the brilliant uniform of a British officer, received the savage chiefs, and, after the proper salutations, he informed them, that being "commissioned by the great and victorious Queen of England, he came to visit them as his friends and brethren, and to reconcile whatever differences had happened since the last treaty."

To this the orator of the savages replied: "We thank you good brother for coming so far to talk with us. The clouds fly and darken, but we still sing with love the songs of peace. Believe my words; so far as the sun is above the earth are our thoughts from war, or the least rupture between us."

In testimony of their sincerity, they presented the governor with a belt of wampum, and invited him to two heaps of stones which had been erected upon a former occasion, and which had been named the two brothers. Here both parties solemnly renewed their pledge of amity by adding more stones to these pillars of witness. This ceremony terminated, guns were discharged by both parties, the savages dancing, singing and uttering wild acclamations of joy.

Negotiations were then entered into respecting trading-houses, the price of commodities, and the employment of an armorer by the English to repair the guns of the savages; presents were exchanged, and, says Penhallow, "everything looked with a promising aspect of a settled peace. And that which afterward seemed to confirm it, was the coming in of Captain Bomazeen and Captain Samuel, who informed that several missionaries from the Friars were lately come among them, who endeavored to break the union and seduce them from their allegiance to the Crown of England, but had made no impression on them, for that they were as firm as the mountains, and should continue so as long as the sun and moon endured."

This action of the savages was reassuring to the colonists, some of whom, alarmed at the threatening aspect of affairs, were preparing to abandon their frontier homes, and they permitted themselves to enjoy for a time a feeling of security; but the story of Bomazeen and Samuel, relative to their rejection of the counsels of the French missionaries, was only intended to deceive them, and was invented for the occasion; at the same time, it shows the part which both parties understood was played by the French missionaries.

Ralé had accompanied his neophytes to the conference, but did not intend to show himself to the English. He tells us, however, that by the precipitate landing of the savages, he found himself, to his chagrin, in the presence of the governor, who, perceiving him, came forward and saluted him. The governor, he proceeds, addressed the savages, telling them that the Queen desired them and the English to live at peace; that he would see that justice was rendered them if they should suffer any wrong, and advised them to remain neutral and not to join the French in case of war between the two crowns; but, says Ralé, "my presence hindered him from saying all that he intended, for it was not without design that he had brought a minister with him."

During the time that the savages were deliberating what to reply, Ralé says, that the governor drew him apart and prayed him not to lead the savages to make war against the English, and that he replied, that his religion and character engaged him to give them only counsels of peace. He says that he should have spoken more, but that he was suddenly surrounded by a score of young warriors, who suspected treachery on the part of the governor, and that, at this juncture, the chiefs advanced to make their reply, which was to the effect, that they should stand by the French and aid them if war broke out between them and the English, a statement totally at variance with the English account, and which must be regarded as incredible, since the design of the savages appears to have been to encourage the colonists to indulge in a feeling of security, that they might accomplish their purposes more completely in the end. Be this, however, as it may, we know that the conference terminated with a show at least of rejoicing on both sides, and it could not have so ended, if the savages had replied to the kind words of the English governor, as Ralé tells us they did; besides, is it possible that Penhallow and others, who were present, would fail to record a reply so important to the welfare of their people? To believe this would be not only to believe that they deliberately falsified, but did so against their own feelings and interests, and for no purpose, unless it were to make their savage foes appear in an agreeable light. "But," says Penhallow, "I should have taken notice of two instances in the late treaty, wherein the matchless perfidy of these bloody infidels did notoriously appear. First, as the treaty was concluded with volleys on both sides, as I said before, the Indians desired the English to fire first, which they readily did, concluding it no other than a compliment; but so soon as the Indians fired, it was observed that their guns were charged with bullets, having contrived (as was afterward confirmed) to make the English the victims of that day. But Providence so ordered it, as to place their chief councillors and sachems in the tent where ours were seated, by which means they could not destroy one without endangering the other. Second, as the English waited some days for Watanummon (the Pigwacket sachem) to complete their council, it was afterward discovered that they only tarried for a reinforcement of two hundred French and Indians, who in three days after we returned, came among them; having resolved to seize the governor, council and gentlemen, and then to sacrifice the inhabitants at pleasure, which probably they might have done, had they not been prevented by an overruling power.

But notwithstanding this disappointment, they were still resolved on their bloody design; for within six weeks after, the whole eastern country was in a conflagration, no house standing, nor garrison unattacked. August 10th, at nine in the morning, they began their bloody tragedy, being about five hundred Indians of all sorts, with a number of French; who divided themselves into several companies, and made a descent on the several inhabitants from Casco to Wells, at one and the same time, sparing none of every age and sex. As the milk white brows of the grave and ancient had no respect shown, so neither had the mournful cries of tender infants the least pity; for they triumphed at their misery, and applauded such as the skilfulest artists, who were most dexterous in contriving the greatest tortures; which was enough to turn the most stoical apathy into streams of mournful sympathy and compassion."[1]

This terrible war, Ralé tells us, was inaugurated by a feast, where two hundred and fifty of his savage neophytes took up the hatchet against the English settlers. Before starting on their bloody errand, he says that he assembled them at confession, and admonished them to observe the laws of war and to abstain from unnecessary cruelty, an admonition which was mockery itself, however masked by moral sentiment. But were this sentiment genuine, the tone which he employs in recounting the prowess of his neophytes is not reassuring, for he tells us, that immediately after receiving his admonition, they rav-

---

[1] *Vide* The History of the Wars of New England with the Eastern Indians, by Samuel Penhallow, Esq., Boston, 1859, p. 16 *et seq.*

aged "more than twenty leagues of country, where there were hamlets and houses," and "in a single day swept away all that the English had there," and "killed more than two hundred of them." One might suppose that these were soldiers that were killed, as he says in a preceding paragraph that a handful of his savages were equal to two or three thousand European soldiers; but no, the larger number of the victims of these heroes, who had so recently partaken of the communion, and received the fatherly admonition to observe the laws of war and abstain from unnecessary cruelty, were helpless women and children. And he continues, after saying complacently that "they carried desolations throughout the land, which belonged to the English," that, "therefore, these gentlemen," using the words with playful sarcasm, persuaded with reason, that in keeping my savages in their attachment to the Catholic faith, I strengthened more and more the bonds which united them to the French, have put in operation all sorts of tricks and artifices to detach them from me."[1]

Could men have had better reason than these afflicted colonists, whose homes were destroyed and wives and children butchered in the most atrocious manner, to resort to tricks and artifices, or even to set

---

[1] *Vide* Letter of Ralé, Oct. 12th, 1723.

a price upon the head of one so destructive to them? Surely not, yet the tricks and artifices, which were uppermost in Ralé's mind, were the sending of a Protestant missionary to the savages with Bibles in their own tongue, and a schoolmaster to instruct them.

Dudley entered into the war with zeal, and carried it into the enemy's country. An expedition was planned against Norridgewock, and Colonel Hilton was dispatched with two hundred and seventy men, in the winter of 1705, to attack it. The weather was severe, and the march on snowshoes laborious, but the party pushed on with persevering energy, and reached the village in good condition, only to find it abandoned. They, however, destroyed it and the chapel which Ralé had built. After the war had raged for four years, Dudley wrote, "Their Priests and Jesuits have gotten the command of all the Inland Indians, and have debauched the Indians of the Province of Mayn, and by their late Trade and discovery of the Messasseppi River, have in a manner made a circle round all the English Colonies, from New England to Virginia, and do every year give the Goverm'ts of New England very great trouble."

And a few months later: "The Post Script of this Letter referring to the Barbarous Method of the French and Indians depending upon them. Scalping the dead that fall into their hands, is upon Account that the French Government have set the Heads of Her Maj^ties Subjects at a Value, sometimes Forty Shillings, sometimes Five pounds, which the Savages cannot challenge without showing the Scalps, as the French have made it in their Order referring thereto. This I have Expostulated and Upbraided Mr. Vaudreuil and Mr. Subercass and every Governour on the French side, and challenged them to tell their own Master if they dare, of such Barbarity used to Christians, but to no effect, and have threatened them to leave their Prisoners in the hands of the Indians as they have done Many of Ours, but have prevailed nothing."[1]

On August 29, 1708, Haverhill was attacked by a band of French and savages, and her only clergyman, the Rev. Benjamin Rolfe, slain.[2] The situation

---

[1] *Vide* Dudley's letters in B. T. New England, vol. 14, S. 26, office of the Public Records, London, Nov. 10, and March 1, 1708.

[2] The Rev. Benjamin Rolfe was born at Newbury in 1662, and graduated at Harvard in 1684, and later was chaplain of a small body of soldiers at Casco. He was married to Mehitabel Atwater, March 12, 1693, just after his call to Haverhill, where he was ordered the January following. It was early on Sunday morning, August 29, 1708, that the savages attacked Haverhill. There were two soldiers in the

was indeed a serious one for New England, and excited grave apprehensions for her future in the minds of the wisest of her people; but after another ten years of war, peace at last came. Ralé heard from Quebec that negotiations for peace were pending, and knowing that news of the signing of the treaty would reach Boston before it could reach Quebec, wrote Capt. Moody as follows:

---

parsonage, but they were panic-stricken and afforded no assistance to Rolfe, who leaping from his bed strove to hold the door against them. Finding this impossible, he fled through the house after being wounded in the arm by a bullet fired through the door, but was overtaken and killed with a hatchet. Mrs. Rolfe was also brained with a hatchet, and her infant torn from her arms and its brains dashed out against a stone near the door. Two children were preserved by being hidden under tubs in the cellar by a faithful servant. Rolfe, his wife and child, were buried in one grave and this epitaph placed upon it: "Clauditus hoc tumulo corpus Reverendi pii doctique viri D. Benjamin Rolfe, ecclesiæ Christi quæ est in Haverhill pastoris fidelissimi; qui domi suæ ad hostibus barbare trucidatus. A laboribus suis requieuit mane diei sacræ quietis, Aug. XXIX, Anno Domini MDCCVIII. Ætatis suæ XLVI. *Vide* History of Haverhill, by George Wingate Chase, Haverhill, 1861, pp. 220, 228 *et passim;* Bancroft's History of the U. S., Boston, 1841, vol. 3, p. 215 *et seq.;* The History of the Wars of New England, etc., by Samuel Penhallow, Esq., Cincinnati, 1859, p. 55.

in New England. 55

"NANRANTSOAK, 18 *Novemb.* 1712.

"SIR — The Governor-General of Canada acquaints me by his letter which has been brought me some days since, that the last vessel of the King arrived at Quebec the 30 Sept., reports that peace is not yet concluded between the two crowns of France & England, but that they talk strongly of it. That is what he tells me about it.

"And other letters that I have received inform me that Monsieur, the Intendent, who has arrived in this vessel, says, that being upon the point of embarking at Rochelle, some one there received a letter from Monsieur Tallard, which asserted that peace had been made, & that it would be published at the end of October.

"Now they cannot know of it in Canada, but can know of it at Boston, where vessels can come at all seasons, if you know anything of it, I pray you let me know of it, in order, that I may send instantly to Quebec upon the ice, to inform the governor-general of it, so that he may prevent the savages from committing any act of hostility." [1]

---

[1] This letter was inclosed in a letter written by Moody to Gov. Dudley, Dec. 10th, in which he says that "The Indians have made us these visits in my absence, and brought several letters from the Friar,

It would seem that Ralé must have known, that Costebelle, six weeks before this, had dispatched a public envoy to Boston under the protection of a passport, with a letter of precisely the same tenor as the above; but be this as it may, the savages were as anxious for peace as the colonists, and must have realized the fact that they were in danger of being ground to pieces between the opposing forces; hence on the 11th of July, 1713, exactly three months after the signing of the Treaty of Utrecht, representatives of the different tribes assembled at Portsmouth to enter into a treaty of peace.

Asking that the war might cease, the savages agreed to forbear all acts of hostility toward the English, and never again to enter into "any treasonable conspiracy with any other nation to their disturbance; and, as in former treaties, not to avenge themselves if they should suffer wrong at the hands of an Englishman, but to appeal to the government for redress. Confirming the rights of the English to the lands, which they had occupied under deeds

---

which are inclosed." This is a translation made by me from the French text in the office of the Public Records, London. There is a translation, also, in Collections of the Mass. Hist. Society, 2d series, vol. VIII, p. 258, and in Goolds' Portland in the Past, p. 162.

from their ancestors, they confessed as follows; "that we have, contrary to all faith and justice, broken our articles with Sir William Phips, Governor, in the year of our Lord God, 1693, and with the Earl of Bellamont in the year 1699.

And the assurance we gave to his excellency, Joseph Dudley, Esq., in the year of our Lord God, 1702, in the month of August, and 1703, in the month of July, notwithstanding we have been well treated by said governors. But we resolve for the future, not to be drawn into any perfidious treaty or correspondence to the hurt of any of her Majesty's subjects of the crown of Great Britain; and if we know any such, we will seasonably reveal it to the English," and, "being sensible of our great offence and folly in not complying with the aforesaid submission and agreements, and also the sufferings and mischiefs that we have thereby exposed ourselves unto, do in all humble and submissive manner, cast ourselves upon her Majesty for mercy and pardon for all our past rebellious hostilities, and violations of our promises, praying to be received into her Majesty's grace and favor." This treaty, dated on the 13th of July, was signed by the heads of the tribes in presence of Governor Dudley, the Counsellors of Massachusetts; Judge Sewall, Jonathan Corwin, Penn

Townsend, John Appleton, John Higginson, Andrew Belcher, Thomas Noyes, Samuel Appleton, Ichabod Plaisted, John Wheelwright and Benjamin Lynde, Esquires," as well as by the Counsellors of New Hampshire; "William Vaughn, Peter Coffin, Robert Elliot, Richard Waldron, Nathaniel Weare, Samuel Penhallow, John Plaisted, Mark Hunkin and John Wentworth, Esquires." The witnesses to it were "Edmund Quincy, Spencer Phips, Wm. Dudley, Shad. Walton, Josiah Willard" and others. That there might be no plea on the part of the savages in the future that they did not understand the agreement made with their chiefs, a delegation of gentlemen proceeded with the treaty to Casco, where it was read by sworn interpreters, article by article, to the assembled tribes in the presence of their chiefs, whose names it bore. No objections were raised by the tribes to any portion of the treaty, and they signified their unanimous approval of all its provisions by acclamation.[1] At the risk of prolixity, the names of the principal gentlemen present at the making of this treaty are given, and they are a sufficient guar-

---

[1] For the treaty made at Portsmouth, *vide* The History of the Wars with the Eastern Indians, etc., by Samuel Penhallow, Esq., Cincinnati, 1859, pp. 78–81.

antee of its correctness. What shall we say then of the following report of the doings at this conference, which Ralé hastened to make to the governor-general of Canada?

"NORRIDGEWOCK, the 9 *September*, 1713.
SIR:—

Touching the propositions which the Englishmen had before made the savages sign by the Governor of Casco Bay, I have so frequently and so forcibly spoken thereupon to them, that they enter into my meaning, and into speaking of them even to the governor of Casco Bay, about which they had great disputes together, of which this governor informed the governor-general, who in effect did not make them to the savages in the assembly.

This is what he said to the savages, who were there in pretty good number: There were of this village 98; of Penobscot 200; of the river St. John 40; of the Micmaks 20; the governor-general spoke to them in this manner: "Thou, Warraeensitt, I am very glad to see thee, what I am going to say to thee I say to all the others; that I am very glad that thou hast returned into my hands the prisoners which thou hast made; if any are found of thine among us I will restore them to thee.

Thou knowest already that the land which is beyond the great lake is fair, and is not bloody. The kings are at peace, and have smoothed the ground, and this was done in the moon during which thou wast fishing; that is, the April moon.

The Frenchman gave us Plaisance, Port Royal and the land about them, reserving only the river where Quebec is situated. The land here is very fair, — showing some papers, — behold these which have caused it to be stained with blood. I put these papers in the earth to the end that they appear no more, I now turn the land upside down that the blood may no more appear. If thou wishest, the English who planted here and there the habitations which have been burned, will rebuild them and will dwell there. I pray thee do not hinder them from hunting game, from taking wood according as they shall have need of it. If by chance some unfortunate affair shall happen, do not avenge thyself, make it known and it shall be remedied. Thou knowest at what price thy beaver was during the peace. It shall be the same price as well as the goods. There shall be three places of trade, Pemaquid for those of Penobscot, and the river St. John, and which they may not go beyond. For thee, thou shalt have two of them, Casco Bay and the river. I warn thee also not to pass the places which I name, because there is a bar there all red with wrath from the blow which thou hast struck at them last autumn. I will try to deaden this fire, and when the bar shall be again cooled, I will notify thee of it, and thou wilt be able to pass. Behold what I have to tell thee."

Two of this village, speaking alternately for all those of the assembly, observe what they replied.

" My brother Englishmen, the king, thou sayest, ours and your queen and the others also have smoothed the land beyond the Great Lake and have effaced the blood with which it was covered. That is well and thou thyself overturnest that here, thou turnest it upside down in order that the blood may no more appear, I do not oppose it, that it may be fair and clean, I find it good. I only know while resting quietly on my mat that suddenly some one comes to tell me that our King strikes the Englishman beyond the Great Lake, and sends me his word which says: My son, strike also the Englishman.

I, who hear thee, I come to strike thee. It is not I who come to strike thee, it is my father who strikes thee by my hands.

My father is now at peace with thee, he ceases from strife with thee and I also, cease from striking thee, that the land may be fair and smooth, I am content.

Thou sayest my Brother, that the Frenchman has given thee Plaisance Port Royal and the land about them, reserving to himself only the river where Quebec is situated. He shall give thee what he will, as for me, I have my land which I have given to nobody, and which I will not give, I wish always to be the master of it. I know the bounds and when anybody wishes to dwell there, he shall pay. Let the English take wood, fish or hunt game, there is enough of them for all, I will not hinder them; and if some wicked affair happens, we will do nothing on one side or the other, and we will deliberate."

After which the English threw their hats into the air, making a cry, perhaps of Long Live the Queen, and the Savages replied to them by their *Sakakois*.

The assembly was terminated by a feast of a great ox, which they had killed, a barrel of pork, two barrels of peas, a barrel of flour, two barrels of beer, a great case of brandy and of wine, one of syrup of molasses, three barrels of biscuit, which two men could not clasp, some knives, and this is what has passed in this country to speak of at the beginning of August.

As it is extremely difficult still to find here workmen and provisions for them, I am compelled to let the Savages act, who have spoken to the English in order to have some. These here having learned that those of Penobscot had left for Quebec, where they went to seek powder which they are accustomed to give them, these leave to the number of 4 or 5 canoes hoping that you will do them the same favor.[1]

It is impossible to reconcile these conflicting accounts of the conference. The treaty which embodies its subject-matter, as a sufficient guarantee of its correctness, bears the names of a large number of the most honorable men of New England; but if this guarantee were wanting, we have, as the result of the conference, the spectacle of the settlers, who survived the war, returning to the desolated country and rebuilding their ruined homes, erecting mills and setting on foot various enterprises, which we may be sure they would not have done had the savages taken the position at the conference which Ralé reports them to have assumed. But this is not all. As soon as the articles of peace were known to have been signed at Utrecht, the savages went to Casco and anxiously requested that a conference should be held there. This request the governor would not accede

---

[1] For the letter in French, of which this is a translation made by the author, *vide* " Lettre du R. P. Rasle a Monsieur le Gouverneur General." Collection de Manuscrits, etc., vol. 11, pp. 562–564.

to, not "being willing so far to condescend," and "ordered" a conference at Portsmouth, to which place the savages submissively went. The reader can form his own conclusion as to which account is entitled to credence.

A few years of peace enabled the hardy English colonists to again take root in the soil of Maine. New hamlets sprang up on the sites of old ones; trading posts were established on the frontiers, and adventurous men planted their rude cabins near by.

Uninfluenced by the fact that Acadia had been ceded back to England, this was regarded by the neighboring French with jealous eyes; and although France and England were enjoying a season of peace and amity, the French rulers of New France ceased not to plot against the welfare of their English neighbors, and to excite the jealousy of the savages against them, by making them feel that the English were usurpers of their territorial rights.

This was easy of accomplishment. The Indians had loose ideas of territorial proprietorship; even tribes had no defined territorial limits. All the land far and near belonged to the wild band, which for the time, could hold it against others, and although Englishmen might possess title deeds to lands from chiefs of tribes, the savages did not feel bound to respect them; indeed, where rights to land were so common, and dependent altogether upon absolute possession, we cannot wonder that men, who had had no part in the conveyance of land held by their tribe, should pay scant respect to titles given by chiefs or others, to whom the common rights had never been ceded.

Listening to Begon, the intendant, and Vaudreuil, the governor of New France, whose treachery and falsehood so conspicuous in his letters will forever doom him to disgrace, Ralé lent his powerful aid in forwarding their plans. "With the savage," wrote Vaudreuil to the French minister, quoting a sentiment of Father de la Chasse, "temporal interest serves as a vehicle to faith;" and he, therefore, bestowed upon them presents, not the least valuable of which were guns and other weapons to be used against the English settlers, with whose government France was then at peace; and in the same letter he adds, "war with the English is more favorable to us than peace."[1] This was the keynote to what fol-

---

[1] Mais comme le marque le Père De la Chasse, la grâce parmi les Sauvages a toujours besoin de la coopération de l'homme, et parmi eux l'intérêt temporel sert de véhicule à la foi. *Je ne doute pas, Monseigneur, que vous fassiez attention à ce que j'ai l'honneur de vous marquer à ce sujet.* . . . Il y a

lowed, and Ralé, who boasted that the savages held no council without calling him to it, and if he approved, responded that it was well, and that, for any considerable wrong done to them, he would tell them they might make war, caught the note and responded to it.¹

The people of New England have been charged with unreasonable enmity to Ralé, but that he might have been received in a friendly manner by his English neighbors, if he had refrained from inciting the savages against them, is probable. Only a few months before the conference at Arrowsic, he visited the place, and was received in a friendly manner. He was suffering from gout and rheumatism in his shoulders, and sought the Rev. Hugh Adams, who not only ministered to the souls, but to the bodies of the poor frontiersmen.

---

longtemps que j'ai prévu ce qui se passe adjourd 'hui, et j'ose dire que par rapport non seulement aux sauvages, mais encore à toutes les nations qui sont dans nos intérêts, que la guerre avec l'Angleterre nous étoit plus favorable que la paix." Lettre de Monsieur de Vaudreuil au Ministre, Québec, le 16 September, 1714. Collection de Manuscrits, etc., vol. 3, p. 5.

¹ *Vide* Lettres Edifiantes et Curieuses, XVII Recueil à Paris, MDCCXXVI, p. 293 *et postea*. He also made the same assertions to Governor Shute, and on other occasions, thereby voluntarily assuming responsibility for their acts.

Some years before, Ralé had fractured his right thigh and left leg by a fall, and suffered from bad surgery, which, perhaps, aggravated his present trouble. The suffering Jesuit was received with friendly interest by his Puritan brother, and not only hospitably entertained, but treated with such skill, that in a short time he was able to return to his people quite restored to his ordinary health.

This kind treatment and cure, Adams firmly believed would effect a revolution in Ralé's feelings toward the English. On his own part he had experienced a change of sentiment. Intercourse with the blackrobed stranger, of whom he had heard so much that was bad, had revealed to him a man like himself, possessed of human sympathies and aspirations for the elevation of mankind, and he had grown to regard him, not only with a considerable degree of respect, but of kindly esteem. Feeling thus he confidently believed that his patient would thenceforth exert his influence for peace, but we shall see that he little understood the motive which dominated the Jesuit's life.

That immediately after leaving the tender care of the sentimental Adams, he resumed his efforts to prevent English settlement on the Kennebec, we know from Flynt, who, under date of Sept. 9th, 1716, records as follows: "the Fryar wrote in the Name of Eastern Indians a Letter to the Govern^t complaining that by building forts in the Eastern Country we acted in peace as tho' 'twere war & o^r Settlements there were on the Indian's Land, Captn Moody & Mr. Wells were sent to them, wch the Fryar understanding dispersed the Indians, and would not appear himself, but left Moxis, Bomozene & some others to talk with Captn Moody at Kenebeck, who said they had talk in the spring to the same purpose, but they did not know the Fryar had wrote the Letter."[1]

Shute succeeded Dudley in the governorship of Massachusetts in 1716, and as soon as he had established himself in his office, he took the necessary steps to have a conference with the Eastern savages. A convention was therefore appointed to be held at Arrowsic Island, at the mouth of the Kennebec, and there the savages of the different Eastern tribes began to assemble early in August, 1717.

On the afternoon of the 9th of August, there lay moored opposite Arrowsic Island a man of war and two other vessels, with the English flag flying at

---

[1] *Vide* the manuscript journal or "Commonplace Book" of Henry Flynt, in Archives of the Massachusetts Historical Society.

their peaks, and on a green slope near Watt's house, the principal mansion of the place, was spread an ample pavilion.

Not far away on another island, were a number of rude booths carelessly constructed of green boughs, amid which was a restless swarm of painted savages, who were awaiting the signal for the conference to begin.

Shute with his councillors and friends, among whom were, Samuel Sewall, a staunch friend of the savages, Andrew Belcher, Edmund Quincy, Samuel Penhallow, John Wentworth, the Rev. Joseph Baxter and wife, and many others, had sailed from Boston on the evening of the 1st, and had crept leisurely along, landing at Falmouth, which had begun again to rise from its ashes, at Cousin's Island and Chebeague, enjoying the summer voyage in spite of the straitened quarters to which they were confined. As they now stood on the fresh lawn in front of Watt's house, Shute and his officers arrayed in brilliant uniforms, a gun was fired, and the English flag flew up the staff and floated over the pavilion.

This was the signal for the opening of the conference, and instantly a number of birch canoes shot out from the bushy shores of Puddlestone Island, and were paddled rapidly toward the place of meeting. The foremost canoe bore the English colors at its prow, and these the savages, when they landed, bore before them in sign of their subjection and loyalty to King George. Shute had seated himself under the pavilion with his suite about him, and as the painted and befeathered chiefs, who had been the terror of the settlers, advanced and "made their reverence" to him, he gave them his hand in token of friendship.

Then Capt. John Giles and Samuel Jordan, laying their hands upon a Bible, were sworn by Judge Sewall to faithfully and truthfully interpret between the parties, and the conference was opened.

Shute began gracefully by expressions of goodwill, and, referring to the treaty at Portsmouth and the ratification of former treaties, assured his savage hearers that he should "build on that foundation," and informed them, that since this good treaty was made, the English crown had descended to King George, and that it was in his name that he now addressed them.

He reminded them of the friendship existing between the French and English, and told them that the subjects of King George were happy in his government, on account of its wisdom, justice and kindness, "His Majesty consulting the common well-fare of His People as to their Religion, Civil Liberties, Trade and every other thing." This good and wise prince, he asserted, was their king as well as the king of the English people, who would always treat them as fellow subjects, and warned them not to listen to "contrary insinuations."

The king and English people he told them were "Christians of the Reformed Protestant Religion," and holding up a Bible, declared it to be the only rule of the Englishman's "Faith and Worship, and Life." Turning to the Rev. Joseph Baxter, who, inspired by the example of Eliot, had left his church at Medfield to become the missionary of the savages, he expressed the hope, that they would treat him with respect and affection, not only "for the sake of the King's Government, but of his own Character. He being a minister of Jesus Christ, our only Lord and Saviour."[1]

---

[1] The following is taken from his Journal: "I was born in Brantry, June 4, 1676. Baptized at Brantry by the Rev. Mr. Moses Fisk, June 11, 1676. Admitted to my first degree, July 5, 1693. Received to full communion with the Church of Christ at Brantry, March 4, 1694. Preached my first sermon at Brantry, Nov. 11, 1694. Preached at Medfield the first time, Nov. 25, 1694. Was called to settle at Medfield, April 26, 1695. Came to live at Medfield, Jan. 14, 1695. Was admitted to a second degree, July

Continuing, he declared that the English settlements were made for their mutual benefit; that the savages would have the advantage of the "Neighborhood and Conversation" of the English, whom he had ordered to be kind and just to them, and if they had occasion to complain of unfair treatment, he would see that justice was rendered them; that he would protect and assist them, for he desired that they should "look upon the English Government as their great and safe shelter."

Giving his hand to the sagamores in token of his sincerity and affection, he held up an English and Indian Bible, and informed his savage hearers that he should leave them with their missionary for their instruction, whenever they desired to be taught, and that the missionary, and the schoolmaster who was to be sent to them, would reside in the vicinity.

Having finished his address, the governor drank the king's health to Moxus, the chief sagamore, in which all the savages joined.

Then Wiwurna gravely arose and said that he was appointed to speak in the name of the other chiefs.

1, 1696. Was ordained at Medfield, April 21, 1697. Was married to Miss Mary Fisk, daughter of Rev. Moses Fisk of Brantry, Sept. 16, 1697. He closed a most busy and useful life in 1745, in the sixty-ninth year of his age, and forty-eighth of his ministry.

"We are glad," he said, "of this opportunity to see your Excellency, when the Sun shines so bright upon us, and Hope the Angels in Heaven rejoice with us; We have been in Expectation of this favor ever since we received your Excellency's Letter in the Winter. We are not now prepared to answer what your Excellency has said to us; But shall wait on your Excellency again to Morrow."

The conference then adjourned, the governor promising the savages an ox for their dinner, for which they expressed thanks. On the forenoon of the next day the flag was again raised on the pavilion, and the savages reassembled before the governor and his attendants.

"It is a great favor of God we have this Opportunity to wait on your Excellency, and we have our Answers ready," said Wiwurna. He then ratified and confirmed former treaties, the governor having the principal articles read to the savages, who declared that they remembered and acknowledged them.

Wiwurna then continued, that the chiefs having considered the governor's expressions in favor of "Love and Unity," they admired them; that their expressions pleased God and they hoped that the governor would act according to them.

Shute, who was a stickler for royal authority, and

like many who were in official position somewhat heady and impatient, broke in to assure the savages, that if they carried themselves properly with respect to " Duty and Allegiance to King George," he should do so, and Wiwurna continuing, hoped that hard feelings might be laid aside, and hearty friendship prevail; that the savages were glad of Shute's appointment to the governorship of New England, and that, though so new a comer, he knew so much about New England affairs; telling him, however, that his predecessors had regarded the savages as under no other government but their own.

Shute, who had interrupted Wiwurna several times, abruptly exclaimed " How is that?"

Wiwurna, praying leave to speak out, explained that the governor had been pleased to say that they must be obedient to King George, and that they should be if they liked the offers made them. To which Shute replied, that they *must* be obedient to the king, and then they would have "all just Offers and Usage."

Wiwurna promised obedience, if the savages were not molested in the improvement of their lands, which Shute declared they should not be, and that the English must not be disturbed in their rights. They were pleased, said Wiwurna, at being permitted to make mention of wrongs suffered; but Shute returning to the principal question at issue, which Wiwurna seemed to be adroitly avoiding, pressed the point that the savages must desist from pretensions to lands belonging by purchase to the English.

Wiwurna, still evading the point, begged leave to proceed in due order with his answer, which request being granted, he promised, that if the savages suffered wrong they would not avenge themselves but apply to the governor for redress, and to acquaint him if they were attacked by foreign tribes, against whom, he hoped, their young men might defend them.

With blunt generosity Shute exclaimed, that when they wanted help his young men should assist them, for which rather hasty offer Wiwurna thanked the choleric governor, but declared that no complaints should be made "without real proof nor for any frivolous matter."

Wiwurna then made a statement, which should be especially remembered, for it was made voluntarily and after mature deliberation by the able spokesman selected by Ralé's savages to uphold their cause, and which so flatly contradicts the position which the priest constantly assumed, and which he employs so much pathos in setting forth in his correspondence, to the effect that the English were trespassers upon the territory of the savages, having thrust themselves upon them against their wishes.

"This place," said Wiwurna, "was formerly Settled and is now Settling at our request; And we now return Thanks that the English are come to Settle here, and will Imbrace them in our Bosoms that come to Settle on our Lands." Again Shute interrupted, taking offense at the word "our," and exclaimed, "They must not call it their Land, for the English have bought it of them and their Ancestors."

"We pray leave to proceed in our Answer, and to talk of that matter afterwards," replied Wiwurna, "We Desire there may be no further Settlements made, We shan't be able to hold them all in our Bosoms, and to take care to Shelter them, if it be like to be bad Weather, and Mischief be Threatened." This objection probably refers to new settlements in places which had not been occupied, for Shute does not appear to have taken notice of it. "All people have a love for their Ministers," continued Wiwurna, "and it would be strange if we should not love them, that come from God. And as to Bibles your Excellency mentioned, We desire to be Excused on that point. God has given us Teaching already, and if we should go from that, we should displease God. We are not capable to make any Judgment about Religion." This last sentence shows the hand of Ralé, who was undoubtedly present but did not show himself to the English. Its counterpart may be found in his letter to Baxter a few days later. Having disposed of the Protestant missionary and his Bibles, Wiwurna skilfully sugared the disagreeable subject with regrets and compliments, like the adroit diplomat that he was.

"Your Excellency," he said, "was not sensible how sick we were yesterday to see the man-of-war ashore. We were so faint we could not Speak out with strength, and we are now very glad the Ship is well. We are very glad to wait on your Excellency and to tell you That we sent our young Men early this Morning to see if the Ship was well, and we were very glad to hear she was."

Shute, doubtless enjoying the humorous prevarication, thanked them for their respect for his majesty's ship, but when Wiwurna began to string together good wishes for fair winds and propitious weather for his return, and a safe passage down the river, Shute thought it time to bring the wily savage back to the main point, namely, the right of the English to occupy the lands purchased of former chiefs, whose deeds he had brought for their inspection, and he pointed his demand with a complaint of their lawless acts. To all this Wiwurna gave no answer but gravely asked for time that the chiefs might consult and frame their reply, which Shute readily granted, but informed them that he should expect a positive answer in the afternoon in relation to the English right of settlement, and as their fierce dogs had done damage to the settlers' cattle, he demanded that they should muzzle them when in the neighborhood of cattle.

The conference reassembled at three o'clock in the afternoon, and Wiwurna gave the result of the deliberation of the chiefs, to the effect that they would cut off their lands "as far as the Mills and the coasts to Pemaquid."

"Tell them," said the governor, impatiently, that "we desire only what is our own, and that we will have it. We will not wrong them, but what is our own we will be Masters of."

Wiwurna, without replying to this, said that at the treaty at Casco it was promised that no more forts should be made, and Shute replied that forts were for their mutual protection, and that King George built forts wherever he pleased in his own dominions as the French king did. That all kings possessed that power, and the governors also whom they appointed.

Wiwurna, now pressed to the point, took up the delicate question of territorial rights, and said that the chiefs did not understand how the lands were purchased; that what lands had been alienated were by gift, whereupon the governor exhibited the Wharton deed, made by former chiefs, which was read to Wiwurna and his associates. To this Wiwurna replied that they had nothing to say about the west side of the Kennebec, but were sure nothing had been sold on the east side. The question of new forts, he said, troubled them. They were willing that the English should continue to possess what they held already, but disliked forts. To this Shute replied that wherever a new settlement was made, he should order the erection of a fort if he thought it proper, and that it was for the security of the savages as well as of the English. "Are any People," he asked, "under the same Government, afraid of being made too strong to keep out enemies?" and he repeated that the English would not take an inch of their land nor part with an inch of their own.

Wiwurna asked if they were to have the privilege of fishing and hunting wherever they wished, and this being answered in the affirmative, the savages, who had grown restive under the sharp interchange of conflicting views, arose abruptly and without taking their English colors left the assembly without the usual courtesies of leave-taking. In the evening, however, they returned bearing a letter from Père Ralé to the effect, that when Vaudreuil, the Canadian governor, was in France, he inquired of the French king if he had ceded the land of the savages to the English, and that he asserted that he had not done so, and would protect them against English encroachments. This was an artful method of influencing the savages against the English, and in view of the articles ceding Acadia to the English crown, was unfair in the extreme. Indignant at his interference in the negotiations between him and the savages, Shute prepared to leave without further attempt to complete a treaty, or as Baxter in his Journal says, he "resolved not to buckle to them, and on ye Lord's Day went aboard, & acted as if he were going away, whereupon the Indians quickly sent on board and desired to speak with ye Governor before he went away," to which the governor replied that he would do so "if they quitted their unreasonable Pretensions to the English Lands, and Complied with what he had said, but not otherwise," and upon receiving their promise to do so, he appointed a meeting on shore at six o'clock in the evening, and, upon their request, restored to them the English colors which they had so carelessly abandoned.

At the appointed hour, the sachems and principal men assembled bearing their English flag, but Wiwurna they had left behind, "because," they said, practicing a little diplomatic fiction, "he has behaved himself so unproperly yesterday."

This time Querebemit was their orator, and he expressed the sorrow of the people for their former rude carriage, and prayed for forgiveness, adroitly reminding his excellency, that he had himself said, that "if anything should happen amiss it should be rectified."

The governor assenting to this, Querebemit confirmed in behalf of his people the former agreements relative to English settlement on the Kennebec, and said, that they desired them to settle as far up the river as they had ever settled, and in token of their sincerity presented a belt of wampum to the governor, with the statement that they desired to live in peace. To this the governor replied, that the English would not begin a quarrel, and the savage orator reiterated fervently the hope that "by the favor of God" they might "always live in Peace and Unity;" a sentiment to which the governor made response "We pray the same."

"If any of our People," continued Querebemit, should happen to be out in Cold and Stormy Weather, we desire the English to shelter them. We shall always do the same for the English, and God Almighty hears us say it." "It is doing like Christians," exclaimed the governor, and Querebemit presenting another belt of wampum, again repeated, "What I have said God Almighty hears:" and responded Shute, "We say the same, what is done is done in the presence of God."

Shute now called the attention of the savages to some of their "miscarriages," but Querebemit's mind was evidently averse to dwelling upon the past, being occupied with thoughts of future advantages, and he became voluble on the theme of liberal supplies of provisions and ammunition; a trading house, and Mr. Minot, "a good natur'd Man" to manage it; "Interpreter Jordan," "a good Lock Smith," and so forth. These were all requested and readily promised by the complacent governor. To the treaty made at Portsmouth several articles were added, and that everything might be understood, the treaty was read to them by Jordan, article by article, "And they all readily & without any Objection Consented to the whole."

The additions made to the treaty at Portsmouth were as follows:

"*George Town on Arrowsick Island in His Majesty's Province of the Massachusetts Bay, in New England, the* 12*th Day of August,* 1717, *in the Fourth Year of the Reign of Our Sovereign Lord George, by the Grace of God, of Great Britain, France & Ireland, K. J. N. G., Defender of the Faith, &c.*

"*We the Subscribers being Sachems and Chief Men of the several Tribes of Indians belonging to Kennebeck, Penobscot, Pigwacket, Saco, and other the Eastern Parts of His Majesty's Province aforesaid, having had the several Articles of the foregoing Treaty distinctly Read and Interpreted to us, by a Sworn Interpreter, at this time, Do Approve of, Recognize, Ratify and Confirm all, and every the said Articles (excepting only the Fourth and Fifth Articles, which relate to the Restraint, and Limitation of Trade and Commerce which is now otherwise managed.*)

"*And whereas some rash & inconsiderate Persons amongst us, have molested some of our good fellow Subjects the English in the Possession of their Lands, and otherwise ill-Treated them, We do Disapprove & Condemn the same, and freely Consent that our English Friends shall Possess, Enjoy, & Improve all the Lands, which they have formerly Possessed, and all which they have obtained a Right & Title unto: Hoping it will prove of mutual & reciprocal Bene-*

fit & Advantage to them & us, that they Cohabit with us.

"*In Testimony, and Perpetual Memory whereof We have hereunto set our Hands & Seals, in behalf of ourSelves, & of the several Tribes of the Indians, that have delegated us to appear for, and Represent them the Day and Year afore mentioned.*"

This instrument was signed by twenty of the sachems and principal savages, and was witnessed by several English gentlemen and young Indians of note in their tribes, after which "the Sachems and Chief Men came with great respect & offered his Excellency their hands; one of them declaring that they Desired the Peace might continue as long as the Sun & Moon should endure." The conference then closed as usual with presents to the savages and dancing by the young men of the tribes present.[1]

The establishment of a Protestant missionary at Arrowsic to teach the savages in the vicinity, or who

---

[1] On the return of the governor to Massachusetts, a report of the conference was made public in a pamphlet having this imprint: BOSTON: printed by *B. Green*, Printer to His Excellency the GOVERNOR & COUNCIL. And sold by *Benj. Eliot*, at his shop below the Town house, 1717. It has been reprinted in the Collections of the Me. Historical Society, vol. 3, pp. 359–375.

resorted there, was enough to intensify the animosity of Ralé against the English, and the savages, understanding the situation, took delight in adding fuel to the flame. Although Ralé well knew the deceptive character of the savages, for "Nothing," he says, is "more dissembling than an Indian's News; he will tell pleasing News for drink or a better bargain," he accepted as true the idle tales, which they carried to him respecting the preaching of the Protestant missionary, and he wrote him what he denominates, "une lettre honnête," stating, in the words used by the savages at the conference a few days before, that his "Christians knew how to believe the truths which the Catholic Faith teaches, but knew not how to dispute about them," and he accompanied his letter with a "memorial of about a hundred pages," in which he says: "I proved by Scripture, by tradition, & by theological reasons the truths which he had attacked by stale enough pleasantries."

Baxter, when he received Ralé's letter, was on the point of returning to Boston. The manner in which he met the priest's unwarranted attack, compares well with what we know of the dignified character of the man. The cause to which he had devoted his life, and for which he toiled until death arrested his labors, was too important in his estimation to permit him to waste precious time in unprofitable theological disputation, and he replied in a letter, the brevity of which elicited a complaint from Ralé, who also affected to find it so illiterate as to be understood only, "by dint of reasoning," a charge which is unsupported by fact.

The dignified course adopted by the Protestant minister, whom Ralé to increase the lustre of his triumph denominates "the ablest of the Boston ministers," in spite of his alleged illiteracy, was not appreciated by the disputatious priest, who promptly returned to the charge, and although the letter which he had received was so brief, he undertook the undignified task of pointing out its blunders, "je relevois les defauts de la sienne." This letter, Ralé informs us, remained unanswered for two years, and then, he says, the writer, "without entering into the matter," was contented to reprove him for having "l'esprit chagrin & critique,— la marque d'un temperament enclin a la colere." The boastful spirit of Ralé, so often exhibited in his writings, is illustrated in the closing paragraph relating to this affair. The Rev. Joseph Baxter was not a resident missionary on the Kennebec, but made temporary visits to that dangerous outpost, a portion of his time being devoted to missionary work farther west; but Ralé would have his nephew believe that he drove Baxter away by overcoming him in theological disputation; for he says, "Thus ended our dispute, which sent away the Minister, & which rendered abortive the project that he had formed of seducing my Neophytes."

The fallacy of this claim is so apparent even in Ralé's own account of the affair as to need no other refutation.[1] That Protestant missionary effort was productive of little result at this period is not strange. The difference between the two forms of worship, Roman Catholic and Protestant, is sufficient to account for this. The Roman ritual with its pomp and glitter, preserved in some degree even in

---

[1] The letters of the Rev. Joseph Baxter to Ralé, which have been preserved, are reproduced in the Collection of Documents at the end of this volume, as well as a *fac simile* page of one of them, that the reader may form an idea of the justness of his adversary's criticism. The neatness and precision of the writing are an indication of a careful and well-trained mind. It would be strange, indeed, if the Latin of a New England minister in the early part of the eighteenth century, did not differ in some particulars from that of a Romanist taught in France, and by whom the language was in daily use; but however great the differences might have been, as the Puritan divine well said, an aptitude in conjugating Latin verbs had little to do in saving savage souls.

the wilderness, was attractive to the savages, and they regarded with contempt the simplicity so dear to New England Protestantism. It may well be doubted, however, if any of the missions among the savages at this time were productive of much sound spiritual fruit. The wild neophyte had no conception of the second of the dual prescripts, for if there was anything which he cherished in his heart of hearts, it was hatred of an enemy. Anything like mercy to a foe was, in his creed, unmanly and degrading; hence, the so-called Christian convert could gloat over the most cruel tortures inflicted upon a helpless prisoner, and immediately participate in religious exercises with apparent zest. This leads us to doubt the genuineness of many of the conversions, which the missionaries of this period claimed to have made, and to ascribe their belief in them to a fervor of sentiment, which gave a fictitious coloring to facts.

This seems not less probable when we consider a prevalent condition of mind, which seriously regarded strange portents, the agency of witchcraft in human affairs, and other unrealities quite as fanciful, a condition of mind not confined to any nationality or religious class, and revealing a credulity in some cases altogether fatuous. The mysterious solitude of vast forests; the presence of a wild and uncouth people, suggestive almost of kinship to infernal powers;· the lack of mental attrition with men possessing well-trained faculties, would, in themselves, influence minds friendly to speculation, and affect judgment in all matters *in penetralia mentis.*

If we may believe his converts, Ralé entertained a belief in omens and visions quite as fantastical as some of his contemporaries on the English side; but little of this nature respecting him has been recorded,[1]

---

[1] This appears from the Journal of Rev. Joseph Baxter, of Medfield. He says under date of Oct. 27, 1717: "I preached at George Town. I had an account from Captn Giles, of his being informed by ye Indians yt the Jesuit still predicted yt ye world would soon come to an end, yt it would be in 49 days." Some weeks before he recorded, that certain Indians had related to him a similar prediction, and April 23, 1718, "I discussed with Three Indians, one of them gave an account likewise of an apparition that the Jesuit at Norridgewock saw, who, Lying alone in his wigwam, awaked in the night, and saw a great Light, as if his wigwam had been on fire, whereupon he got up & went abroad, and after some time he returned to his wigwam & went to sleep again, and after a while he awaked, and felt as it were a hand upon his throat, yt almost choaked him, & saw a great light again, and heard a voice saying: "It is vain for you to take any pains with these Indians, your children, for I have got possession of them. The Jesuit likewise said, yt there was a Letter brought to him,

and this comes from savage sources too unreliable for evidence. Knowing the superstition of the savage mind he may have bent it to a useful purpose.

Although peace between the French and English continued, the situation of the frontier settlers was painful in the extreme. They were continually harassed by rumors of savage outbreaks, and after getting their rude cabins erected, and the land about them cleared, many would abandon them and seek safer places of abode. Many of the savages were friendly and desired the English to settle near them. One of them remarked to Capt. Giles at Brunswick, that he did not understand what the French governor meant "by hindring ye English from settling here unless he is afraid y^t we shall live too happy together."[1]

A short time after, Capt. Westbrook, at the block house at St. George, showed a number of Kennebec which was written in the name of an Indian yt was dead, wherein he declared yt he was now burning in a most horrible fire. He shewed this Letter to the Indians, but first tore off the name yt was subscribed, & did not let them know who he was. The letter was written in ye Indian Tongue. This Apparition, he said, was about forty days ago." A copy of this Journal made by the Hon. Joseph Williamson may be found in the archives of the Me. Historical Society.

[1] *Vide* Journal of the Rev. Joseph Baxter of Medfield, archives of the Me. Historical Society.

savages the letter written by Ralé to Governor Shute, already spoken of, and which was written in the names of all the savages, and he read to them the threats made to burn the settlers' houses; "whereupon they said y^t Patrahows, *i. e.*, the Jesuit Lied, and he was very wicked, &c., and y^t They desired always to live in friendship and Brotherhood with the English." Soon after, Westbrook had an opportunity to show this letter to some Penobscot chiefs, who, also, expressed ignorance of it, and declared their desire to live with the English "as Brothers." But this was not to be permitted. In the spring of 1719, John Minot and Joseph Heath were sent by Governor Shute with a message to the natives of Norridgewock, and after their return, affidavit was made that the natives asserted that they were continually urged by Ralé to attack the English settlements; that King George was not the right king, that he came in at the back door, and that there was "Another, who was the right heir to the crown."[1]

---

[1] *Vide* Maine Historical Quarterly for 1890, p. 372; Depositions of Lewis Bane, Esq., and John Minot, mercht.; also, Collection Mass. Historical Society, 2d series, vol. VIII, p. 265; Letter of Joseph Heath and John Minot to Gov. Shute as follows: "After the Jesuit had talk't with us as before inserted in the name of the Indians (as he said we told the

This report, with the threatening attitude of the savages, alarmed the English, and awakened animosity, for awhile dormant, toward Ralé, and the General Court passed a resolve to send a hundred and fifty men to Norridgewock to compel the savages to make amends for their depredations upon the settlers, and to arrest Ralé and take him to Boston. The Council, however, wishing to avoid war if possible, did not assent to this resolve, and it was set aside.

Though fickle and unreliable, the savages dreaded war with the English, whose power they realized; but Ralé was advised by Vaudreuil to urge them to prevent English settlement. Their naive reply was a request for the French king to do so, and that they

---

principall Indians thereof, who said the Jesuit had told us wrong storeys, and calling a councell declaired they did not consent to what the Jesuit said, and that he spoke his mind and not theirs, and that they did not imploy him to write any letter for them, and that if he sent any letters at any time, they desire your Excellency would receive them as his letters and not theirs. Its our humble oppinions that the Fryer is an incendiary of mischief amongst these Indians and that were it not for his pernicious suggestions, your Excellency would not meet with any trouble from them." This statement is in harmony with repeated utterances of the savages to others who have left similar records.

had granted to the English the privilege of coming "half way from Sagadahock to Norridgewock." But they were not permitted to remain at peace even if they would. Vaudreuil and Begon were especially instructed by the king, to hinder traffic between them and the English. The cattle of the frontiersmen were killed, and when one of them complained, Ralé wrote Vaudreuil the savage's reply, which he had doubtless inspired. "Complain as much as you wish to the governor; he is not my judge and has nothing to do with me. For the payment of your cattle you should ask him who has told you to build there."[1] The action of the French in exciting the

---

[1] "Pour ce qui regarde ceux de Narantsouaks, je vois par les lettres du Père Raslé qu'ils ne se démentent point. Ce missionnaire me marque par sa lettre du 15 Septembre qu'il avoit reçu, en la finissant, une lettre d'un Anglois qui s'est bôti dans la Rivière de Narantsouak, par laquelle il se plaint que les Sauvages tuent ses bestiaux et demande qu'ils les payent et cessent de les tuer, autrement qu'il s'en plaindra au Gouverneur; et que pour réponse il avoit marqué à cet Anglois qu'il avoit fait assembler les Sauvages pour savoir ceux qui avoient tué ces bestiaux et délibérer du payement; que c'éstoit tout ce qu'il pouvoit faire, et qu'il lui envoieroit la réponse de ces Sauvages, cette réponse est en ces termes:

'Plains-toi tant que tu voudras au Gouverneur, ce n'est point mon juge, et il n'a rien à voir sur moi. Pour le payment de tes bestiaux, tu le demanderas à

savages to prevent the English from settling in Eastern Maine was a terrible wrong. They certainly had as much right to settle there as the French had to settle along their own frontiers, a right which the English did not have the hardihood to question; nevertheless, they persisted in their ungenerous course, and Vaudreuil and Begon wrote home on the 26th of October, 1720, " Father Ralé continues to excite the savages of the Norridgewock mission not to suffer the English to spread over their lands." And the king replied, " His Majesty is gratified with the pains which Father Ralé continues to take to excite the savages of the Norridgewock mission not to suffer the English to establish themselves on their lands." [1]

---

celui qui t'as dit de te bâtir là.' Voilà une reponse vigoureuse, mais il est à craindre que ces Sauvages et ceux de Panaowamské et de la Rivière St Jean ne puissent pas se soutenir contre les Anglois, s'il est vrai comme la Père Raslé me marque que le Gouverneur de Baston va envoyer 200 familles anglaises pour habiter la Rivière Ponaowamské, etc." *Vide* Rapport de Monsieur de Vaudreuil au Conseil. Québec, le 31 Octobre, 1718. Collection de Manuscrits, etc., vol. 3, p. 32.

[1] " Le Père Rálle continue à exciter les Sauvages de la mission de Narantsouak à ne point souffrir les Anglois de s'ôtendre sur leurs terres." "Sa Majesté est satisfaite des soins que le Père Raslé, jésuite, continue de se donner pour exciter les Sauvages de

The church at Norridgewock was completed in the autumn of 1720. Funds had been furnished by the French king to build it, and the work was performed by English workmen. It was at this time that Père Charlevoix wrote to the Duke of Orleans, that Ralé, who had made attempts to prevent the English from settling on the lower Kennebec, had not thought it possible to employ all his authority, since this would have uselessly exposed his life, and would not have prevented the settlement of the English, who, finding out what the Jesuit had done to hinder them, would not fail to put a price on his head, as they did in the case of Father Aubrey, at the beginning of the former war, for the same reason.[1] Yet he was not inactive. A letter which

---

sa mission de Narantsouak, et ne point souffrir que les Anglois s' établissent sur leurs terres. — Sa Majesté approuvera qu'on ne laisse par manquer de munitions les Sauvages de ces trois missions, et qu'on les soutienne en cas qu'ils soient attaqués contre raison par les Anglois." Lettre de Messieurs Vaudreuil et Begon au Ministre. A Québec, le 26, 8 bre, 1720; and Memoire du Roy Aux Sieurs de Vaudreuil et Begon. Versailles, le 8 juin, 1721. Collection de Manuscrits, etc., vol. 3, pp. 48, 54.

[1] *Vide* Collection de Manuscrits, etc., vol. 3, p. 52. Memoire sur les limites de l'Acadia envoyé à Monseigneur le Duc D'Orleans par le Père Charlevoix, Quebec, le 29 Octobre, 1720.

he wrote to Capt. Moody near the close of the year 1719, greatly aroused the indignation of the English. Judge Sewall, under date of March 7, 1720, says that it was read in Council on that date, and calls it "Friar Ralle's railing Letter."[1] The principal portion of the letter has been preserved, which is as follows:

"*Feb.* 7, 1720.

"The Governor (Shute) solicits some Indians to go to England. If they do I shall drive them forever from the Church & the Indians would then remove them from being of their Kindred, for mere External Consenting to it, through Complaisance. I will not receive them in a year: You must know a Missionary is not a Cipher like a Minister. The Indians hold no Council but they call me to it & when they have deliberated ask my thoughts. If I approve, I say that's well, If not, I say so & give my reasons, for we must give them reasons. 'Well,' say they, 'Let it be as our father says,' they in their Councils always having my presence & admitting my correcting, hence the Treaty at Arrowsick could not be admitted in this Village, much less with those at Canada, who, when they heard of it, their people that Live in two

---

[1] *Vide* Sewall Papers, 5th Series, Mass. Historical Society's Collections, vol. 3, p. 245.

great Villages & the Mohawks, the Algonkins, the Hurons, &c., sent two young men hither to disallow & reject it.

"They approve of Nothing but what Ouaourene[1] spoke; he had the word of the Nation & said to the Governor, 'this is what I send thee: thou shalt not go beyond that mill, which I see from hence & among the habitations thou shalt build no fort.' Says the Governor, 'I'll build a hundred If I please.' Then said Ouaourene to his people, 'Let us begone, it's vain talking here.'

"This only that passed at that Treaty was received by the Indians of Canada & this Village, this is also what I govern myself by.

"If the Indians kill Cattle below the Mill towards the seaside they must absolutely pay for them, but from the Mill on this side, I exhort them not to do it,

---

[1] This is the same chief called by the English Wiwurna, and Ralé, artfully assumed that all that took place after Wiwurna left the conference with Shute on the afternoon of August 10th was null; nor did he fail to exercise all his power to prevent the cementing of friendship with the English, even to the extent of excommunication. No wonder that the indignation of the English was deeply aroused at such an extraordinary assumption, although they were not perhaps fully aware of his efforts to prevent friendly relations between them and the Savages.

because you improve the Land against the Consent of the people of the Land, So that whatever was said after the breaking up is Null although it be printed.

"The Indians have Wit for everything which regards them, they speak in their Councils well without studying. The reason is, the Indian has none but his own affairs in his head, the Europeans have many. All Boston is not so certainly informed as I am of every considerable thing that passeth in Europe, so that I am not in pain to refute the false News which the English tell the Indians. When the Governor said to the Indians at Piscataqua, that he had been in the army, and was always victorious, the Indians diverted themselves with it, saying, 'he thinks to fright us;' some said, 'we wish war was begun presently, that we might see If he be such a warrior.'

"The Governor told the Indians at Piscataqua that King George, 'my king' or 'ours' had so Conquered the King of France that he could not Live, If he had not granted him some part of his Land to Live on. The Indians whom I had instructed about the Terms of the peace were Scandalized saying, he would by this take us off from the King of France, that he might attach all to his King, and only scorned him. I should blush to relate their words; for my part, I accuse the interpreter, for you have not one interpreter that can Explain faithfully in the Indian Language: they speak nothing but Gibberish.

"They Enquire about my words: do they intend to unite against me to drive me from my Mission? that would be a retirement from misery, both by the Indians who can't furnish me with Butter or Cheese, but Indian Corn; besides, I shall have the same Merit before God as if I had finished my Life in the misery to which I consented at my coming among the Indians, but, upon my quitting my Mission, It may happen, 'deficiente uno non deficit alter aureus et Simile frendescit virga metallo'. You may likewise think that I sha'n't be made to Leave it for such trifles: whatever you may think you can't move me.

"1. All debates in Indian's Councils, If I approve, it Stands. If not It's changed or Nulled.

"2. Any Treaty with the Governor, particularly that of Arrowsick is Null, If I don't approve it, though the Indians have consented, for I bring them so many reasons against it that they absolutely condemn what they have done.

"3. The English tell them, I have bought of the ancient Indians such and such Lands. I tell them 'twas after this manner, the Englishman offers a bottle of rum for such a tract of Land; the Indians agree; the English ask the Indian's name and writes it down and so the bargain is made, and shown to dazzle the Indian's Eyes; the Indian and English, too, knows this is not buying: furthermore by the Laws of all Kingdoms the Guardians of pupils can't sell or alienate the Estates of the pupils. I say to the Indians you are masters of the Land which God has given you to Live on, but though the English should give all their treasures they can't buy it, because your Children whose Guardians you are, will forever reenter into their Estates: this is a Law established all the world over.

"Moreover if the English had bought the Land in form, you having retaken it three times by force of arms are become masters of it. All this I wrote to Mr. Dudley.

"4. The Indians will that presently & absolutely those that are settled in the river quit it; because I have shown them Evidently, that If they did not make them retire they would Lose their Lands, and, by greater misfortune, their prayers; they are convinced of it now, having added to them that If they did not do it, I would go away from them. I say, then that from the Mill on this side, I will not that there should remain so much as one habitation where several are, only because John Giles bid them sit down there. He does such fine actions; he Loves Ketermogus,[1] a Cipher in the Village, but he's hated by the greater part, wherefore according to my thoughts, the Governor will do well to cause them to withdraw before the Treaty, to save them the shame of being driven away by the Indians, for assuredly, there shall not one remain there.

"The Traders in Brandy to the Indians had by their declarations in Canada a fine set upon them of a thousand Crowns, and he that could not pay it was condemned to the Chain and to be whipped through

---

[1] The reason of Ralé's animosity against this chief was caused by his desire to maintain peaceful relations with the English settlers. He appears to have been an old man at this time, and, in common with many of the older men, to have endeavored to dissuade the younger and more violent men from listening to the bad counsels of the French, foreseeing that war would ultimately be disastrous to his people. He was on friendly terms with Capt. John Giles, the commander of the fort at Brunswick. Taken a captive when a lad by the savages, and having lived with them for a period of eight years, Giles had acquired a knowledge of their language, and, understanding their idiosyncracies, was in a position to exercise a considerable influence over them. This rendered him particularly obnoxious to Ralé, whose declaration that he spoke nothing but gibberish, must be taken with allowance, or placed in the category of statements shown in this work to be unsupported by facts.

the Town. There is no Justice among'st the English, who have never given them any, Even under this Governor, I think to do it myself.

"If Rum drinking continues, the drinker of Rum shall find wherewithall to eat, by suffering him to kill one of the cattle belonging to him that shall have given him drink. And if he won't kill it for fear of being refused it another time, another that is not a drinker shall kill it; this I think to propose to the men, when they come home, and I am sure they'll hear me with pleasure.

"I can't by my Character carry them forth to war, I can absolutely hinder them when they haven't solid reasons for it, but when they have any, I sha'n't hinder them, as for example, to preserve their Land whereon depends their prayers, or any considerable wrong that's done to them, in these cases I'll tell them they may make war.

"The views of your Governor are fine & generous; he desires war, and being a warrior he must not wonder at it, but I'm sure he would be astonished at an Indian war, five forts and many houses in Arrowsick were reduced to ashes in one day.

"The English say it's the Fryer or Mr. Vaudreuil that stirs up war, but 'twi'l be said at the Conference (where I shall be & upon their desire, perhaps, speak for the Indians) 'tis you English, you seize our Lands against our will & thereby take away our prayers, more valuable than our Lands or bodies; you would govern us; I desire your Governor may know this. I am actually composing an ample writing about these things to send to the King of France, that he see what I do to preserve my Indians in their Lands & prayers, which depend thereon; herein I heard the King's designs reported to me by Mr. Vaudreuil, Last fall, and three years before that I should assist the Indians to preserve their Lands & prayers; to move me he has assigned me a considerable pension of 6,000 francs till my death; all this goes away in Good Works; this I suppose comes because your Governor has threatened he will have me taken up, or cause me to quit by writing to his King against me; the Indians told it to Mr. Vaudreuil who wrote it to the Court, since which I am more and more strengthened here.

"I'll cause my book to be printed, presented to the King & the public, that it may be seen what I do for my Children. Shall they be Cheated, driven from their Lands & prayers, & shall not I counsel & defend them; they shall sooner take away my Life than hinder me. The book shall be Embellished with figures of Rhetoric, Epigrams, Poetry, &c. A

Jesuit is not a Baxter or a Boston Minister. I'll describe how the English treat the Indians, killing them & their dogs, dearer to him than his Oxen; would govern him & possess all his Land without his Consent, to his own great profit, and when the Indian says to the English, 'why do you thus' the answer is, 'you offend me, your father bid you say it.'"

This letter, so threatening, so arrogant and so vain, was read by the sober magistrates of Boston with surprise. No men were less likely than they to be intimidated by threats, or moved to regard priestly assumption with respect. They understood now, if they had not before, what they had to expect and the source of their peril was plainly revealed to them.

The method of reasoning, which rendered it impossible for men once in possession of land to ever alienate it under any conditions; no matter if their tenure were by recent conquest, as in this case, or, if alienation were legal, that they possessed the right of taking it back again by force; the proposition to make it lawful, in this instance equitable, for one who purchased intoxicants of another to despoil him of his property or to procure a virtuous friend to do so, that he might secretly continue to profit by the nefarious business as long as possible, might surprise one not familiar with that remarkable body of similar reasonings, long ago formulated and still sanctioned by casuists of Ralé's order; but some of the men who read this "railing letter," though surprised at its assumptions, were as familiar with these reasonings as we are, and as fully realized their significance as we can realize them to-day. Point had been given to this letter not long before its reception at Boston, by the destruction of a house belonging to a venturesome settler on the Kennebec, and the slaughter of cattle, and Ralé had dispatched two chiefs from Norridgewock to inform Vaudreuil of the belligerent attitude of his savages, and that Governor Shute had threatened to send in the spring five hundred men to protect the settlers.

This was communicated to the king at once with the intimation that Shute's threat was probably made to intimidate the savages, who now appeared determined to drive out the English.[1]

Yet as already remarked, the reluctance of the savages to another war with the English could not

---

[1] *Vide* Extract de la Réponse en datte du 26 8bre 1719, faite par Mrs. Vaudreüil Et Begon, cydevant Gouverneur general Intendant en Canada, au Memoire du Roy en datte du 23, May de Ladte anné, in the author's collection of manuscripts.

be readily overcome. This is illustrated by an event which occurred about this time. Their chief Taxous died, and it was necessary to elect his successor.

A council was called at Norridgewock, and thither the wild people, tricked out in barbaric paint and feathers, flocked in large numbers. Should they have war or not, was the uppermost question with the fickle and restless crowds, gathered under the spreading trees, and thronging the open glades about Norridgewock. There were two parties; one, composed of the older and wiser men, was for peace, the other for war. The election of a chief from one or the other of these parties would determine the question.

When the council assembled, the acts of the English, which had been placed in the worst light by the French, were made the pretext for immediate hostilities by the younger and more violent men, but wiser counsels prevailed, and Wissememet, a champion of peace, was elected. A short time after, a friendly conference was held at Georgetown, at which was present not only the chief, whom Ralé calls "Ketermogus, a cipher in the Village," because of his love of peace; but, also, Ouaourene, whom he praises for his hostility to the English, and both not only declared themselves to be friends of peace, but moreover delivered hostages to confirm this declaration.

One who studies carefully the history of the transactions between the English and savages, cannot fail to be impressed with the apparent desire of both for friendly relations; but a treaty was no sooner concluded between them, than the active agents of the French began to make the savages dissatisfied with it.

Ralé, in evident chagrin, wrote Vaudreuil the result of the election. The reply to this letter reveals the odious character of Vaudreuil. He was indignant at the faintheartedness of the savages in making pledges to the English, and thought that active efforts should be made to obtain the aid of the Canadian tribes to awaken their zeal. The new chief was made to feel the displeasure of the French at his pacific attitude; and Ouaourene was flattered and rewarded for displaying his opposition to them. A number of "degraded" savages, friendly to the English, were sent to Quebec by Ralé, and their reception by the governor may be imagined from this passage from his letter to the priest, "You may depend I will make the *degraded*, sensible how much I am discontent with their conduct."[1]

---

[1] *Vide* Begon's letter to Ralé, Quebec, the 14th June, 1721; Board of Trade Papers, New England, bundle T, vol. 17, and Vaudreuil to Ralé, Quebec,

The reception by Gov. Shute of a letter from the savages, in the summer of 1721, increased the public indignation against Ralé. It was in French, signed by the head of the Norridgewocks and eight other chiefs, his allies, so called, and was a threatening protest against English settlement, along the Kennebec. It was certainly, on the face of it, an alarming document, for it represented not only the tribes of Maine, but the Micmacs, Iroquois, Algonkins, Hurons and other more remote tribes, the signatures of whose chiefs had been obtained by the French, and it so plainly revealed the hand of Ralé, that he was believed not only to have instigated, but to have been the author of it. De la Chasse was, however, quite as prominent in its production as his confrère.

We now know, from the correspondence of the chief actors in the affair, the secret history of this document, much of which was concealed from the knowledge of our forefathers. The formation of a peace party among the Norridgewock savages, already spoken of, aroused Ralé to action, and a conference with the English having been determined upon, he planned to prevent the peace party from having a too

---

the 25th September, 1721. *Ibid.*, bundle 10, vol. 16, Office of the Public Records, London, printed by the author in Me. Hist. Quarterly for 1890, pp. 373-377.

prominent part in the conference. As he wrote Vaudreuil, he deemed it necessary to have the peace delegates to the conference outnumbered by the "well intentioned" or in the words of the practical politician of our day, to pack the meeting. Fearing defection even among those who were for war, he dispatched six savages to Canada, to invite their countrymen residing there, and the Hurons of Lorette, "to find" themselves at the proposed conference. Ralé's runners were received by Vaudreuil, who brought them to the villages of St. Francis and Becancourt, to impress upon the savages how injurious to them was English settlement on the frontier. This mission was successful, and they all agreed to join in the conference.

To strengthen affairs at Norridgewock Vaudreuil dispatched thither Father de la Chasse, Superior of the Jesuits, who had served among the Abnakis for a score of years, in order to bring the people there "to one mind," a task which was rendered easier by the vigorous measures which Ralé had adopted at the outset. Having accomplished this task, De la Chasse then returned to Canada, where he assembled his savage neophytes and again set out for Norridgewock, gathering on his way a wild band from the Penobscot and other savage villages; in fact, to the surprise of the English, he succeeded in getting recruits from their dangerous neighbors on the Piscataqua. Having gathered these savages of different tribes to the number of two hundred and fifty; on the 28th of July, 1721; when, be it remembered, France and England were at peace, the two priests, with Castin and Croisel, the latter a French officer, appeared with them opposite Arrowsic,[1] and formally presented the letter in question, which was as follows:

---

[1] La Père Râlé, missionaire à Narantsouak, a informé les Sieurs de Vaudreuil et Begon, le printemps dernier, que sur les représentations qu'il avoit faites aux Sauvages de sa mission de ne pas souffrir que les Anglois continuassent de s'établer au bas de leur revière, ils avoient tué il y a deux ans un grand nombre de bestiaux appartenant aux Anglois et depuis les avoient menacé que s'ils ne se retiraient ils augmenteraiént les actes d'hostilité pour les y forcer; que l'automne dernier it s'est formé deux partés dans ce village dont la moitié a été d'avis de continuer de s'opposer aux établissements des Anglois, et l'autre gagné par eux dans la volanté de souffrir qu'ils s'y établissent. Le sentiment de ces derniers a prévalee; et quatre ôtages ontété envoyés à Baston.

Il leur a aussi donné avis que les Anglois leur ayant indiqué un pourparler pour engager le reste du village à souffrir leur etablissement, il *etait nécessaire que dans ce pourparler le parti des Sauvages bien intentionné fut la plus numbreux* afin de faire revenir à leur sentiment ceux qui avoient été gagnés

" Great Captain of The English :

" Thou seest by the treaty of peace of which I send thee a copy, that thou shouldst live peaceably with me. Is it to live in peace with me to take my land

par les Anglois, et qu'ils fussent tous ensemble parler avec fermeté à l'Anglois pour l'obliger à se retirer de dessus leurs terres.

Comme il y a à craindre que les Sauvages de ce village parlant seuls à l'Anglois ceux que avoient tenu bon jusques à présent ne se laissent gagner par les présents, caresses, menaces et mensonges des Anglois pour parvenir à leur fin, il a engagé six des Sauvages de venir ici inviter les Abénakis et les Hurons de Lorette de se trouver au pourparler. Pour faciliter le succés de cette invitation, le Sieur de Vaudreuil les a mené aux villages de St. François et de Bécancourt où ils ont expliqué combien l'enterprise des Anglois étoit préjudiciable aux intérêts de la nation. Le Sieur de Vaudreuil leur a aussi fait connaître qu'il étoit important que l'Anglois juge par lui même qu'il se les attiroit tous contre lui.

Ces deux villages convinrent d'envoyer à ce pourparler trois canots de St. François et trois de Bécancourt auxquels s'est joint un canot de Hurons de Lorette.

Il a cru aussi devoir engager avec eux le Père La Chasse, Supérieur des Jésuites, qui ayant été pendant 20 ans missionaire des trois villages Abenaquis de l'Acadie les connait bien.

Ce Père a été d'abord à Narantsouak, et après avoir réuni les esprits de tous les Sauvages de cette nation il invita les Sauvages du village de Pan-

despite me ? My land that I have received from God alone, my land of which no King nor strange power has been able, nor can dispose of despite me, that which thou nevertheless hast done for several years, by establishing and fortifying thyself therein against

---

aouamské d'où il a fait aussi avertir ceux de Medocteh et de Penondaky.

Il est revenu ensuite à Narantsouak accompagné de plus de 100 Sauvages de Panouamské et des députés des villages de Medocteh et de Penondaky. Il a fait venir aussi ceux de Pegeonaky qui sont les plus proches des Anglois du côté de Baston.

Ces Sauvages ainsi rassemblés et au nombre de 250 qui représentoient toute la nation Abénaquise et leurs alliés, après avoir tenu Conseil, se sont rendus le 28 juillet dernier, armés devant le Fort Anglois de Menaskous où le pourparler étoit indiqué.

Le Gouverneur de Baston informé du grand nombre de Sauvages qui vouloient lui parler, n'ayant pas osé s'y trouver après s'etre fait attendre pendant 50 jours, les Sauvages sommèrent les principaux officiers des cinq forts et environ 50 des habitants anglois les plus considérables de s'y trouver au défaut du Gouverneur, et y étant venus, ils leur dirent qu'ils eussent à se retirer de leurs terres leur jettèrent les 200 castors par eux promis pour les bestiaux tués et en même temps leur demandèrent où étoient les quatre hommes qu'ils avoient amenés à Boston pour sûreté de ce paiement.

Des Anglois répondirent qu'ils ne pouvoient se retirer des terres sans l'Ordre du Gouverneur qui les y avoit envoyés ; que pour les ôtages ils ne croyoient

my will, as thou hast done in my River of Anmou-kangan, of Kenibekki, in that of Matsidouanoussis, and elsewhere and recently in my River of Anmou-kangan, where I have been surprised to see a fort which they tell me is built by thy orders.

"Consider ; Great Captain ; that I have frequently

---

pas que le Gouverneur les rendît à moins qu'ils n'en envoyessent quatre autres pour gage de leur fidélité à la Couronne d'Angleterre.

Surquoi les Sauvages se recrièrent protestant que c'étoit une imposture ; qu'ils n'avoient donné ces ôtages que pour sûreté des 2co castors, et qu'ils n'avoient jamais consenti de donner des hommes pour quelques bêtes qu'ils avoient eu le droit de tuer pour les obliger de se retirer sur leurs terres.

Après de grandes contestations les Sauvages prièrent le Père de la Chasse de lire leurs paroles déclarant aux Anglois qu'ils les avoient mis en écrit pour envoyer au Gouverneur de Boston puis qu'ils ne pouvoient pas lui parler.

Ouaourné et Pehonuret dirent cette parole, le premier en Sauvage et le second en Anglois, Elle fut dite aussi en latin par le Père de la Chasse, ministre, qui l'expliqua en Anglois ; après ça le Sieur Penhalo un des principaux officiers du Fort de Menaskouk et d'autres officiers reçurent cet écrit signé des marques des Abénakis et des Sauvages leurs alliés dont copie est ci jointe ; ils promirent de l'envoyer au Gouverneur de Baston, ce qu'ils ont fait." *Vide* Collection de Manuscrits, etc. Rapport de Messieurs de Vaudreuil et Begon au Ministre, vol. 3, p. 57.

told thee to retire from off my lands, and I repeat it to thee now for the last time. My land belongs to thee neither by right of conquest, nor by gift, nor by purchase. It is not thine by right of conquest.

"When hast thou driven me from it? and have I not always driven thee from it, every time that we have had war together, which proves that it is mine by many titles.

"It is not thine by gift, The King of France, thou sayst has given it to me; but has he power to give it to thee? am I his subject? The Indians have given it to thee. Some Indians that thou hast over-reached by making them drink, have they power to give it thee to the predjudice of all their nation, who very far from ratifying this gift, which would be necessary to give thee some right, declares it to be vain and illusory? Some have lent thee some places, but know that all the nation revokes these loans, because of the abuse which thou hadst made of them. When have they permitted thee to build forts and to advance thyself as much as thou hast done in their River?

"It is not thine by right of purchase. And thou tellest me a thing that my grandfathers and my fathers have never told me. That they had sold my land when some of them would have sold certain places, which is not so since thou canst not say that thou hast fully paid for the least of the islands which thou wishest to possess. I have the right of recovering property which has not been alienated to my predjudice, and that I have so many times reconquered.

"I wait then thy reply within three sabbath days; if within this time thou dost not write me, that thou hast retired from my land, I will not tell thee again to withdraw, and I shall believe that thou wishest to make thyself master of it in spite of me.

"Furthermore this is not the word of four or five savages, whom by thy presents, thy lies and thy tricks thou canst easily make fall into thy opinions, this is the word of all the Abnaki nation spread over this continent and Canada, and of all the other christian Indians their allies who are expressly assembled at Pemster in order to speak to thee thus about my land, and who, after having awaited thee more than 50 days and my people, that I am surprised that thou hast not sent back to me, contrary to thy word, summon thee alltogether to withdraw thyself from off the land of the Abnakis, that thou wishest to unjustly usurp, and which has for bounds the River Kenibequi, the River which separates it from the land of the Iroquois. I should have the right to reclaim from thee all the space which is between that

River and me, since thou possessest nothing of it only by deceit, but I am quite willing to leave thee in this place, on condition that absolutely no more English shall dwell within a league of my River Pegonakki, nor from this bound along the borders of the Sea which corresponds to all the extent of my land, nor at the mouth of my Rivers, nor in any of the islands, which correspond to my land, which are adjacent and where my canoe can go. If some individual savages addicted to drink tell thee to dwell where thou didst formerly dwell, Know that all the nation disavows this permission and that I will go to burn the houses after having pillaged them.

"By my people who are in Boston, I await thy reply in my village of Nanrantsouak, in French as I write thee. If thou writest me in English I shall believe that thou dost not wish to be understood and that thou wishest to retain my land and my people in spite of me, which I then tell thee to restore to me, because the land is mine, and that for my 4 men I have given ransom for which we are assembled to acquit myself of my word although I owe thee nothing. This is the word of all the Abnaki nation, spread over this continent and Canada and of all the Catholic Indians, Hurons, Iroquois, Micmaks, and other allies of the Abnakis of which the old men and deputies have appeared and spoken at the place called Menaskek, at the river, July 28-1721.

"Know further Great Captain that all the Abnaki nation pronounces void all the deeds which thou hast passed heretofore with the Indians and because they have not been avowed nor received from all the nations, and because they have only been the effect of thy impositions, as in the case of Peskadoe, upon which thou establish thyself so strongly, where thou didst so falsely make the savages understand that thou wast sole master of the land, that the King of France had given thee their country as if a king could give that which is not his.

"Mark the effect of the drink which thou has given in plenty to the Indians, after which they promise thee all that thou wishest.

"Mark the effect of the violence which thou hast exercised against them on several occasions, and quite recently the last winter, when after having called six to speak with thee, on the subject of the cattle which they had killed for thee, and which they had a right to kill for thee in order to oblige thee, by that to withdraw from the land which is not thine, thou madest them enter into a house and immediately surrounded it with near two hundred Englishmen armed with pistols and swords and compelled 4 of them to remain for the cattle killed. Thou hast conducted these 4 men to Boston. Thou hast promised to restore these 4 men by giving thee 200 beavers. The beavers have been given and now thou retainest these men. By what right?

"Signatures of the Abnaki Nation and of the Indians, its allies."[1]

The Rev. Hugh Adams, who had befriended Ralé at Arrowsic, joining in the common indignation, experienced an extraordinary revulsion of feeling. With that mental bias peculiar to the age already alluded to, he prayed that his former patient might be confounded in his wicked designs, and publicly predicted his overthrow.[2] So much in harmony, however,

---

[1] This document has the character, 8, employed by the French Jesuits to represent the sound of the French *ou*. The employment of this character indicates its authorship. I have thought best to omit it and to substitute the letters *ou*.

[2] The Rev. Hugh Adams was graduated at Harvard College in the class of 1697, and the year following removed to South Carolina, where he remained until 1706. In 1707 he settled at Braintree and resided there until 1711, when he removed to Chatham, Cape Cod. In 1716 he was at Arrowsic, but remained there but one year, when we find him settled at Dover, N. H. He died in 1750. *Vide* Proceedings Mass. Hist. Society, vol. 3, pp. 322–326. Collections N. H. Society, vol. 5, p. 135. The History of Cape

Those of Narrantouak

Those of Pentagouet

Those of Narakamigou

Those of Anmissoukanti

Those of Muanbissek

Those of Pegouakki

Those of Medokteck

Those of Kouupahag

Those of Pesmokanti

Those of Arsikantegou

Those of Ouanouinak

Their Allies

The Iroquois of the Falls

The Iroquois of the Mountain

The Algonquins

The Hurons

The Mikemaks

The Montagnez of the Northside

The Papinachois and other neighboring nations

was this with the current thought of the age, that it excited no surprise, a fact which should not be overlooked in our estimate of men and acts connected with the events under consideration.

So bitter had the feeling against Ralé become, that the General Court voted to send a force of three hundred men to Norridgewock to demand his surrender, but owing to the opposition of Judge Sewall, it was not carried into effect. Castin and his son, a half breed, the English had good reason to believe to be conspirators with Ralé in his plots against them. Castin himself still claimed to be in the French service, if we may judge from his application to the king at this time for arrears of pay as a lieutenant, and his son sported the uniform of a French officer. The frequent outbreaks of the savages, and the well known influence of the Castins, made them objects of suspicion, and, an opportunity offering, the young Castin was arrested and taken to Boston, where he was detained for several months, and questioned relative to his participation in recent hostilities; but as nothing could be proved against him, he was returned to his people. There is nothing on record to show

---

Cod, by Frederick Freeman, Boston, 1862, vol. 2, pp. 593-595. The prediction alluded to, may be found in the Massachusetts Courant for December, 1722.

that he was not treated with due consideration, yet some writers would have us believe that his arrest was the cause of subsequent acts of hostility, which, in fact, were but a continuance of similar ones. Ralé, however, was a too conspicuous fomenter of mischief, to be permitted by the English to continue his dangerous designs against them, and in the winter of 1721-22, Colonel Thomas Westbrook was dispatched to Norridgewock, to apprehend and take him to Boston. As Westbrook was painfully making his way up the river, he was discovered by Indian hunters, who, divining his purpose, struck across the forest to alarm the village.

Unsuspecting danger, Ralé was alone in the village with the old men, women and children, the young men being absent, when he was startled by the sudden appearance of the savages, who had discovered Westbrook's approach.

Not a moment was to be lost. Seizing the consecrated host, the pious missionary swallowed it in haste, and then packing the church vessels in a small chest, he fled to the forest where the frightened people, who had been left in the village, had betaken themselves. Night was approaching when Westbrook and his men cautiously made their way through the thickets which surrounded Norridgewock. All was ominously silent as they drew near the village and surrounded it. Surprised at the dead silence, they drew nearer, keeping on the alert for a foe, whose cunning they well knew. There was no sound, no movement in the village, and finally the secret was disclosed; it had been deserted. A diligent search was made the next day for Ralé, but although Westbrook's men passed near his hiding place, they did not discover him, and at last abandoned the search. Westbrook secured, however, a valuable prize, a small box containing letters from Vaudreuil and Begon, which disclosed to the English the perfidy of their French neighbors. In the box was also a dictionary of the Abnaki language,[1] the labor of Ralé for many years, and when we consider how precious this manuscript was to him, we cannot but sympathize with him for its loss, for in the hands of his enemies, whom he regarded as ruthless vandals, he supposed it forever lost to the world; yet Providence seems to have employed this method for its preservation. On the door of the church was found the following paper in Ralé's handwriting:

---

[1] This valuable relic is now the property of Harvard College. It was published in 1833, by John Pickering, LL. D.

"*Englishmen.*

"I that am of Norridgwock have had Thoughts that thou wil't Come and Burn our Church & Our Fathers House to Revenge thy self without Cause for the Houses I have Burnt of thine. It was thou that didst force me to it, why didst thou build them upon my Land without my Consent.

"I have not yet burnt any, but what was upon my own Land; Thou mayest burn it, because thou knowest that I am not there such is thy Generosity, for if I were there, Assuredly thou shouldst not burn it, altho thou shouldst Come with the number of many hundred Men.

"It is Ill built, because the English dont work well; It is not finished, altho five or six Englishmen have wrought there during the space of four years, and the Undertaker who is a great Cheat, hath been paid in advance for to finish it. I tell the Nevertheless, That, if thou dost burn it in Revenge upon my Land, thou mayest Depend upon it, That I will Revenge myself also and that upon thy Land in such a manner as will be more sensible and more disadvantageous to the, for one of thy Meeting houses or Temples is of more value beyond Compare than our Church. And I shall not be Satisfied with Burning only one or two of thine, but many; I know where they are, and the Effect shall make the know that I have been as good as my word.

"This shall Certainly be done sooner or later, for the War is but just beginning ; And if thou wouldst know where it will have an End I tell the it will not have an end but with the World. If thou Canst not be driven out before I Dye, Our Children and Nephews will Continue it till that time, without thy being able to Enjoy it peaceably.

"This is what I say to the, who am of Norridgewock in the Name of all the NATION."[1]

The discovery of Vaudreuil's duplicity, as his correspondence with Shute had been such as would naturally pass between men in their position, whose governments were nominally friendly, astounded the English, and Shute at once dispatched copies of the letters found in Ralé's box to the government, and himself wrote a letter to the French governor, so manly in tone, that he must have always respected

---

[1] This letter was copied by me from the one in the office of the Public Records, London, and bears the following indorsement : "*Translated from the French. The foregoing was found upon the Church Door at Norridgewock & in the hand Writing of Father Rallé, the Jesuit.* Examined pr. J. Willard, Sec'y." The box containing the correspondence of Vaudreuil is now the property of the Maine Historical Society.

its author, in spite of the bitter reproofs which it contained. In this letter he said :

" Sir :—

"In the month of September last I did myself the Honor of writing to you a Letter by the way of Albany, which I hope came Safe to your hand ; however, for fear of a Miscarriage, I have now sent you a copy of it. Therein you will observe the great Confidence I had at that time in your Justice and Friendship with respect to the Indians at Norridgewock, but I am sorry to find I was so much mistaken ; You have convinced me by Letters under your own hand, that I was in the wrong to Expect the least Service from you upon that occasion, For it appears over & over again, That the Hostile appearance and Insolent Behaviour of the Indians at Arowsick in the Summer last past, was not only with your Allowance, but even with your projecting from the beginning ; And your Approbation of it afterwards, That you excited them to it, Supplyed them in it, with Officers and Stores of War, and after all was done, mightily applauded and Rewarded them, And least they should be at a loss what to say, to the English you even put Words into their Mouths, & prepared Instructions for their Conduct in that Affair; I must needs say, Sir, I should not easily have been brought

RALÉ'S BOX CONTAINING THE FRENCH CORRESPONDENCE.
Captured by Westbrook in the winter of 1721-22, now in possession of the Maine Historical Society.

to believe these things of a Gentleman, a Christian, and a Governor of a French Colony, and who, as such, is Obliged to live in Peace and Friendship with the English Government; But what shall I say? I have your Original Instructions, and Letters now before me, as you may See by the Copies of some of them, which I now Inclose; The Originals I shall send home to his Majesty, my Great Master; You do indeed suggest, That you have Orders for what you have done or shall do further in this Affair; His Majesty will soon Discover the Truth and Validity of that pretence, and how Agreeable Your Conduct has been, both to the Letter and Spirit of the Treaty of Utrecht, more especially to the twelfth and Sixteenth Articles; Is it thus We are to Imitate the Examples of Our Masters at Home, who live in such strict Allegance and Friendship? Should I have offered to stir up the Indian Tribes at St. Francois or Besancourt, or any other within the Bounds of Your Government to commit such Affronts and Hostilities to the Government and People of Canada, would you not justly & greatly have Complained of it? I do not Judge it necessary to Enter far into an Argument upon this Head, But I Could Easily Convince you how very much you are in the wrong to Concern yourself with an Indian Tribe that are settled upon one of the Principal Rivers of New England, that live in the Neighborhood of Our English Towns & Garrisons, & until very lately have Constantly Conversed and traded with them, and pass by the English settlements every time they Come to the sea for their Fishery, And their Lands or place of Settlement must of necessity fall within the English Pale or Territory, inasmuch as the Crown of Great Britain have now the Right & Dominion of Nova Scotia, formerly called L'Accadie, with all its Dependencies, But above all, and what I very much Insist on, This Tribe of the Indians, as well as that of Penobscot, have for a great number of years last past, by Frequent and Solemn Treaties, willingly and Joyfully put themselves under the Protection of the Crown of Great Britain, & the Government of New England, and on these Occasions have had Tokens of His Majesties kindness & Friendship presented to them; And you may Depend upon it His Majesty will never quit His right and Interest with respect to those Indian Tribes, but Insist upon it to the last, And while I have the Honour to be His Governour here, I shall Endeavor to do my Duty in Defending and Maintaining it, and shall take Just and proper Measures to prevent such Insults and Injuries to His Majesties good subjects for the future; I suppose Mr. Rallé, who has been the great Incendiary in all this Affair has acquainted you with his narrow Escape; he will do well to take warning by it & return to his own Countrey, or at least to Canada, and no longer abuse his profession by Stirring up the Indians of this Country to Acts of Hostility, which if Continued in, will finally end in their ruin.

"I shall be glad if upon this Remonstrance Your future conduct towards this Government and the Indian Tribes Dependent thereon, Especially those of Norridgewock and Penobscot may be such as to give me Occasion to say, what I would willingly do, That I am Sir

"Your very humble Servt.

"Samll. Shute."[1]

This expedition of Westbrook, coupled with the arrest of Castin's son, acts fully warranted by existing circumstances, furnished the savages with a sufficient pretext to extend their depredations, and we are told by Ralé, that they resolved to destroy the English habitations near them. "They chanted the war," he says, "among the Hurons of Lorette, and in

---

[1] This letter is a copy made by the author from the original in the office of the Public Records, London.

all the villages of the Abnaki nation," and "Norridgewock was the place appointed to assemble the warriors in order to concert their project together."

In June, 1722, all was in readiness, and the first blow was struck. The savages, proceeding to the mouth of the Kennebec on the 13th, destroyed some small buildings of the English, and then continuing up the river, says Ralé, "plundered and burnt the new houses which the English had built." They, however, abstained from slaughter and liberated all their captives but five, whom they retained as hostages.

Doubtless in this act they followed the advice of their older men, who ever counseled moderation; but moderation is not a savage virtue, and, intoxicated with success, they soon entered upon a wholesale destruction of the English settlements. On the following July, Capt. Harmon, who was stationed at Arrowsic with a small force, having discovered that the settlement of Brunswick was on fire, at once proceeded in two whale boats to its relief. As he made his way through the darkness with muffled oars, he perceived lights on Pleasant Point, and landing cautiously, he came upon eleven canoes of the savages, who had been engaged in the destruction of Brunswick. They had been enjoying one of their infernal orgies, the torturing of a prisoner, Moses

Eaton, of Brunswick, whose tongue they had cut out, and whose legs and arms they had also severed from his body, and now exhausted by the exercise of their ferocious passions, they were lying about their fires unsuspicious of the proximity of an avenger of their victim.

The moment was opportune, and Harmon, cautiously advancing his small force, the chief reliance of the settlers of the vicinity, came suddenly upon them; indeed, Penhallow tells us that he " stumbled over them as they lay asleep." The attack was sudden, yet in the darkness most of them escaped. A large body of savages, however, were encamped not far away, and aroused by the sound of guns, they fired upon the English in the darkness but without execution. Deeming it prudent to avoid risking a battle so far from his base of supplies, and upon ground where the savage was at home, after burying the mutilated body of Eaton, Harmon hastened back to the defense of Arrowsic.

Let us see Ralé's account of this transaction. He says, after relating the first attack of the savages, in which they burnt a number of dwellings and released all of their prisoners but five, suppressing all allusion to the destruction of Brunswick and the murderous work which followed, " This moderation of the Indians, however, had not the desired effect. On the contrary, a party of English having found sixteen Abnakis asleep on an Island, made a general discharge on them, by which five were killed and three wounded."

So strong were Ralé's prejudices against the English, that it was impossible for him to relate fairly any incident respecting them. The savages, who slowly tortured to death their English prisoners, he saw through a mist, which gave them an appearance of primeval simplicity, while the English heretics, seen through the same medium, took on the shape of ugly satyrs. This is but a single instance of the manner in which Ralé described the events connected with the wars between his savages and the English, and it is no exaggeration to say, that hardly an incident of these wars involving the character of the English related by him and Charlevoix, the latter of whom cooked without question everything which came to his net, will bear critical analysis, or a comparison with historical documents of the times.

This act of Harmon has been criticised by several of our writers, who have listened too readily to Charlevoix, as impolitic and cruel, but they certainly cannot have considered the existing conditions. Harmon's act was cruel only because all war is cruel. The

English settlers were surrounded by terrible perils, and knew, from years of bitter experience, the merciless nature of the foe with whom they had to deal; a foe who surprised sleeping hamlets, and destroyed old and young with fiendish cruelty. Though in their first attack there had been no blood shed on either side, no resistance having been made, the imperiled settlers realized that war had begun with a pitiless foe, and self preservation was the question uppermost in their minds. In this condition of affairs we should not expect them to weigh questions of ethics with the same care which we, in the seclusion of our closets, bestow upon them. That injury might not be done to those savages friendly to the English, Governor Shute in his proclamation of war, issued on the 25th of July, 1722, notified them, that none would be molested, who reported within forty days to the nearest military post, and those within the English lines were ordered to remain peaceably at home and not to harbor the enemy.

Although the French could not openly enter into the conflict, they secretly supplied the savages with arms, and encouraged them to pursue the war. The result was, that along the English borders the same scenes of desolation and cruelty were enacted, that had characterized former savage wars.

Ralé, by his own testimony, accompanied his neophytes on some of their bloody raids, and was not always careful to keep in the background, but exhibited himself to the English for the avowed purpose of exciting their rage against him. The following letter written by him is proof of this:

"My people returned in the spring having learnt what had passed in the winter, made a party of forty men against the English not with a design to kill, but to put them in mind of their word, and to make them draw off. In one night they ranged near ten leagues of the countrey where the English had settled, broke into their houses, bound their men, which they made prisoners to the number of sixty-four, pillaged their houses and burnt all, and this party being returned, another fitted out to pillage and burn many houses, with we hear a stone fort, and at length they took up the hatchet against the English and carried it to a village of Canada. The warriors set out on their way and being arrived here, I embarqued with them to go to war, being in all 160, we arrived at the village they went to attack, which consisted of fifty fair houses, supported by five forts, two of stone and three of wood. At break of day ten Englishmen coming out of their stone fort with their arms, seven of my people set upon them, killed

some, but one of ours being wounded in the thigh
was brought to the camp, and the English dare not
after that come out of their stone fort any more,
where all the inhabitants had sheltered themselves to
the number of near 600 men, besides women and
children.

My people still inviting them to come out and
nobody appearing they fell upon the houses, supposing the inhabitants had been there, which they
found empty, and pillaged and burnt them all with
their three forts of wood ; they burnt all their works
of wood, filled up their wells, killed their cattle, oxen,
cows, horses, sheep, swine ; and these 600 miserable
Englishmen saw all this without daring to come out ;
and as for myself to pleasure the English I made my
appearance and shewed myself to them several times
which, perhaps, increased their fury against me,
while they saw me, but dare do nothing to me, although they knew that the governour had set my
head at a thousand livres sterling, I shall not part with
it, nevertheless, for all the sterling money in England. But that which I see most perplexing and
pittiful in all is, that the English still keep their forts
and the Indian arms not being able to do anything
against them, they remain still masters of the land,
and unless the French join with the Indians the land

is lost. This is what now discourageth the Indians for which reason they have left Norridgewock fort for to people the villages of Canada, they would have carried me with them, but I bid them go. But as for me I remain, and they are gone and about eight or nine stays here with me. We know what the court shall judge concerning this countery and the Indians have quitted being perswaded that the English to revenge themselves for the damage we have done will come and burn Norridgewock."

Regarded by the English as one of the chief causes of their sufferings, they were determined to drive Ralé from the Kennebec, or secure his person. His life must have been one of constant alarms, situated as he was in an exposed position, in the midst of a fickle and excitable people. It was at this time that he found time to address a lengthy letter to his nephew across the sea, giving an account of his life and labor among the savages.

This letter is of a most interesting character, as it gives us vivid pictures of his daily life and surroundings, in fact, almost brings the bodily presence of the man before us.[1]

---

[1] This letter and another which appears further on, were published in a collection of letters from Jesuits stationed in different parts of the world, at

"NORRIDGEWOCK,
This 15*th October*, 1722.
"Monsieur, my dear Nephew,
The peace of Our Saviour :
" During the more than thirty years that I have lived in the heart of these forests with the Savages, I have been so occupied in instructing them and forming them to christian virtues, that I have but little leisure to write many letters, even to those who are most dear to me. Nevertheless I cannot refuse the little details of my various duties which you desire. I owe it in acknowledgment of the friendship, which makes you so strongly interested in everything that concerns me.

"I am in a district of that vast extent of land which lies between Acadia and New England. Two other Missionaries are occupied with me among the Abnaki Savages, but we are far removed from each other. The Abnaki Savages, beside the two villages which are in the center of the French colony, have three others, each villages of considerable size,

---

Paris, in 1726, by Nicholas LeClerc. The translation is the author's, and was nearly completed before he was aware that one had already been made by Bishop Kip, which, although more elegant, is not so literal as the one here given.

situated on the bank of a river. The three rivers empty into a sea south of the Canada river between New England and Acadia.

"The village where I live is called Nanrantsouak;[1] it is situated on the bank of a river, which discharges itself into the sea about thirty leagues hence. I have built a Church,[2] which is neat and very ornamental. I thought nothing ought to be spared neither for its decoration, nor for the ornaments which are used at our holy ceremonies; Vestments, chasubles, copes, sacred Vessels, everything appropriate, and would be so esteemed in our Churches of Europe. I have formed a little Brotherhood of about forty young Savages, who assist at divine Service, in their cassocks and surplices; each have their duties, so many to assist at the holy Sacrifices of the Mass, & to chant the divine Office for the Consecration of the Holy Sacrament, & for the processions which they make with a great crowd of Savages, who often come from long distance to attend them. You would be edified at the good order which they keep, & the piety which they show.

---

[1] So in the French, which is doubtless a misprint, and should be *Narantsouak*. Later it crystallized into Norridgewock.

[2] The church he here speaks of was really the third edifice erected by him.

"They have built two Chapels at about three hundred paces from the village; the one dedicated to the most holy Virgin, & where may be seen her Image in relief, is above the river; the other dedicated to the guardian Angel, is at the lower end of the same river. Since they are both on the road which leads either to the woods or into the open country, the Savages never pass them without offering their prayer. There is a holy emulation among the women of the Village as to who shall the better decorate the Chapel, of which they have the care, when the procession repairs thither. All that they have, jewels, pieces of silk, or calico and other things of that kind are used to adorn it.

"The abundance of light adds not a little to the beauty of the church and Chapels; I have no need to be saving of wax, as this country furnishes it to me in abundance. The islands of the sea are bordered with wild laurels,[1] which in autumn bear berries a little like those of the Juniper. They fill their kettles with them and boil them with water. As soon as the water boils, the green wax rises & remains on the surface of the water. From a measure of three bushels of this berry, one obtains nearly four

---

[1] The bayberry.

pounds of wax; it is very pure and very good, but neither soft nor manageable. After several attempts, I have found that by mixing as much tallow, either of beef, mutton or moose as of the wax, fine, hard & serviceable candles may be made. With 24 pounds of wax and as much tallow, one can make two hundred long candles of more than a foot in length. One finds an infinity of these laurels on the islands & along the sea coast: A single person will easily pick four measures in a day. The berry hangs like grapes from the branches of the tree. I have sent a branch to Quebec with a cake of wax: it has been found excellent.

"None of my neophytes fail to repair twice a day to the Church; in the early morning to attend Mass, & in the evenings to assist at the prayers which I offer at sunset. As it is necessary to fix the imagination of the Savages, too easily distracted, I have composed suitable prayers to make them enter into the spirit of the August Sacrifice of our Altars; they chant them or properly recite them in a loud voice during Mass. Besides the sermons that I give them on Sundays & Holy Days, I scarcely allow a week day to pass, without giving a short exhortation, to inspire horror of the vices to which they are most inclined, or to strengthen them in the practice of some virtue.

"After Mass I teach the Catechism to the children and young people; a large number of old persons assist at this and reply with docility to the questions which I ask them. The rest of the morning until noon, is devoted to hearing all who wish to speak to me. It is then that they come in crowds to make me share their pains and their inquietudes, or to communicate to me subjects of complaint against their countrymen, or to consult me about their marriages, & other particular affairs. It is necessary for me to instruct some, to console others, to re-establish peace in families at variance, to calm troubled consciences, to correct others by reproofs mingled with gentleness and charity; in short, as much as it is possible, to render them all contented.

"After noon I visit the sick and go around among the cabins of those who have need of particular instruction. If they hold a council, a frequent occurrence among the Savages, they depute one of the principal men of the assembly, to beg me to assist at the decision of their deliberations. I go as soon as possible to the place where the council is being held; if I judge that they are taking a wise course, I approve it; if on the contrary I find anything to say, against their decision, I declare to them my opinion, which I support by solid reasons, & they conform to it. My advice always fixes their resolutions. They do not even hold their feasts without inviting me; those invited bring each a dish of wood or bark: I give the benediction on the food; they put in each dish the portion prepared. The distribution being made, I say grace, & each retires; because such is the order & custom of their feasts.

"In the midst of these ceaseless occupations, you will not find it difficult to understand with what rapidity the days slip by. There has been a time when it was with difficulty that I found time to recite my Office, & to take a little repose during the night; for discretion is not the virtue of the Savages. But for some years I have made it a rule to speak to no one, from the evening prayer until after Mass the next morning, & I have forbidden them to interrupt me during this time, unless it is for some important reason, as for example, to assist a dying person, or for some other affair which cannot be put off. I employ this time to pray and to repose from the fatigue of the day.

"When the Savages go to the seashore, to pass some months hunting ducks, bustards & other birds which are found there in great quantities, they build on an island a Chapel which they cover with bark, near which they prepare a little hut for my dwelling.

I take care to carry there part of the ornaments, & the service is performed there with the same propriety and the same crowds of people as at the village.

"You see, my dear nephew, what are my occupations. For as to what regards me personally, I will tell you that I only see, only hear, only speak to Savages. My food is simple and light. I was never able to adapt my taste to the meat & to the fish smoked by the Savages; my only nourishment is maize,[1] which they pound and of which I make every day, a kind of pudding which I cook with water.

"The only sweetening which I have here, is to mix with it a little sugar to correct the insipidity. This is not wanting in these forests. In the spring time the Maples hold in store a liquor similar to that which the sugar cane of the Islands contains. The women occupy themselves in collecting it in bark dishes, when the trees distil it; they boil it and obtain from it a fairly good sugar. The first distilled is always the best.

"All the Abnaki Nation is Christian, & very zealous to preserve their Religion. This attachment to the Catholic Faith, has made them up to this time choose rather our alliance, to the advantages that they had

---

[1] *Bled de Turquie* in the original.

drawn from the alliance with the English their neighbors. These advantages are very attractive to our Savages; the ease which they have of trading with the English, from whom they are not farther away, than a journey of one or two days, the convenience of the road, the great market which they find for the purchase of the goods which suit them; nothing can be more capable of attracting them. Instead of which going to Quebec, more than fifteen days are necessary to get there, besides they have to provide provisions for the journey, while they have a number of rivers to cross, and frequent portages to make. They feel these inconveniences, & they are not indifferent to their interests, but their faith is infinitely more dear, & they think that if they withdrew themselves from our alliance, they would soon find themselves without Missionary, without Sacraments, without Sacrifice, without almost any exercise of Religion, and in manifest danger of being plunged again into their former infidelity.

"This is the tie which binds them to the French. It has been tried in vain to break it, either by traps which have been held out to their simplicity, or by acts of trespass, which could not help irritating a Nation infinitely zealous of its rights & of its liberty. These beginnings of misunderstandings fail not to alarm me, & make me fear the dispersion of the flock, which Providence has confided to my care so many years & for which I would willingly sacrifice that which remains of my life. Observe the various artifices which they employ to detach them from our alliance.

"The Governor General of New England, several years ago sent to the lower part of our river the most able of the Ministers of Boston, for the purpose of holding a school there, to instruct the children of the Savages, & to maintain them at the expense of the Government. As the allowance of the Minister was to increase in proportion to the number of his scholars,[1] he forgot nothing to draw them to him; he went to find them ; he caressed them; he made them little presents ; he pressed them to come and see him ; in fine he gave himself up for two months to many useless movements, without gaining a single child. The contempt which they showed for his caresses & his invitations did not repulse him; he addressed himself even to the Savages, he put to them various

---

[1] This statement was without foundation in fact. It was written to a man who could not verify its incorrectness, for the sole purpose of belittling a brother missionary, and making it appear that he was governed in his self-sacrificing labors by mercernary motives.

questions touching their creed; & upon the replies which were made to him, he turned into ridicule the Sacraments, Purgatory, the Invocation of Saints, the Beads, the Crosses & Images, the lighting of our Churches, & all the pious customs so sacredly observed in the Catholic Religion. I believed it my duty to oppose these first seeds of seduction; I wrote a civil letter to the Minister, wherein I pointed out to him that my Christians knew how to believe the truths which the Catholic Faith teaches, but knew not how to dispute about them; that not being skillful enough to solve the difficulties which he proposed, he had apparently the design that they should be communicated to me; that I seized with pleasure this opportunity, which he offered me to confer with him either personally, or by letters; that I would send him with this a memorial which I prayed him to read with serious attention. In this memorial which was about a hundred pages, I proved by Scripture, by tradition, & by theological reasons, the truths which he had attacked by stale enough pleasantries. I added in finishing my letter to him, that if he was not satisfied with my proofs, I would await a refutation from him precise and supported by theological reasons, & not by vague arguments which proved nothing, still less by injurious reflections which belonged neither to our profession, nor to the importance of the matters with which he struggled.

Two days after having received my letter, he started to return to Boston, & he sent me a short reply, which I was obliged to read several times in order to comprehend the sense, so obscure was the style, & so extraordinary the latin.[1]

[1] The best refutation of this is the *fac simile* portion of the original letter here produced, revealing in its neat handwriting the careful and painstaking scholar that its author was; the entire Latin letter in the appendix, and the following translation of this letter.

Reverend Sir:

I received your letter in which you say that perhaps it will seem strange to me that you send me this letter. Now I tell you frankly that if you desire to have friendly intercourse with me, it will be very acceptable to me. Let us send letters back and forth freely. I wonder indeed that you who are thought by some to be a man of exalted piety and sanctity, write with so much feeling and without any provocation or reason accuse me of being guilty of deceit, and assert that you and others also know that I am guilty. Yet you do not show and therefore it is clear that you cannot show in what I am deceitful. Is it not strange that you desire to frighten me from laboring for the benefit of immortal souls? Even if the work is especially laborious and difficult, is it not worth while to accomplish a very difficult and

"I understood nevertheless by dint of reasoning, that he complained that I attacked him without

---

laborious work in order to persuade men to flee to Christ and walk in the way of salvation and thus receive life everlasting? And what if there are not with us magnificent furnishings and decoration of churches and splendor and beauty of priestly robes to attract the men of the forest! Neither were there these things in the time of the Apostles to attract the men to whom the Apostles were sent, and yet they persuaded many to believe in Christ and receive eternal life. Now it is clearly stated that the Gospel or the word of God is the power of God unto salvation (Rom. 1. 16) and that it pleased God to save men by the foolishness of preaching (1 Cor. 1. 21). Although this is a work difficult of accomplishment among men of the woods, still the love of Christ and of souls constrains us. Although we do not expect to merit salvation by accomplishing this work — for after we have done all we can we are still unprofitable servants (Luke 17. 10) and trust wholly in the merits of Christ — yet where the love of Christ is, there is the desire to extend Christ's Kingdom, and this desire moves men to accomplish a very difficult and laborious work in persuading and bringing men into the Kingdom of Christ. Hence your arguments are puerile and ridiculous.

You say that you desire to answer for the men of the forest, but it is not necessary for you to take that labor upon yourself. I will work as I shall have opportunity to bring them into the straight path of salvation, and to give them satisfaction in all things. If there is any hope that it will be for the benefit of

Reverende Domine

Delectaris Procul dubio Reprehendendo, Ideoque ea culpas Quæ non sunt Reprehensione digna. Et in culpando, Tu ipse Crimina admittis. Dicis enim mihi; Tu Anglice Loqueris, utendo verbis Latinis. In his verbis Domine Tibi ipsi contradicis, Si Quis enim verbis Latinis utitur, Quamvis non Rhetorice tamen Latine, & non Anglice Loquitur. Quisquis ... est verbum vere Latinum.

Dicis, Amicum est Substantivum, nec potest esse Adjectivum. Sed non Recte dicis. Certissime datur Tale Adjectivum Apud Latinos. Amicus Animus, est Latina Locutio, & valet Amicum, & Humor Pratis Amicus &c.

Ais, Commercium in hoc est Barbarum Quid. Sed Quis Tuæ Dictioni credet absque Probatione. Ipse Dixit non valet.

De multis Aliis etiam dicis non sunt Latina sed Barbara At non valet Authoritas Tua. Certissime Talia verba sæpe inter Latinos adhibentur.

Dicis, merere est solæcismus, illud verbum est Deponens, non Activum scribe mereri. Sed aiunt Docti datur mereo merere, æquæ ac mereor mereri. Merere culpam in infinitivo est Latina Locutio, & merere salutem &c.

Dicis Mola est Lapis, non ædificium. Sed Docti aiunt Mola est ædificium, Lapis qui ponitur in mola Lapis Molaris est.

Dicis, Domus habet in Accusativo Plurali Domos, non Domus. Sed Quæ non habet Domos, & Domus.

Multa Alia etiam reprehendis Quæ non sunt vituperanda. Et si Te mirarer Jossem dicere, Tu Minister! Tu è societate Jesu, & hæc non intelligis. Dicis verba mea non sunt intelligibilia. Quare non intelligis sequi male ... consiliis ... conjidebatur ... illis afficeretur ... nominabatur Gen. Pet. 2. 23. & isti monitioni, vel Mandato Auscultaso in Prov. 20. 4. Ne Responde stulto secundum stultitiam ejus ne adæqueris ei Tu quoque.

Manifeste patet, Te reprehendere multa Quæ non sunt culpanda. Tamen concedo Errata sunt in Scriptione mea Quam Propostere scribebam. viz existimaris virum pro vir, & movent pro movet vel ...

Et in Tuis Scriptionibus equidem multa sunt Errata (Quamvis Tu isti (ut inquis) Professor Rhetorices, & Linguæ Græcæ in urbe nemini ... Egi nunquam sui Professor Rhetoricæ, & Tamen Errata video Quæ Errata in nossa Criticus & Iordocus reperiet in Epistolis Tuis, Imo in Epistola Quam gloriosissime scribebas Falsissime me accusabas dicendo Tu Te jactitas Apud Silvestres Scire linguam Latinam. Nunquam enim jactita ... super Silvestres non unum verbum locutus sum sylvestribus De Lingua Latina. Si Tu maxime jactabas in secunda Epistola, & Tamen indo scribebas Intelligit, & accurate scribit Latina. An hac Dictione ... non Accurate scribit Latine nam Accusativus Casus sequi ... verbum scribit. Scripsisse Te oportuit Accurate scribit Linguam Latinam, vel Accurate scribit Latine.

reason; that zeal for the salvation of souls had led him to show the Savages the way to Heaven; that for the rest my proofs were ridiculous & childish. Having sent him a second letter to Boston, in which I pointed out the blunders in his, he answered me at the end of two years without entering into the matter, that I had a jealous and critical spirit, & that this was the mark of a temperament inclined to anger.[1]

---

you who ought to believe, and act and walk according to the word of God which is the perfect rule of doctrine and morals, I will cheerfully reply to your arguments but your messenger says that he will hasten to you to-morrow, and so I have not at this time an opportunity of replying to your long letter.
      Farewell, sir.
          J. BAXTER.
 To the Rev. Sebastian Ralé in the town called Norridgewock.

[1] The following translation of this letter will convince the reader that the overcritical priest did not have the best of the argument, as he tries so ostentatiously to make his kinsman believe.

Reverend Sir:

You doubtless take delight in fault finding and so find fault with things that do not deserve censure, and in your fault-finding you admit the truth of the charges. For you say "You write English using Latin words." In these very words, Sir, you contradict yourself; for if any one uses Latin words, although not in a rhetorical manner, he still speaks Latin, not English. Whoever speaks English, uses English words. What if an expression has a decided English ring, it is truly a Latin expression.

You say *amicum* is a substantive and cannot be an adjective, but you are not correct. It is most certainly used by Latin writers as an adjective in the following : *amicus animus ; vale, lumen amicum* & *humor pratis amicus* &c.

You say *commercium* (intercourse) in this sense is a foreign or unpolished word. But who will believe your statement without proof. *Ipse dixit* has no weight.

Concerning many other things also you say, "they are not Latin but foreign." Your opinion is of no avail. Most certainly such words are used by Latin writers.

You say, "*merere* is a solecism ; that verb is deponent not active; write *mereri.*" Learned men, however, say it is given, *mereo, merere,* as well as *mereor, mereri. Merere culpam* in the infinitive is a Latin expression and so *merere salutem,* &c.

You say "*mola* (mill) is a stone not a building." Learned men, however, say that *mola* is the building and the stone that is placed in the mill (in mola) is the mill-stone (lapis molares).

You say "*domus* has in the accusative plural *domos* not *domus,*" but why has it not both *domos* and *domus ?*

You also find fault with many other things that are not to be blamed, and if I were to imitate you, I might say "You a minister! You, a member of the Society of Jesus, and not know these things!" You say that my words are unintelligible. Why, pray, are you ignorant of words often used by Latin writers? But

I prefer to follow the example of Christ who when he was reviled, reviled not again; when he suffered threatened not, &c. (1 Pet. 2. 23), and I will also give heed to the warning or command in Proverbs 26. 4, "answer not a fool according to his folly lest thou also be like unto him."

It is clearly evident that you find fault with many expressions that ought not to be criticized. I grant that there are errors in my writing which I wrote very hurriedly, viz.: *Existimaris virum* for *vin, movent* for *movet*, &c. In your writings also there are many errors, although you were, as you say, a Professor of Rhetoric and Greek in the city of Nismes.

I was never Professor of Rhetoric and yet I see errors. How many errors then might a critic and a very learned man find in your letters? Moreover in the letter which you wrote in a most boastful strain,' you falsely accused me in saying, "you boast among the men of the forest that you know Latin very well," for I have never spoken a single word to them about Latin, but you were especially boastful in your second letter and yet in *that* you wrote *intelligit et accurate scribit Latina*. Even in this expression you do not write Latin accurately, for the accusative case follows the verb *scribit*. You ought to have written *accurate scribit linguam Latinam* or *accurate scribit Latine*. You also wrote *ut emendatur in scolis*. Scolus is a mountain in Bæotia and a town in Macedonia. You should have written *in scholis*. You also wrote *substantium et adjectium*. No such Latin words are given. You ought to have written *substantivum et adjectivum*. You wrote "you do not quote Paul faithfully. Paul says 'for it is the virtue of God unto salvation to every one that believeth'" (*omni credendi*). If I were to imitate you I might say "What do you mean by these words *omni credendi?*" You should have written "for it is the power of God unto salvation to every one that believeth" (*cuivis credenti*).

You wrote *merere est sollescismus*. What do you mean by this word? No such word is given among the learned. *They* write *soloecismus*. Your *sollescismus* is indeed a solecism.

I might speak of many other things and exclaim "Your words are foreign and unintelligible, &c.," but of what use are such exclamations? I will not imitate you. I see that you are moved by anger and I would not provoke you. I exhort you in the words of the Apostle (Eph. 4 26–27): "Let not the sun go down upon your wrath, neither give place to the devil," and in verse 31: "Let all bitterness and wrath and anger and clamor and evil speaking be put away from you with all malice." It is written in Tit. 1. 7. "For a bishop must be blameless as the steward of God; not self-willed, not soon angry, &c.," and in Eccles. 7. 9, "Be not hasty in thy spirit to be angry; for anger resteth in the bosom of fools."

You say, "Is this conclusion of yours correctly drawn: I have not made known to you, and therefore I cannot make known in what you are deceitful." I reply: "Indeed the inference is rightly made and it is proved thus: if you had been able to show it you would certainly have made it known, for you were very angry with me and earnestly desired to show that I was at fault.

You have taken *this* upon yourself, viz.: to prove that I am deceitful, in the following manner: 1st: You say "I have shown openly and have made it clearer than light that you (plural) neither have nor

follow the correct standard of religious belief and
that no one among you is able to make answer to
arguments that assert this. Therefore by endeavor-
ing to persuade a different rule of faith upon the
men of the forest you become an unfaithful custo-
dian of their souls and aim to plunge them more
deeply into hell." I reply that you have not proved
this nor can any of you prove it. How often have
professors of the reformed religion made answer to
all your arguments and shown them to be empty!
I was not unfaithful for all my teachings were in harmony with the Holy Scriptures which teach nothing
except truth and right. 2d : The men of the forest
say " The Englishman is very eager to be able to
teach our children letters and under cover of letters
gradually to persuade them all to embrace the Angli-
can faith when they are men, and being thus united in
faith and friendship, no further war may break out
between them, &c." If the men of the forest say
this, I think *you* first said it for them. I have never
heard them speak in this way. Some of them speak
differently. But whoever says this, only substitutes
it fraudulently for the truth, and neither fraudulent
substitution nor a foolish imagination proves the
thing.

You say: "I know that you cannot present formal
arguments," but how do you know it? Afterwards
you say "Your replies to theological arguments are
circumlocutions, &c.," but how do you know *this?*
You have never, I think, seen my replies to any
theological arguments. I did not reply to such arguments in the letter I sent you and because I did not,
you seem to draw this conclusion, viz.: that I cannot
reply to any formal arguments. The arguments of
which I spoke are contained in the opening of your

long letter where it is stated: "Fifty years ago some of the men of the woods went to the city of Quebec to make purchases. When, however, they saw the furnishings of the churches, the priests clad in their priestly robes performing the sacred rites, and others richly clad waiting upon them, and the ceremonies performed by them, &c., they were so moved by these things as to be carried away in admiration. With you, however, they would not be moved by the magnificent furnishings and ornaments of your churches, &c." These are not theological arguments, only *argumenta ad homines*, and certainly what you say is more pleasing to boys than to men. In such words you do not present formal arguments.

You pride yourself very much on the statement, "In the course of my letter there are many arguments thorny, pungent, &c. I say and maintain that neither you nor any one of you can answer them." But is it not written in Proverbs 27. 2, "Let another man praise thee, not thine own mouth; a stranger, and not thine own lips," and in 1 Kings 20. 11, "Let not him that girdeth on his harness boast himself as he that putteth it off." There are many of us who can reply to your arguments and show them to be empty and vain. Although you say that I will not find that you speak in anger, still I have found that you speak in anger and write in bitterness, not only in the letters you sent me, but also in the one you wrote our governor. It is said in Proverbs 22. 24, "Make no friendship with an angry man," and in Proverbs 29. 20, "Seest thou a man that is hasty in his words? There is more hope of a fool than of him." When all bitterness and wrath and anger are put aside by you, and you receive with meekness the

"Thus ended our dispute which sent away the Minister, & which rendered abortive the project that he had formed of seducing my Neophytes.

"This first attempt having had so little success, they had recourse to another artifice.[1] An Englishman asked permission of the Savages to build on their river a kind of storehouse, to trade there with them, & he promised to sell them goods at a much greater bargain, than they had bought them even at Boston. The Savages who would find it for their profit, & who would save the trouble of a journey to Boston, consented to this willingly. Another Englishman asked soon after the same

---

ungrafted word which is able to save your soul, I will answer your arguments.
    Farewell, sir,
     I am yours,
      J. BAXTER.
(The Latin of this letter may be found in the appendix.)

[1] Trading posts, or truck-houses, as they were called, had been established among the Abnakis long before the arrival of Ralé among them, and were purely mercantile enterprises, which were alike beneficial to both buyer and seller, except in instances where rum was sold to the savages by unprincipled traders, to the scandal of the authorities and more thoughtful men of New England, who were not slow in condemning it, but powerless to prevent it.

permission, offering conditions even more favorable than the first. It was accorded him equally. This readiness of the Savages emboldened the English to establish themselves along the river, without asking permission; they built houses there, & raised forts of which three were of stone. This proximity of the English gave at first pleasure enough to the Savages, who did not perceive the trap which they laid for them, & who only looked at the pleasure which they had, in finding their new guests all that they could desire.

"But at last, perceiving themselves insensibly as it were, surrounded by the habitations of the English, they began to open their eyes, & to entertain distrust. They asked the English by what right they had established themselves on their lands, & even built forts there. The reply which was made them, that the King of France had ceded their country to the King of England, threw them into great alarm; for there is no Savage Nation, which does not suffer impatiently what they regard as subjection to any Power whatever it may be; they will be called allies and nothing more. This is why the Savages immediately sent some of their number, to M. le Marquis de Vaudreuil, Governor General of New France, to learn if it were true, that in effect the King had thus disposed of a country of which he was not the master. It was not difficult to calm their inquietude; it was only necessary to explain to them the articles of the treaty of Utrecht which concerned the Savages, & they departed content.[1]

---

[1] It would indeed be interesting to know the exact words in which the wily Vaudreuil made this impossible explanation. One has only to turn to the French king's patent conveying Acadia to De Monts in 1603, to see just what the French had always claimed as belonging to them prior to the cession of their claims to the English by the treaty of Utrecht. This patent defined Acadia as comprising all the territory between the forty-third and forty-sixth parallels of latitude, and empowered De Monts to "establish the authority of the French king *and thereunto subject, cause to submit and obey, all the people of said land.*" The treaty of Utrecht conveyed Acadia to the English "*by its ancient limits;*" that is, as described in the patent of De Monts, as well as all the rights which they possessed therein; yet, it would seem by this statement of Ralé, that the French governor was so skillful in the use of words as to be able to send the anxious and jealous savages away, satisfied with the French, who had conveyed Acadia to the English by solemn treaty, and inflamed against the English who had received the conveyance. of Gerard's Peace of Utrecht, Bolari's Importance and Advantage of Cape Breton; The Hardwicke Papers, and the Actes, Memoires, etc., concernant la paix d'Utrecht. Also, mémoire pour servir

"About this time a score of Savages entered into one of the English houses, to trade or to rest. They had been there but a short time, when they saw the house suddenly surrounded by a troop of nearly two hundred armed men. *We are dead men* suddenly cried one of them, *let us sell our lives dearly.* They prepared to throw themselves upon this troop, when the English perceiving their resolution, & knowing besides of what the Savage is capable in the first access of fury, strove to pacify them, by assuring them that they had no evil designs, & that they had come only to invite some of them to go to Boston, to confer there with the Governor, on the means of keeping peace and good understanding, which should exist between the two Nations. The Savages a little too credulous, deputed four of their fellow countrymen who repaired to Boston; but when they arrived there, the conference with which they were diverted, ends in retaining them prisoners.[1]

---

d'eclaricissement sur le droit que les françois ont dans le proprieté des pays de l'Amerique Septentrionale de L'Accadie depuis Pentagöuet jusque a la Rivière de quinibequi.

[1] Ralé does not agree with himself in relating this transaction. The evidence is clear that these men were voluntarily delivered to the English as hostages, and were so recognized by both parties in their cor-

"You will doubtless be surprised that so small a handful of Savages, should pretend to make head against a troop so numerous as that of the English. But our Savages have done an infinitude of deeds which are much more hardy. I will relate to you one only from which you may judge the others.

"During the last wars, a party of thirty Savages returned from a military expedition against the English. As the Savages, & above all the Abnakis, do not know what it is to put themselves on their guard against surprises; they fell asleep at the first resting place, without even thinking to post a sentinel during the night. A party of six hundred English, commanded by a Colonel, followed them to their Encampment, & finding them plunged in sleep, surrounded them with his force, resolving that not one of them should escape him. One of the Savages being awakened, & having perceived the English troops, suddenly warned his Companions, crying

---

respondence. Vaudreuil and Begon, as well as others on the French side, always denominated them *otages*, and a reference to Ralé's correspondence, a portion of which will be found in Note 1, p. 161, will show that Ralé fully understood the transaction, and reported it to the French governor quite accurately; yet in this familiar letter to his nephew, he places the transaction in very different light.

according to custom, *we are dead men let us sell ourselves dearly.*

"The resolution was immediately taken; they formed on the instant, six little platoons of five men each; then with hatchet in one hand & knife in the other, they threw themselves on the English with such impetuosity & fury, that after having killed more than sixty men, among whom was the Colonel, they put the rest to flight.[1]

"The Abnakis no sooner learned in what way their comrades were treated in Boston, than they complained bitterly of this, that in the midst of the peace in which they rejoiced, the right of the nation was violated to the utmost. The English replied that they only retained the prisoners as hostages for the wrong which had been done them, in killing several cattle which belonged to them; that as soon as they

---

[1] One can hardly understand how Ralé could have listened to this boastful story, and then have gravely recorded it as true. Neither Englishmen nor Frenchmen shrunk from encountering bodies of savages outnumbering them; indeed, the European ever held the prowess of the savage in contempt, except when he was in ambush or hidden by the shadows of night. In a fair fight he was no match for the civilized man, yet Ralé would have his nephew believe that the English were a race of cowards. History renders a sufficient answer to this.

would repay this damage, which amounted to 200 pounds of Beaver, the prisoners would be released. Although the Abnakis were not convinced of this pretended damage, they did not omit to pay the 200 pounds of Beaver, not wishing that for so small a thing, they could be reproached for having abandoned their brothers. Meanwhile, notwithstanding the payment of the disputed debt, they refused to liberate their prisoners.

"The Governor of Boston, fearing that this refusal would force the Savages to venture upon a bold stroke, proposed to treat this affair amicably in a conference; they agreed on the day & the place where it should be held; the savages repaired there with P. Ralé, their Missionary; the Père de la Chasse, Superior General of these Missions, who was then making his visit, was there also, but M. the Governor did not appear. The Savages argued ill from his absence.[1] They formed the resolution to

---

[1] Shute well answered this in a letter to Vaudreuil, April 23, 1722, as follows: "They have also misinformed you in saying that I had appointed to meet them the last year; for, on the contrary, I sent them word by an express that some of the principal gentlemen of this government would see and treat with them at Arrowsick, who accordingly went thither, but finding no Indians, returned."

make him understand their sentiments by a letter written in the savage tongue, in English & in Latin; & the Père de la Chasse, who understood these three languages, was appointed to write it. It seemed useless to use any other than the English language, but the Father was very glad, because on the one hand the Savages would know themselves, that the letter contained nothing but what they had dictated; & on the other, the English could not doubt that the English translation was faithful. The sense of this letter was 1st., That the Savages could not comprehend why their fellow countrymen were held after a promise had been given to return them as soon as 200 pounds of Beaver were paid; 2nd., That they were not less surprised to see that their country was seized upon without their consent; 3rd, That the English should leave it as soon as possible & set at large their prisoners; that they would expect their reply within two months, & that if after that time they refused to satisfy them, they knew well how to get justice.

"It was in the month of July of the year 1721 that this letter was carried to Boston by some Englishmen who had assisted at the Conference. As the two months rolled by without a reply from Boston, & besides, the English ceased to sell powder, shot,

& food to the Abnakis as they had done before this trouble; our Savages prepared to make reprisal. It needed all the influence of M. la Marquis de Vaudreuil upon their minds, to make them suspend for a while the vows already made.[1] But their patience was at last pushed to the extreme, by two acts of hostility which the English committed at the end of December of the year 1721, & in the beginning of the year 1722. The first was the seizure of M. de St. Castin. This officer is Lieutenant in our troops; his mother was an Abnaki & he has always lived with our Savages, among whom he has so merited their esteem and confidence that they have chosen him for their Commander General; in this capacity he could not help assisting at the conference at which I spoke, where he endeavored to regulate the interests of the Abnakis his brethren.

---

[1] Ralé's report of this sham conference, planned and arranged most artfully by himself, de la Chasse and Vaudreuil, when compared with Vaudreuil and Begon's report, which fortunately has recently come to light and is printed in note 1, page 110, shows well his method of writing history. As for Vaudreuil's magnanimity in striving to prevent the savages from attacking the English, it did not exist, as Ralé's correspondence with him shows. Let us examine some of the French correspondence bearing on the subject. In a report made to the Duke of Orleans by

"The English thought it a crime; they dispatched a small Vessel towards the place of his abode. The captain took pains to conceal him, and with the ex-

---

Père Charlevoix, Oct. 29 1720, after treating of the limits of Acadia, Charlevoix relates a conference between Vaudreuil and the savages of Norridgewock. The latter complained to him respecting the terms of the peace made by the French with the English, when he replied, "My children, I will send you underhand, *sans mains*, hatchets, powder and lead. 'Is it thus, then,' replied the savage, 'that the father helps his children, and have we helped thee in this fashion?' 'A father,' he added, 'when he sees his son contending with an enemy stronger than himself, comes forward, makes his son withdraw and tells the enemy that it is with him that he has to deal.' 'Eh bien, my children,' said Monsieur, the Governor, 'I will engage the other savage nations to help you.' To these words the deputies with a mocking laugh replied: 'Know that whenever we all wish, inasmuch as we are of the nations of this vast continent, we will unite together to drive out of it all foreigners, whoever they may be."

"This declaration surprised Monsieur de Vaudreuil, who, to quiet them, protested that rather than abandon them to the mercy of the English, he would march himself to their aid. * * * Monsieur the Marquis de Vaudreuil asserts that he has among the Abnakis of Norridgewock, an accredited man, '*homme accrédité*,' who is wholly devoted to him. Monsieur Begon is of the opinion that it is necessary that some rattle brain of the savages should strike a blow at the English which should bring about war."

ception of two or three men whom he left on deck, they invited M. de St. Castin, among whom he was well known, to come on board to refresh himself.

This state of affairs continued, and on the 8th of June, 1721, Vaudreuil and Begon were informed by the king that he was satisfied with Ralé's efforts to incite the savages against the English

On the 8th of October, Vaudreuil and Begon reported to the king what had taken place in Canada for several months past. Although this report is given in the original French under note 1, page 110, it may not be considered out of place to translate a portion of it here. Vaudreuil and Begon reported that they had been informed by Ralé, that upon the representations he had made to the savages not to permit English settlements on the lower Kennebec, they had during the past two years killed a large number of the settlers' cattle; but that there had grown up a peace party, whose sentiments had so far prevailed, as to cause the tribe to send four hostages to Boston.

Ralé had also, they say, informed them "*that the English having appointed a conference to engage the rest of the village to permit their settlement, it was necessary that in this conference the party of the Savages well intentioned;* 'that is, the war party,' *should be the more numerous, in order to compel those who had been gained by the English to return to their former feeling, so that they should all together speak emphatically to the English to oblige them to retire from their lands.*" In other words, Ralé deemed it necessary to pack the conference with men whom he had encouraged to make war upon the English, which

M. de St. Castin, who had no reason for holding himself on the defensive, went alone & unattended. But hardly had he appeared there when

---

with his greater skill in diplomacy he could easily accomplish.

The report continues, that as Ralé fears that others of the war party may be won over by the English, "*he has engaged six Savages to come here,*" that is to Quebec, "*to invite the Abnakis and the Hurons of Lorette to find themselves at the conference. To facilitate the success of this invitation, the Sieur de Vaudreuil has brought them to the villages of St. Francis and Bécancourt, who have explained how much the enterprise of the English was prejudicial to the interests of the nation. The Sieur de Vaudreuil has let them know that it was important that the Englishman may see for himself that he will draw them all against him.*

"*These two villages agreed to send to this conference three canoes from St. Francis and three from Bécancourt to which is to be joined a canoe of the Hurons of Lorette.*

"*He has thought it also his duty to engage with them, the Father de la Chasse, Superior of the Jesuits, who having been for 20 years missionary of the three Abnaki villages of Acadia, knows them well.*

"*This Father went first to Norridgewock and after having brought all the savages of that nation to one mind, he invited the savages of the village of Penobscot, from whence he also notified those of Medocteh and Pemondaki.*

"*He returned immediately to Norridgewock, accompanied by more than* 100 *savages of Penobscot, and* they seized & carried him to Boston. There they cross-questioned him & interrogated him like a criminal. Among other things they asked him why

deputies from the villages of Medocteh and Pemondaky. He also made those of Piscataqua come, who are nearest to the English on the coast of Boston.

"*These Savages thus assembled and to the number of 250 who represented all the Abnaki nation and their allies, after having taken counsel, presented themselves the* 28*th of July last, armed before the English fort of Menaskous where the conference was appointed.*" On the 10th of November, Vaudreuil in another letter to the Council of State, says, that he "*is persuaded that if his Majesty permits him to join the French with the Abnakis, the English will be forced to abandon all the settlements which they have on the lands of these Savages, he feels certain of the result by the long experience that he has, that the Abnakis supported by the French have always made the English tremble, who have been obliged in the last war to abandon nearly a hundred leagues of country.*"

It is unnecessary to quote from the French correspondence at greater length to show how far from the true picture is this which Ralé presents to his nephew. Charlevoix's account of this conference so artfully prepared by Vaudreuil, Ralé and de la Chasse, presents an equally false picture to the world, and should be carefully compared with the detailed reports of Vaudreuil and Begon to the French government. *Vide* Collection de Manuscrits, etc., vol. 3, pp. 49–70, *et passim;* Histoire et Description Generale de la Nouvelle France, etc., à Paris MDCCXLIV, Tome quatrieme, pp. 113–115.

& in what capacity he had assisted at the conference which was held among the Savages; what was signified by the Military uniform in which he was clothed; & if he had been sent to that assembly by the Governor of Canada. M. de St. Castin replied that he was an Abnaki on his mother's side; that he had passed his life among the Savages; that his Countrymen having chosen him Chief of their Nation, he was obliged to enter into their assemblies to support their interests; that it was in this capacity alone that he had assisted at the last conference; as for the rest the coat which he wore was not a Military uniform, as they thought it; that in truth, it was his own & well enough decorated, but was not above his rank, even independent of the honor which he had in being an Officer in our troops.

"M. our Governor, having learned of the detention of M. de St. Castin, wrote at once to the Governor of Boston to make complaint.

"He received no reply to his letter. But near the time the English Governor expected to receive a second, he restored liberty to his prisoner, after having kept him confined during five months.

"The enterprise of the English against myself, was the second act of hostility, which served to irritate to excess the Abnaki Nation. A missionary could not fail to be an object of hatred to these Gentlemen. The love of Religion, which he strives to engrave in the hearts of the Savages, holds these Neophytes strongly to our alliance, and alienates them from that of the English.

"They also regard me as an invincible obstacle to the design which they have to spread themselves over the Abnakis' territory, & little by little to seize the continent which is between New England and Acadia. They have often sought to carry me off from my flock, & more than once my head has been put on sale.[1] It was toward the end of January in the year 1722, that they made a new attempt,

---

[1] Charlevoix, who almost literally quotes Ralé, says: "They set a price on his head and promised a thousand pounds sterling to anyone who brought it to them." Our own writers have copied and repeated this without taking the trouble to ascertain the facts relative to the transaction. This statement of Charlevoix fairly exhibits the percentage of truth to be found in his entertaining history. The following is the act which passed the General Assembly July 13, 1720: "This court being credibly informed that Mons. Rallé, the Jesuit, residing among the Eastern Indians, has not only, on several occasions of late, affronted His Majesty's government of this Province, but has also been the incendiary that has instigated and stirred up those Indians to treat His Majesty's subjects settling there in the abusive, insolent, hostile manner that they have done.

which had no other success than to show their ill will in regard to me.

"I had remained alone in the village with a small number of the old and infirm, while the rest of the savages were off hunting. The time seemed favorable to them to surprise me, & with this in view they sent out a detachment of 200 men. Two young Abnakis who were hunting on the seashore, learned that the English had entered the river; they immediately turned their steps that way in order to watch their progress; having perceived them at ten leagues from the village, they outran them in crossing the country to give me warning, & to cause the old men, women & children to retire in haste.

"I had but time to swallow the consecrated Wafers, to put the holy Vessels into a little chest, & to save

---

"*Resolved*, That a premium of One Hundred Pounds be allowed and paid out of the Public Treasury to any person that shall apprehend the s^d Jesuit within any part of this Province and bring him to Boston and render him to justice."

It will be seen that no price was put upon his head, and that the sum offered was one-tenth the sum Ralé and Charlevoix state it to have been. (*Vide* Shea's Charlevoix, New York, 1871, vol. 5, p. 275; Council Records, Massachusetts Archives, vol. 8, p. 71.)

myself in the woods. The English arrived in the evening at the Village, & not having found me, they came the next day to search for me, even to the place of our retreat. They were in gunshot when we discovered them; all that I could do, was to bury myself in haste in the depths of the forest. But as I had not the time to take my snowshoes & besides as there remained to me considerable weakness from a fall from which several years since I had a broken leg & thigh, it was impossible for me to fly very far. The only resource left me, was to conceal myself behind a tree. They immediately traversed the different paths made by the Savages, when they went to gather wood, & when they came within eight steps of the tree which concealed & where naturally they ought to have seen me, as the trees were stripped of leaves; still as if they had been restrained by an invisible hand, they all at once retraced their steps & repaired again to the village.

"It was thus as by an especial protection of God that I escaped their hands. They pillaged my Church & my little dwelling, whereby they almost reduced me to death by hunger in the midst of the woods. It is true that when they knew of my adventure at Quebec, they immediately sent me provisions, but they could not arrive until very late, & during that time I found myself deprived of all succor and in extreme need.

"These repeated insults made the Savages judge that they had no further answer to expect, & that it was time to repel violence, & to make open force succeed peaceful negotiations. On returning from the hunt, & after having sown their lands they took the resolution to destroy the newly constructed dwellings of the English and to remove far from them these unquiet & redoubtable guests, who little by little encroached on their lands & who meditated enslaving them. They sent a deputation into the different villages of the Savages, to interest them in their cause & to engage them to lend a hand in the necessity wherein they were making a just defence. The deputation was successful. They chanted the war among the Hurons of Lorette, & in all the villages of the Abnaki Nations. Norridgewock was the place designed for the assembling of the Warriors, that they might concert their plans together. Meanwhile the Norridgewockians descended the river; arrived at its mouth, they seized three or four little Vessels belonging to the English. Then reascending the same river they pillaged and burned the new houses which the English had built. They abstained nevertheless from all violence toward the inhabitants; they even permitted them to withdraw to their people, excepting five whom they retained as hostages until their countrymen had been given up who were detained in the prisons of Boston.

"This moderation of the Savages had not the effect which they hoped; on the contrary a party of English having found sixteen Abnakis sleeping on an Island, made a general discharge on them, by which five were killed and three wounded.[1]

"This is the new signal of the war, which is being lighted between the English and the Savages. The latter expected no help from the French, because of the peace which reigns between the two Nations; but they have one resource in all the other Savage Nations, who will not fail to enter into their quarrel, and to take up their defense.

"My Neophytes, touched by the peril in which I found myself exposed in their Village, often press me to retire for a while to Quebec. But what will become of the flock, if it is deprived of its Shepherd? There is nothing but death that can seperate me from it. They have well represented to me, that in

---

[1] This relates to Harmon's act at Pleasant Point and is another strange perversion of facts, perhaps caused by a too ready confidence in savage *raconteurs*.

case I should fall into the power of their enemies, the least that can befall me is to languish the rest of my life in a hard prison; I close their mouths with the words of the Apostle, which Divine goodness has engraved deep in my heart, "Do not trouble yourselves, I say to them as to what regards me; I fear not the threats of those who hate me without a cause & *I count not my life dear unto myself that I might finish my course, & the ministry which I have received of the Lord Jesus.* Pray him my dear Nephew that he will strengthen in me this sentiment which springs only from his mercy, to the end I may live and die without ceasing to labor for the salvation of these neglected souls, which are the price of his Blood, & which he has deigned to commit to my care.

"I am, &c."

We can but admire the calm reliance of Ralé upon the protection of a higher power, and his entire devotion to what he considered his duty. The spirit which he exhibits in his religious work largely compensates for his arrogant assumptions of superiority over religious workers in other fields, and the weakness which he displays in recounting the prowess of his savage people, and accepting their relations of transactions with the English as facts to be recorded as history. Nor, regarding him as a fallible Christian of a fallible age, should we be surprised that he did not love the English, though as a disciple of Christ, we should admire him more if he had displayed more charity toward them. This lack, however, was to prove his bane. He had taken the sword figuratively, and was to perish by it.

In the winter of 1723, another expedition against Norridgewock was planned. It was led by the intrepid Harmon, but he found the country impassable, and returned to camp without accomplishing his purpose. This failure but strengthened the self-confidence of the savages, and increased their audacity. The Rev. Joseph Willard was surprised on the highway and killed after a struggle in which he manfully defended his life.[1] The Abnaki converts had killed three of New England's Christian pastors, who had

---

[1] He was a graduate of Yale College, in 1714, and was settled in the ministry at Southerland for several years after leaving college. In the summer of 1721 he moved to Rutland. On the 14th of August, 1723, a party of five savages fell upon Deacon Joseph Stevens and his four sons while making hay on their farm at Rutland. Two of the sons were killed, and two made prisoners; but the father escaped by concealing himself in some bushes. Two of the savages then concealed themselves in ambush to surprise some other haymakers in the vicinity, but

taken no part in the war, nor done anything to make themselves conspicuous. To many it seemed as if the war was a religious one, and that the cause of it could be traced to the Jesuit missions, established in defiance of a law of England, which prohibited even the residence of a Jesuit within her territorial possessions.

Ralé and Lauverjeat, his confreré on the Penobscot, were certainly encouraging their neophytes in the war, and glorying in their successes. About this time he penned the following interesting letter to his brother in France.[1]

"At Nanrantsouak, this 12th. of October 1723.

"Monsieur and very dear brother:

"The peace of Our Lord:

"I can no longer refuse the kind requests which you make me in all your letters, to inform you a little in detail of my occupations and of the charac-

---

not wanting to be too long separated from their companions, who had gone on with the prisoners, they started to join them, when they encountered Mr. Willard, who was armed, and fired upon him. Willard returned the fire, and wounded one of them. The other would probably have been overpowered had not the three others, hearing the firing, come to his assistance and slain the brave minister.

[1] *Vide* Lettres Edifiantes et Curieuses, Paris, 1726. The translation is the author's.

ter of the Savage nations, in the midst of which Providence has placed me for so many years. I do it the more willingly, because in conforming in this regard to wishes so urgent on your part I satisfy yet more your affection and curiosity.

"It was the 23 of July of the year 1689 that I embarked at Rochelle; and after three months of a pleasant enough voyage, I arrived at Quebec the 13 of October of the same year. I applied myself at first to learning the language of our Savages. This is difficult; because it is not sufficient to study the terms and their signification and to make a collection of words and phrases, it is still necessary to know the turn and the arrangement which the savages give them, which one hardly acquires except by intercourse and association with these people.

"I went then to dwell in a village with the Abnaki nation, situated in a forest, which is only three leagues from Quebec. This was inhabited by two hundred savages nearly all Christians. Their cabins were arranged a little like the houses in the towns; an inclosure of stakes, thick and high, form a kind of wall which shelters them from the incursions of their enemies.

"Their cabins are very soon set up; they plant poles which they join at the top; and they cover them with great sheets of bark. The fire is made in the middle of the cabin; they spread all round rush mats, on which they sit during the day; and take their repose during the night.

"The clothing of the men consists of a cassock of skin, or else of a piece of red or blue stuff. That of the women is a blanket; which hangs from the neck quite to the middle of the legs and which they adjust quite properly. They put another blanket on the head, which descends even to the feet and which serves them for a cloak. Their stockings extend only from the knee to the ankle. Socks made of elks' hide and lined inside with hair or wool serve them in place of shoes. This sock is absolutely necessary to them in order to be adjusted to the snow-shoes, by means of which they walk upon the snow. These snow-shoes are made lozenge shape, are more than two feet long and a foot and a half wide. I did not believe that I could ever walk with such machines; when I made trial of them I soon found it so easy that the savages could not believe that it was the first time that I had made use of them. The invention of these snow-shoes is of great use to these savages not only to travel on the snow, with which the ground is covered a great part of the year, but also to go in pursuit of beasts and above all of the moose; these animals, larger than the largest oxen of France walk only with difficulty upon the snow; thus it is not difficult for the savages to overtake them, and they often kill them with a common knife attached to the end of a stick, they feed upon their flesh and after having well dressed their skins in which they are skillful they trade them with French and English who give them in exchange cassocks, blankets, kettles, guns, hatchets and knives.

"To give you an idea of a savage, picture to yourself a large man strong, agile, of a swarthy tint, without beard, with black hair, and whose teeth are whiter than ivory. If you wish to see him in his acoutrements you will only find for his whole adornment what is called beads; this is a kind of shell or stone which they fashion into the form of little grains, some white and others black, and which they string in such a manner, that they represent divers very regular figures which are agreeable to them. It is with this bead that our Savages knot and plait their hair above their ears and behind, make collars, garters, belts, five or six inches wide and with this sort of ornaments they estimate themselves a great deal more than an European does with all his gold and his jewels.

"The occupation of the men is hunting or war, that of the women is to remain in the village and to make there out of bark, baskets, bags, boxes, dishes, plates etc. They sew the bark with roots and make of them various utensils very appropriately wrought, the canoes are likewise made solely of bark, but the largest can scarce hold more than six or seven persons.

"It is with these canoes made of a bark which has hardly the thickness of a crown, that they cross the arms of the sea, and that they navigate the most dangerous rivers and lakes of four or five hundred leagues around. I have thus made many voyages without having run any risk. Only once, that in crossing the river Saint Lawrence I found myself suddenly surrounded with masses of ice of enormous size and the canoe was wedged in them; at once the two savages who conducted me cried out; "we are dead men; it is done, we must perish," in the mean time making an effort, they leaped upon the floating ice. I did like them, and after having drawn up the canoe we carried it to the extremity of this ice. Then it was necessary for us to place ourselves again in the canoe to gain another ice cake, and thus then leaping from ice cake to ice cake, we arrived at last at the bank of the stream without other inconvenience than being very wet and numb with cold. Nothing equals the affection which the savages have for their children. As soon as they are born, they place them on a little piece of board covered with cloth and a little bear skin in which they envelope them, and this is their cradle. The mothers carry them on their back in a manner convenient for the children and for them. Hardly do the children begin to walk when they are trained to draw the bow. They become so adroit in this, that at the age of ten or twelve years they do not fail to kill the bird that they shoot at. I have been surprised at it, and I should have hardly believed it, if I had not been witness of it.

"That which I most revolted at when I began to live with the savages was to find myself obliged to take my repast with them; nothing is more disgusting. After having filled their pot with meat they make it boil at the most three quarters of an hour, after which they take it from the fire, serve it in bark porringers and divide it with all those who are in the cabin. Each one bites into this meat as he would into a piece of bread. This spectacle did not give me much appetite, and they very soon noticed my repugnance. 'Why dost thou not eat,' they asked. I replied to them that I was not accustomed to eat meat thus, without adding to it a piece of bread. 'It is necessary to conquer thyself,' they replied, 'is it so difficult as to be a patriarch who knows prayer perfectly? We overcome a great deal to believe that which we cannot see.' After this there was no more to consider. It was best to bring one's self to their manners and customs in order to merit their confidence and gain them to Jesus Christ.

"Their meals are not regular as in Europe, they live from hand to mouth, whilst they have somewhat from which to make good cheer, they profit by it, without troubling themselves about having anything to live on the following days.

"They passionately love tobacco; men, women, children smoke almost continually. To give them a piece of tobacco, is to give them more pleasure than to give them their weight in gold.

"In the beginning of June, and when the snow is nearly all melted, they sow the *skamgar*, this is what we call Turkey or Indian wheat. Their style of sowing is to make with the fingers or with a little stick, different holes in the ground, and to throw in each eight or nine kernels, which they cover with the same earth which they have withdrawn to make the hole. Their harvest takes place at the end of August.

"It is in the midst of these people, who pass for the least coarse of all our savages, that I passed the apprenticeship of a missionary. My principal occupation was the study of their tongue: it is very difficult to learn, above all when one has no other masters than savages. They have many sounds which they only utter from the throat, without making any movement of the lips; *ou*, for example is of this number, and this is why in writing it, we make it by the figure 8, to distinguish it from other sounds. I passed a part of a year in their cabins and heard them talk. It was necessary for me to maintain extreme attention, to gather what they said, and to conjecture the signification of it. Sometimes I guessed right, more often I deceived myself, because not very able to manage their guttural letters. I repeated only part of the word, and this made them laugh. At last, after five months of continual application, I reached the point of understanding all their terms, but that was not sufficient for me to express myself according to their taste. I had still a good way to go to catch the scope and genius of their tongue, which is altogether different from the genius and scope of our European languages. To shorten the time and to put myself sooner in a state to exercise my functions, I made choice of some savages who had more wit and spoke better. I told them roughly some articles of the catechism, and they rendered them to me in all the delicacy of their language. I put them at once on paper, and by this means I made myself in a little while a dictionary and a catechism which contained the principles and the mysteries of religion.

"One cannot deny that the language of the savages has true beauties, and I know not what of energy, in the turn and manner in which they express themselves. I am going to give you an example of it. If I should ask you, Why God has created you? You would reply to me, that it is to know him, to love him and to serve him, and by this means to merit eternal glory. But should I put the same question to a savage, he would reply to me thus in the term of his language; The great Spirit has thought of us; let them know me, let them love me, let them honor me, and let them obey me for then I shall make them enter into my glorious felicity. If I should wish to tell you in their style, that you would have much difficulty in learning the savage tongue, see how it would be necessary to express myself; I think of you my dear brother, that he will find difficulty in learning the savage tongue. The language of the Hurons is the master language of the savages; and when one possesses it in less than three months one can make himself understood by the five Iroquois nations. It is the most Majestic and the most difficult of all the savage tongues. This difficulty does not come alone from their guttural character, but still more from the diversity of accents, because two words composed of the same characters have significations quite different. Father Chaumont, who has dwelt fifty years among the Hurons, has composed a grammar of it, which is very useful to those who newly arrive in that mission, nevertheless a missionary is most happy when, with those helps, after ten years constant labor, he expresses himself elegantly in this language.

"Each savage nation has its particular tongue; thus the Abnakis, the Hurons, the Iroquois, the Algonkins, the Illinois, the Miamis, etc., have each their language. They have no books to learn these languages, and, when they shall have them, they will be useless enough. Practice is the only master which can instruct us. While I have labored in four different missions of savages, namely among the Abnakis, the Algonkins, the Hurons and the Illinois, I have been obliged to learn these different languages. I am going to give you a specimen, to the end that you may know the little relation which there is between them. I choose the strophe of a hymn of the Holy Sacrament, which they ordinarily chant during the Mass at the elevation of the sacred host and which begins in these words, O Salutaris, hostia ; Such is the translation in verse of this strophe in the four languages of these different nations.[1]

En langue abnakise.

Kighist oui- nuanuiouinns
Spem kik papili go ii damek
Nemiani oui kouidan gha benk
Taha saii grihine.

En lan langue algonkine.

Kouerais Jesus teousenam
Nara oueul ka stisian
Ka rio vllighe miang
Vas mama vik umong.

En langue huronne.

Je ous outo etti xichie
Outo etti skuaalichi-axe
J chierche axeraouensta
D'aotierti xeata-ouien.

En langue illinoise.

Pekiziane manet oue
Piaro nile hi Nanghi
Keninama oui ouKangha
Mero ouinang ousianghi.

---

[1] The author has substituted *ou* in place of the figure 8, as given by Ralé.

which signifies in French : 'O saving sacrifice who art continually offered, and who givest life ; thou by whom we enter heaven, we are continually assaulted ; come strengthen us.'

"It was nearly two years that I lived with the Abnakis, when I was recalled by my superiors; they destined me to the mission of the Illinois, who had lost their missionary. I went then to Quebec, where, after having employed three months in studying the Algonkin tongue, I embarked the 13th. of August in a canoe, to go to the Illinois; their country is distant from Quebec more than eight hundred leagues. You may well judge that so long a voyage in these barbarous lands cannot be made without running great risks, and without suffering great inconvenience. I had to traverse lakes of immense extent, and where storms are as frequent as on the sea. It is true that one has the advantage of setting foot on land every night; but one is fortunate when one finds some flat rock where one may pass the night. When the rain falls, the only means of protection is to place oneself beneath the turned over canoe.

"One runs still greater dangers on the rivers, principally in places where they flow with extreme rapidity. Then the canoe flies like an arrow, and if it comes in contact with rocks, which one finds there in abundance, it breaks into a thousand pieces. This misfortune happened to some of those who accompanied me in other canoes, and it is by a singular protection of divine goodness that I did not suffer the same fate; because my canoe struck several times against the rocks, without receiving the least damage. In fine, one risks suffering from hunger that which is most cruel. The length and the difficulty of these kinds of voyages only permits bringing with one a sack of Indian corn. One would suppose that the chase would furnish on the route something to live upon; but if the game fails, one finds oneself exposed to many days of fasting. Then all the resource which one has is to search for a kind of leaves, which the savages call *Kingnessanach*, and the French *tripes de roches*.[1] One would take them for Cerfeuil, of which they have the shape, if they were not much larger; they serve them either boiled or roasted; those which I have eaten are not so bad.

"I did not suffer much from hunger as far as the lake of the Hurons, but it was not the same with the companions of my voyage; the bad weather having

---

[1] Literally rock tripe. A bitter and purgative fungus found growing on rocks, and used extensively by the inhabitants of the far north for food.

scattered their canoes, they could not join me. I arrived the first at Missilimakinak, from whence I sent them food, without which they would have died of hunger. They had passed seven days without any nourishment but that of a crow, which they had killed rather by chance than by skill, for they had not strength to support themselves.

"The season was too far advanced to continue my route as far as to the Illinois, from whence I was yet distant about four hundred leagues. Thus it was necessary for me to remain at Missilimakinak, where there were two of our missionaries, one among the Hurons, and the other with the Outaouacks. The latter are very superstitious and much attached to the jugleries of their medicine men. They attribute to themselves an origin as senseless as ridiculous. They pretend to spring from families, and each family is composed of five hundred persons.

"Some are of the family of Michabou, that is to say of the great hare. They pretend that this great hare was a man of prodigious size, that he could spread nets in the water at eighteen feet in depth, and that the water came hardly to his armpits; that one day, during the deluge, he sent the beaver to discover the land; but as this animal did not return he sent out the otter, who brought back a little earth covered with foam; that he repaired to the place in the lake where he found this earth, which formed a little isle; all around which he walked in the water, and that this island became extraordinarily large. This is why is attributed to him the creation of the earth. They add that after having accomplished this work he flew up to heaven, which is his ordinary abode, but before quitting the earth, when his descendants came to die, that they should burn their bodies and throw their ashes into the air, so that they should more easily raise themselves towards heaven; that if they should fail in this, the snow would cease to cover the earth, that their lakes and their rivers would remain frozen, and that, not being able to angle for fish, which is their common food, they would all die in the spring.

"In fact, a few years ago, the winter having continued longer than ordinary, there was a general consternation among the savages of the family of the great hare. They had recourse to their accustomed jugleries; they assembled many times in order to advise on the means of dissipating this snow enemy who seemed obstinate to remain upon the earth; when an old woman approached them. 'My children,' said she, 'you have no wit, you know the orders that the great hare has left to burn the bodies of the dead and to throw their ashes to the wind, to the end that they should return more promptly to heaven, their country; and you have neglected his orders by leaving some days journey from here a dead man without burning, as if he was not of the family of the great hare. Repair forthwith your fault, take care to burn him if you wish that the snow should disappear.' 'You are right our mother' replied they, 'thou hast more wit than we and the council which thou givest us restores life to us.' They immediately deputed twenty-five men to go and burn this body. They employed about fifteen days in this journey. During that time the thaw came and the snow melted. They loaded with praises and presents the old woman who had given the advice; and this event, quite natural as it was, served much to confirm them in their folly and superstitious credulity.

"The second family of the Outaouacks pretend to have sprung from the *Namepick*, that is to say from the carp. They say that a carp having laid his eggs upon the bank of the river, and the Sun having darted its rays there, he formed a woman from them from whom they are descended. Thus they call themselves of the family of the carp.

"The third family of the Outaouacks attributes its origin to the paw of the *Machova*, that is to say, of a bear, and they call themselves of the family of the bear, but without explaining in what manner they are sprung from it. When they kill any of these animals they make a feast to him of his own flesh; they speak to him, they harangue him; 'do not have any design against us,' they say to him, 'because we have killed thee; thou hast wit, thou seest that our children suffer for hunger, they wish to make thee enter into their bodies, is it not glorious for thee to be eaten by the children of the chief?'

"It is only the family of the great hare which burns dead bodies, the two others bury them. When any chief dies they prepare a vast coffin, where, after having laid the body clothed in its finest garments, they enclose with him his blanket, his gun, his supply of powder and lead, his bow, his arrows, his kettle, his platter, some provisions, his tomahawk, his pipe, his box of vermillion, his mirror, some collars of beads, and all the presents which were made at his death according to usage. They imagine that with this outfit he will make his journey more happily to the other world, and will be better received by the great chiefs of the nation, who will conduct him with them into a place of delights.

"While all is being adjusted in the coffin the relatives of the dead assist at the ceremony by mourning after their fashion, that is to say, by chanting in a lugubrious tone and beating time with a stick to which they have attached many rattles.

"Where the superstition of these people appears the most extravagant is in the worship that they render to that which they call their *manitou*. As they scarcely know anything but the beasts with which they live in the forests, they imagine within these beasts, or within their skin, or within their plumage, a kind of spirit which governs all things, and which is the master of life and death. There are, according to them manitous common to all the nation, and there are particular ones for each person. *Oussakita*, say they, is the great manitou of all the beasts which walk upon the earth, or which fly in the air. It is he who governs them; thus when they go to chase, they offer him tobacco, powder, lead, and skins well dressed, which they attach to the end of a pole, and elevate it in the air. '*Oussakita*,' they say to him, 'we give thee to smoke, we offer thee of that to kill the game, deign to accept these presents, do not permit that they should escape our arrows, let us kill a great number of the fattest of them, so that our children shall neither fail of clothing, nor of nourishment.

"They call *Michibichi* the manitou of the waters and of the fish, and they make a sacrifice to him nearly similiar when they go to fish or when they undertake a journey. This sacrifice consists of throwing into the water some tobacco, food, kettles, and asking him that the waters of the river should flow more slowly, that the rocks should not break their canoes, and that he accord to them fish in abundance.

"Besides these common manitous, each has his own particular one, which is a bear, or a beaver, or a bustard, or some similar beast. They carry the skin of this animal to the war, to the chase, and on their journeys, persuading themselves that they preserve them from all danger and that they will make them successful in their undertakings.

"When a savage wishes to get a manitou, the first animal which presents itself to his imagination during his sleep is commonly the one upon which his choice falls. He kills a beast of this kind; he puts his skin, or his plumage, if it is a bird in the most honorable place in his cabin; he prepares a feast in his honor, during which he makes to him his harangue in terms the most respectful, after which he is known as his manitou.

"As soon as I saw the spring arrive, I left Missilimakinak to go to the Illinois. I found on my route many savage nations, among others Maskoutings, Jakis, Omikoues, Iripegouans, Outagamis, etc. All these nations have their peculiar language but for all the rest they differ in nothing from the Outaouacks. A missionary who dwells at the bay of the Puants, makes from time to time excursions among these savages to instruct them in the truths of religion.

" After forty days walking, I entered the river of the Illinois, and having advanced fifty leagues I arrived at the first village, which was of three hundred cabins, all of four or five fires. One fire is always for two families. They have twelve villages of their nation. On the morrow after my arrival I was invited by the principal chief to a grand repast, which he gave to the more considerable persons. He had caused to be killed for this a number of dogs ; such a banquet passes among the savages for a magnificent feast ; it is why they call it the feast of the chief. The ceremonies which they observe are the same among all the nations. It is common in these sorts of festivals that the savages deliberate upon their most important affairs, as, for example, when it is agitated, either to undertake war against their neighbors, or to terminate it by a proposition of peace.

"When all the guests have arrived, they range themselves all around the cabin, seating themselves either on the bare earth, or on mats. Then the chief arises and begins his harangue. I avow to you that I admired his flow of words, the justice and the force of reasons which he displayed, the eloquent turn that he gave them, the choice and delicacy of the expressions, with which he adorned his discourse. I am persuaded that if I could put in writing what this savage said to us on that moment and without preparation, it would convince you without difficulty that the most able European, after much meditation and study, could scarcely compose a discourse more solid and better termed.

"Their harangue finished, two savages who performed the function of carvers, distributed the plates to all the assembly, and each plate was for two guests, they ate conversing together of indifferent things; and when the repast was finished, they retired, carrying, according to their custom, that which they had remaining in their plates.

"The Illinois do not give those feasts which are customary with many other savage nations, where one is obliged to eat all that has been served to him, should one burst by it. When it happens that any one has not the power to observe this ridiculous rule, he addresses himself to some one of the guests, whom he knows to be of a better appetite; 'My brother,' says he to him, 'have pity on me, I am dead if thou dost not give me life, eat that which remains to me, I will make thee a present of something.' It is the only means to escape from embarrassment.

"The Illinois only cover themselves about the waist, and as to the rest, they go all naked; different compartments of all sorts of figures, which they engrave on the body in a way which is ineffaceable, hold for them the place of garments. It is only in the visits which they make or when they assist at church, that they wrap about them a covering of dressed skin during the summer, and during the winter, of a skin, with the hair on, which they leave to retain more warmth. They adorn the head with feathers, of different colors, with which they make garlands and crowns, which they adjust quite properly; they take care to paint the face with different colors, but above all with vermillion; they wear collars, and pendants from the ears made of different stones which they cut in the form of precious stones;

some are blue, red and white like alabaster, to which it is necessary to add a plate of porcelain which finishes the collar. The Illinois persuade themselves that these fantastic ornaments give them grace and attract respect.

"When the Illinois are not occupied in war or in the chase, the time is passed either in sport, or in feasts, or in the dance. They have two sorts of dances; some which are used in token of rejoicing, and to which they invite the most distinguished women and girls; the others are used to mark their grief, the death of the more important of their nations. It is by these dances, that they pretend to honor the deceased, and to dry the tears of their relatives. All have the right to mourn in this way the death of their relations, providing they make presents for this purpose. The dances last more or less time, in proportion to the price and value of the presents and they immediately distribute them to the dancers, their custom is not to bury the dead; they wrap them in skins and attach them by the head and feet to the tops of trees. Excepting their times of sports, of feasts and dances, the men remain quietly on their mats, and pass their time in sleeping, or in making bows, arrows, pipes, and other things of this nature. As for the women, they work from morning till night like slaves. It is for them to cultivate the land, and to sow the corn during the summer; and from the beginning of winter they are occupied in making mats, in dressing skins, and in many other kinds of work; because their first care is to provide the cabin with all that is necessary therein.

"Of all the nations of Canada, there are none who live in so great abundance of all things as the Illinois. Their rivers are covered with swans, with bustards, with ducks, and with teals. Hardly can one go a league, but he finds a prodigious multitude of turkeys, which go in flocks, sometimes to the number of two hundred. They are bigger than those which one sees in France. I had the curiosity to weigh some which were of the weight of thirty pounds. They have at the neck a kind of wattle of hair a half a foot in length. The bears and the stags are there in very great quantity; one also sees there an infinite number of buffaloes and deers; there is not a year that they do not kill thousands of deers, and more than two thousands of buffaloes; one sees on the prairies till lost to view from four to five thousand buffaloes which feed there. They have a hump on the back, and a head extremely large. Their hair, except that on the head, is curled and soft as wool, their flesh is naturally salt, and is so light, that although one eats it quite raw, it does not cause indigestion. When they have killed a buffalo, which appears to them too lean, they are contented to take the tongue, and go to seek one fatter.

"Arrows are the principal arms which serve them, in war and in the chase. These arrows are armed at the end with a cut stone and sharpened in the form of a serpent's tongue; lacking a knife they serve them also to skin the animals which they kill. They are so adroit in drawing the bow, that they hardly ever miss their stroke, and they do it with so much swiftness that they will have sooner discharged a hundred arrows than another will have charged his gun. They put themselves to little trouble in working with the proper nets to fish in the rivers, because the abundance of animals of all sorts which they find for their subsistence, renders them quite indifferent to fish. However, when they take a fancy to have them, they embark in a canoe with their bows and their arrows, standing upright the better to discover the fish, and as soon as they have perceived him, they pierce him with an arrow.

"The only means among the Illinois to public esteem and veneration is, as with other savages, to make the reputation of a skilful hunter, and yet more of a good warrior; it is principally of that which they make their merit consist, and it is that which they call to be truly a man. They are so passionate for this glory that they will undertake journeys of four hundred leagues, in the midst of forests, to make a slave, or to take the scalp from a man whom they have killed. They count for nothing the fatigues and the long fasts which they have to sustain, above all when they approach the enemy's land; because then they no longer dare to hunt, from fear that the beasts, being only wounded may fly with the arrow in the body, and warn their enemy to put himself in state of defense, because their manner of making war, the same as among all savages, is to surprise their enemies; this is why they send out scouts, to observe their number and their march, or to note if they are on their guard. According to the report which is made them, they either put themselves in ambush, or make an irruption into their cabins, tomahawk in hand, and they do not fail to kill some of them before they had dreamed to defend themselves.

"The tomahawk is made of a stag's horn, or of wood in the shape of a cutlass, terminated by a large ball. They hold the tomahawk in one hand and the knife in the other. As soon as they have dealt their blow on the head of their enemy they encircle it with their knife, and remove the scalp with a surprising rapidity.

"When the savage returns to his country laden with many scalps he is received with great honors; but it is for him the height of glory when he makes prisoners, and brings them alive. As soon as he arrives all the people of the village assemble and range themselves in a line on the road where the prisoners should pass. This reception is very cruel; some tear out their nails, others cut off their fingers or ears; while others deal them blows with clubs.

"After this first reception, the old men assemble to deliberate if they shall accord life to their prisoners or if they shall put them to death. When there is some dead person to revive, that is to say, if some one of their warriors has been killed, and whom they judge should be replaced in his cabin, they give to this cabin one of their prisoners, who holds the place of the deceased and this is what they call reviving the dead.

"When the prisoner is condemned to death, they plant immediately in the earth a great post, to which they attach him by both hands; they make him sing the song of death, and all the savages being seated around the post, they kindle a few steps from it a great fire, where they heat hatchets, gun barrels, and other irons. Then they come one after the other, and apply them all red upon different parts of the body, there are those who burn him with fire brands; some who gash his body with their knives; others who cut off a piece of flesh already roasted, and eat it in his presence; one may be seen filling his wounds with powder, and rubbing it all over his body, after which they set it on fire. In fine each torments him according to his caprice, and that during four or five hours, sometimes even during two or three days. The more shrill and piercing the cries which the violence of these torments make him utter, the more agreeable and diverting is the spectacle to these barbarians. It was the Iroquois who invented this frightful kind of death, and it is only by way of retaliation that the Illinois, in their turn, treat their Iroquois prisoners with an equal cruelty.

"That which we understand by the word christianity, is known only among all the savages by the name of prayer. Thus, when, I shall say to you in the remainder of this letter, that such a savage nation has embraced prayer, it is saying, that it has become christian, or that it is disposed to be so. One would have had less trouble in converting the Illinois, if the prayer had permitted polygamy among them. They avow that prayer is good, and they are pleased when it is talked to their women and children; but when one speaks of it to themselves; one finds how difficult it is to fix their natural inconstancy and to persuade them to have but one wife and to have her always.

"At the hour when they assemble, morning and evening, for prayer, all repair to the chapel. There are none even among their greatest medicine men, that is to say, among the greatest enemies of religion, who do not send their children to be instructed and baptized. Here is the greatest fruit which one finds at first among the savages, and of which one is the most certain; because among the great number of infants, not a year passes but many die before they reach the age of reason;[1] and among the adults, the most part is so fervent and so attached to prayer, that they would suffer the most cruel death rather than abandon it.

"It is a blessing for the Illinois to be far removed from Quebec, because they cannot carry to them the fire-water as they do others. This drink is among the savages the greatest obstacle to christianity and the source of an infinite number of the most shocking

---

[1] The idea here is, that those dying before the age of reason were saved if they had received baptism.

crimes. We know that they only purchase it in order to plunge themselves into the most furious intoxication; the disorders and the sad deaths of which one is witness every day should much overbalance the gain which one can make by traffic in so fatal a liquor.

"It was two years that I abode with the Illinois, when I was recalled to consecrate the rest of my days to the Abnaki nation. It was the first mission to which I had been destined at my arrival in Canada, and it is that apparently, where I shall finish my life. It was necessary then for me to return to Quebec, to go from there to rejoin my dear savages. I have already described to you the length and difficulties of this journey; therefore, I will speak to you only of a very consoling adventure to me four leagues from Quebec.

"I found myself in a kind of village, where there are twenty five French houses, and a curé, who had care of it. Near this village appeared a cabin of savages, where was found a girl of the age of sixteen years, whom a sickness of many years had reduced to extremity. M. the curé, who did not understand the language of these savages, prayed me to go to confess the sick girl, and conducted me himself to her cabin. In the conversation which I had with this young girl, on the truths of religion, I learned that she had been very well instructed by one of our missionaries, but that she had not yet received baptism. After having passed two days to put to her all the questions proper, to assure myself of her disposition; 'Do not refuse me, I conjure thee,' said she to me, 'the grace of the baptism that I demand of thee; thou seest how much my breast is oppressed and that but little time remains to me to live; how unfortunate it would be to me; and what reproaches wouldest thou not have to make to thyself, if I should die without receiving this grace?' I replied to her that she should prepare for it on the next day, and retired. The joy which my reply caused her, worked in her a change so immediate that she was in a state to repair early in the morning to chapel. I was extremely surprised at her arrival and immediately I solemnly administered baptism to her. After which she returned to her cabin where she ceased not to thank the divine mercy for so great a blessing; and to sigh for the happy moment which should unite her to God for all eternity. Her desires were granted, and I had the happiness to assist at her death. What a stroke of providence for this poor girl, and what consolation for me to have been the instrument which God had well wished to use to place her in heaven.

"You do not require from me, My dear brother, that I should enter into the detail of all that which has happened to me during the many years that I am in this mission; my occupations are always the same, and I should expose myself to wearisome repetitions. I will content myself by reporting to you certain facts, which appear to me the most to merit your attention.

"I can tell you in general that you would find it difficult to restrain your tears if you found yourself in my church with our assembled savages, and if you should be witness of the piety with which they recite their prayers, chant the divine offices and participate in the sacraments of penance and the eucharist. When they have been illumined with the lights of faith, and when they have sincerely embraced it they are not the same men, and the most part preserve the innocence which they have received from baptism. It is this which fills me with the sweetest joy, when I hear their confessions, which are frequent; whatever the questions which I put to them, I can often hardly find matter to absolve them from.

"My occupations with them are continual. As they only expect help from their missionary and as they have in him complete confidence, it does not suffice me to fulfill the spiritual functions of my ministry for the sanctification of their souls, it is still necessary that I enter into their temporal affairs that I may always be ready to comfort them, when they come to consult me, and that I should decide their little differences, that I should take care of them when they are sick, that I should bleed them, that I should give them medicines, etc. My days are sometimes so full, that I am obliged to shut myself up in order to find time to devote to prayer, and to recite my office.

"The zealous spirit with which God has filled me for the welfare of my savages was much alarmed in the year 1697, when I learned that a nation of Amalingan savages were coming to establish themselves a day's journey from my village. I had ground to fear that the jugleries of their medicine men, that is the sacrifices which they make to the demon and the disorders which ordinarily follow, might make an impression upon some of my young neophytes; but thanks to the divine mercy, my fears were very soon dissipated by what I am going to tell you.

"One of our captains, celebrated for his valor, having been killed by the English, from whom we are not distant, the Amalingans sent several of their nation into our village, to dry the tears of the relatives of this illustrious deceased, that is to say, as I have already explained to you, to visit them, to make presents to them, and to testify to them by their dances the part which they take in their affliction. They arrived on the eve of Corpus Christi. I was then occupied in hearing the confessions of my savages, which continued all that day, the night following, and the next day until noon, when began the procession of the Consecrated Host. It was done with much order and piety, and, even in the midst of these forests, with more pomp and magnificence than you yourself could imagine. This spectacle, which was new for the Amalingans, attracted them, and struck them with admiration. I thought it my duty to profit by the favorable disposition in which they were, and after, having assembled them, I made them the following discourse in savage style. 'It is a long time, my children that I have wished to see you; now that I have this happiness, it wants but little that my heart should burst. Think of the joy that a father has who tenderly loves his children, when he again sees them after a long absence in which they have run the greatest dangers, and you will conceive a portion of mine; because although you pray not yet, I cease not to regard you as my children, and to have for you a father's tenderness, because the children of the great Spirit, who has given you being as well as those who pray, who has made heaven for you as well as for them, who thinks of you as he thinks of them and me, that they may rejoice in eternal happiness. That which gives me pain, and lessens the joy that I have in seeing you is the reflection which I actually make, that one day I shall be separated from one part of my children, whose lot will be eternally unhappy, because they do not pray; while the others who pray will be in the joy which never ends. When I think of this sad separation can I have a contented heart? The happiness of some does not give me so much joy, as the unhappiness of others afflicts me. If you had insurmountable obstacles to prayer, and if abiding in the state where you are I could make you enter into heaven I would spare nothing to secure you this happiness, I would push you in, I would make you all enter there, so much I love you, and so much I desire that you should be happy; but it is this which is not possible. It is necessary to pray, it is necessary to be baptized, in order to enter into this place of delights.'

"After this preamble, I explained to them at great length the principal articles of the faith, and I continued thus:

"'All the words which I come to explain to you are not human words; they are the words of the great Spirit; they are not written like the words of a man upon a collar, which they make to tell all that they wish; but they are written in the book of the great Spirit, where a lie cannot have access.'

"To make you understand this savage expression, it is necessary to remark, my dear brother, that the custom of these people when they write to any nation, is to send a collar, or a large belt, on which they make different figures with porcelain beads of different colors. They instruct him who carries the collar, telling him, this is what the collar says to such a nation, to such a person, and they send him forth. Our savages would have trouble in understanding what was said to them, and would be but little attentive if one did not conform himself to their manner of thought and expression; I continued thus:

"'Courage, my children, hear the voice of the great Spirit who speaks to you by my mouth, he loves you; and his love for you is so great, that he has given his life to procure for you an eternal life. Alas! perhaps he has only permitted the death of one of our captains in order to draw you to the place of prayer, and make you hear his voice. Reflect that you are not immortal. A day will come when they will likewise wipe away the tears for your death; what will serve you to have been in this life great captains, if, after your death, you are cast into eternal flames? He, for whom you come to mourn with us is happy to have listened a thousand times to the voice of the great Spirit and to have been faithful to the prayer. Pray like him, and you shall live eternally. Courage, my children, we will not separate that some should go to one side, and others to another; let us all go to heaven, it is our country, it is that to which the sole master of life calls you of whom I am only the interpreter; think of it seriously.'

"As soon as I had done speaking, they conversed together some time, afterwards their orator made me this reply on their part; 'My Father, I am glad to listen to thee. Thy voice has penetrated even into my heart, but my heart is yet closed, and I cannot open it at present, to make you know what is there, or on what side it will turn; it is necessary that I should wait a number of chiefs and other considerable people of our nation who will arrive the next autumn, it is then that I will disclose to thee my heart. Behold, My dear father, all that I have to say to thee at present.

"'My heart is content,' replied I to him; 'I am very glad that my word has given you pleasure, and that you demand time to think of it; you will only be more firm in your attachment to the prayer when you shall have once embraced it. In the meantime I shall not have ceased to address myself to the great Spirit, and to ask of him that he should regard you with eyes of pity, and that he should strengthen your thoughts to the end that they should be turned to the side of prayer.' After which I quitted their assembly and they returned to their village.

"When autumn had come, I learned that one of our savages would go to the Amalingans to seek corn to sow their lands. I made him come to me and charged him to say to them on my part that I was impatient to see my children again, that I had them always present in mind, and that I prayed them to remember the word that they had given me. The savage acquitted himself faithfully of his commission, and this is the response that the Amalingans made him.

"'We are much obliged to our father for thinking of us without ceasing. On our side, we have thought much on that which he has said to us. We cannot forget his words, while we have a heart because they have been so deeply graven there, that nothing can efface them. We are persuaded that he loves us, we wish to listen to him, and to obey him in that which he desires of us. We accept the prayer which he proposes to us and we see nothing in it but what is good and laudable; we are resolved to embrace it, and we should already have gone to find our father in his village, if there had been sufficient provisions for our subsistence during the time that he should devote to our instruction; but how can we find it there? We know that hunger is in the cabin of our father, and it is this which doubly afflicts us, that our father should be hungry and that we should not be able to see him that he may instruct us. If our father could come here to pass some time with us he would live and would instruct us. This is what you shall say to our father. This answer of the Amalingans was returned at a favorable juncture; the greater part of my savages had been gone for some days to seek wherewith to live upon until the gathering in of corn; their absence gave me leisure to visit the Amalingans, and on the next day I embarked in a canoe to repair to their village. I was no more than a league distant, when they perceived me; and immediately they saluted me with continual discharges of guns which ceased only at the landing of the canoe. This honor which they rendered me assured me of their present dispositions. I lost no time and as soon as I arrived I caused a cross to be planted, and those who accompanied me very soon raised a chapel which they made of bark in the same manner as their cabins were made, and erected an altar in it. While they were occupied with this work, I visited all the cabins of the Amalingans, to prepare them for the instruction which I should give them. As soon as I commenced they became very assiduous to understand. I assembled them three times a day in the chapel; namely, the morning after my mass, at midday, the evening after prayer. The rest of the day I went about the cabins where I gave them more particular instructions.

"When after several days of continual work, I judged that they were sufficiently instructed I fixed the day when they should come to regenerate themselves in the water of the holy baptism. The first who repaired to the cabin, were the chief, the orator, three of the more considerable of the nation, with two women. After their baptism, two other bands, each of twenty savages, succeeded them, who received the same grace. In fine all the others continued to come there on this day, and the morrow.

"You can judge well enough, my dear brother, that however the missionary labors, he is well recompensed for his fatigue by the sweet consolation that he receives in leading an entire nation of savages into the way of salvation. I prepared to leave them, and return to my own village, when a deputy came to tell me on their part that they had all assembled in the same place, and that they prayed me to repair to their assembly. As soon as I appeared in the midst of them, the orator addressed these words to me in the name of all the others. 'Our father,' said he to me, 'we have not words to testify to thee the inexpressible joy that we all feel in having received baptism. It seems to us now that we have another heart; everything which gave us trouble is entirely dissipated, our thoughts are no more wavering, the baptism interiorly fortifies us, and we are fully resolved to honor it all the days of our life. Behold what we say to thee before thou quittest us."[1] I replied to them in a little discourse, wherein I exhorted them in the singular grace which they had received, and to do nothing unworthy of the character of a child of God, with which they have been honored by the holy baptism. As they prepared to depart for the sea, I added that on their return, we should determine what would be most proper, either that we should go to dwell with them or that they

---

[1] Of course we are not to suppose that the savages ever uttered these fine sentiments. They but expressed their good will in their savage way, and their rude sentiments were transfused in the glowing imagination of the poetic Frenchman into this splendid *flux de bouche.*

should come to form with us one and the same village.

"The village where I dwell is called Nanantsouack, and is placed in a country which is situated between Acadia and New England. This mission is about eight leagues from Pentagouet, and they count it a hundred leagues from Pentagouet to Port Royal. The river of my mission is the greatest of all those which water the lands of the savages. It should be marked on the chart, under the name of Kinibeki; which has brought the French to give to these savages the name of kanibals. This river empties into the sea at Sankderank,[1] which is only five or six leagues from Pemquit. After having ascended forty leagues from Sankderank, one arrives at my village which is on the height of a point of land. We are only the distance of two days at the most from the English habitation; it takes more than fifteen days for us to reach Quebec, and the journey is very painful and difficult. It would be natural that our savages should do their trading with the English, and there are no advantages which the latter have not offered them to attract and to gain their friendship; but all their efforts have been use-

---

[1] That is, at Sagadahoc.

less and nothing has been able to detach them from alliance with the French. The only tie which has so closely united us with them is their firm attachment to the Catholic faith. They are convinced that if they gave themselves up to the English, they would very soon find themselves without a missionary, without a sacrifice, without a sacrament, and nearly without any exercise of religion, and that little by little they would be plunged into their first infidelity. This firmness of our savages has been put to all sorts of tests on the part of their powerful neighbors, without their ever having been able to gain anything.

"In the time when the war was on the point of being kindled between the powers of Europe, the English governor newly arrived at Boston, requested of our savages an interview on the sea-shore, or an island which he designated.[1] They consented to it, and prayed me to accompany them there, to consult me on the artful proposals which might be made to them, in order to be assured that their replies should have nothing contrary neither to religion, nor to the interests of the king's service. I followed them, and my intention was to keep myself simply in their

---

[1] The island of Arrowsic.

quarters, to aid them by my counsels, without appearing before the governor. As we approached the island, to the number of more than two hundred canoes, the English saluted us by a discharge of all the cannons of their ships, and all the savages responded to this salute by a light discharge of all their guns. Afterwards the governor appearing on the island, the savages landed there with precipitation; thus I found myself where I desired not to be and where the governor desired not that I should be. When he perceived me, he came some steps toward me, and after the ordinary compliments, he returned to the midst of his people, and I to the savages.

"'It is by order of our queen,' said he to them, 'that I come to see you; she desires that we should live in peace. If some English man should be imprudent enough to do you wrong, do not dream to avenge yourself for it, but address your complaint immediately to me, and I will render you prompt justice. If it happens that we should have war with the French, remain neutral, and do not mix yourselves in our differences. The French are as strong as we, therefore let us settle our quarrels together. We will supply all your needs; we will take your furs, and we will give you our goods at a moderate price.' My presence hindered him from saying all that he intended, for it was not without design that he had brought a minister with him.[1]

"When he had ceased speaking, the savages retired, to deliberate together on the reply which they had to make. During this time, the governor drawing me apart 'I pray you sir' said he to me, 'not to lead your Indians to make war against us.' I replied to him that my religion and my character engaged me to give them only counsels of peace. I should have spoken more, when I saw myself suddenly surrounded with a score of young warriors, who feared lest the governor wished to carry me away. In the meantime the savages came forward, and one of them made the following reply to the governor.

"'Great chief, thou didst tell us not to join with the French. Supposing that thou shouldst declare war against him; know that the French man is my brother; we have the same prayer he and I, and we are in the same cabin at two fires; he has one fire and I the other. If I see thee enter into the cabin on the side of the fire where the French man is seated I should watch thee from my mat, where I am seated at the other fire; if, in watching thee, I should perceive that thou carriest a hatchet, I should have the

---

[1] The Rev. Joseph Baxter, of Medway, mentioned elsewhere.

thought what does the Englishman intend to do with this hatchet? I should raise myself then upon my mat, to observe what he will do. If he raises the hatchet to strike my brother the Frenchman, I take mine, and I run to the Englishman to strike him. Is it that I should be able to see my brother struck in my cabin, and remain quietly on my mat. No, no, I love my brother too much, not to defend him. Thus I would say to thee, great chief; do nothing to my brother, and I will do nothing to thee; remain quiet on thy mat, and I will remain in repose on mine.'

"It is thus that this conference ended. A little time after some of our savages arrived from Quebec, and reported that a French vessel had brought there the news of war kindled between France and England. Our savages immediately, after having deliberated according to their custom, ordered the young men to kill the dogs, to make the war feast, and to learn there those who wished to engage themselves in it. The feast took place; they hung a kettle, they danced, and two hundred and fifty warriors met there. After the feast they fixed upon a day to come to confess themselves. I exhorted them to be as attached to their prayer as they were in the village, to well observe the laws of war, not to exercise any cruelty, not to kill anybody except in the heat of combat, to treat humanely those who surrendered themselves prisoners, etc.

"The manner in which these people make war, renders a handful of their warriors more formidable than a body of two or three thousand European soldiers would be. As soon as they have entered into the enemy's country, they divide themselves into different parties, one of thirty warriors, another of forty, etc. They say to the first; 'to you is given this hamlet to devour,' this is their expression 'to you others, is given this village, etc.' At once, the signal is given to strike all together, and at the same time in different places. Our two hundred and fifty warriors, spread themselves over more than twenty leagues of country, where there are villages, hamlets, and houses; on the day mentioned they struck all together early in the morning; in a single day they swept away all that the English had there, and they killed more than two hundred of them, and they made more than one hundred and fifty prisoners, and had on their part only a few warriors slightly wounded. They returned from this expedition having each one two canoes loaded with booty which they had taken.

"During all the time that the war lasted, they carried desolation throughout all the land which belonged to the English; they ravaged their villages, their forts, their farms, carried away a great number of cattle and made more than six hundred prisoners. Therefore these gentlemen persuaded with reason, that in keeping my savages in their attachment to the Catholic faith I strengthened more and more the bonds which united them to the French, have put in operation all sorts of tricks and artifices to detach them from me.[1] There are no offers nor promises which they have not made them, if they would deliver me into their hands, or at least send me back to Quebec, and take in my place one of their ministers. They have made several attempts to surprise me and carry me off; they have gone even so far as to promise a thousand pounds sterling to him who would carry my head to them. You may well believe, my dear brother, that these menaces are not capable of intimidating me, nor to diminish my zeal; too happy if I should become their

---

[1] After such cruel destruction as Ralé describes so lightly, and it must be remembered that those killed and taken prisoners were largely the women and children of the poor settlers, it is not surprising that they did greatly desire the removal from their midst of the aggravating cause of their sufferings. Ralé's own statement here sufficiently justifies their course. The thousand pounds sterling for his head is rhapsody.

victim, and if God should judge me worthy of being loaded with irons and to pour out my blood for the salvation of these savages.

"At the first news which came of the peace made in Europe, the governor of Boston caused our savages to be told that if they would properly assemble in a place, he would confer with them on the present juncture of affairs. All the savages presented themselves at the place indicated, and the governor spoke to them thus.

"'To the men of Naranhous, I inform thee that peace is made between the King of France and our queen, and that by the treaty of peace, the King of France ceded to our queen, Plaisance and Portrail with all the lands adjacent. So, if thou wishest, we will live in peace thou and I. We have done so formerly; but the suggestions of the French have made thee break it, and it was to please him that thou hast come to kill us. Let us forget all these wicked doings and cast them into the sea, to the end that they shall appear no more and that we shall be good friends.' 'That is well,' replied the orator, in the name of the Savages, that the Kings should be at peace, I am very glad of it, and I have no more trouble in making it with thee. It is not I who struck thee during twelve years, it is the Frenchman who has used my arm to strike thee. We are at peace, it is true, I have even thrown away my hatchet, I know not where, and while I was in repose on my mat, thinking of nothing, some young men brought me word, which the governor of Canada sent me by which he said to me; My son the English man has struck me, help me to avenge myself on him, take thy hatchet, and strike the Englishman. I who have always listened to the word of the French governor, I sought my hatchet, I found it at last all rusted, I burnished it, I hung it at my belt to come to strike thee, now the Frenchman tells me to put it down; I throw it far away, that one may no longer see the blood with which it is red. I consent to it.

"' But thou sayest that the French man hast given thee Plaisance and Portrail which is in my neighborhood, and all the lands adjacent; he shall give it to thee as much as he will, for me I have my land which the great Spirit has given me to live on as long as there shall be a child of my nation, he will fight to preserve it.' All ended thus pleasantly. The governor made a great feast to the savages, after which each withdrew. The happy expectations of peace, and the tranquillity which they began to enjoy, gave birth to the thought among our savages to rebuild what has been ruined in a sudden eruption which the English made, while they were absent from the village. As we are very distant from Quebec and much nearer Boston, they deputed some of the principal men of their nations to demand workmen, with the promise to pay liberally for their work. The governor received them with great demonstration of friendship, and bestowed upon them all sorts of blandishments. 'I wish myself to rebuild your church,' said he to them, 'and I will use you better in it than the French governor has done whom you call your father. It should be for him to rebuild it, since it was he who in some sort has ruined it, in leading you to strike me; as for me, I defend myself as I can; as for him, after being served by you for his defence, he abandons you. I shall act much better with you, for not only do I grant you workmen, I wish moreover to pay them myself, and to bear all the expense of the building which you wish to construct; but as it is not reasonable that I, who am an Englishman should build a church without putting into it an English minister to keep it, and to teach prayer in it, I will give you one with whom you will be contented and you shall send back the French minister to Quebec, who is in your village.'

"'Thy word astonishes me' replied the deputy of the savages, 'and I wonder at the proposition that thou hast made me. When thou camest here, thou didst see me a long time before the French governor; neither those who preceeded thee, nor thy ministers have ever spoken to me of prayer, nor of the great Spirit. They have seen my furs, my skins of the beaver, and the moose, and it is on them alone they have thought; it is these that they have sought with eagerness, I could not furnish them to the French governor, my father, to send them to me.'

"In effect, M. the governor had no sooner learned the ruin of our church, than he sent his workmen to rebuild it. It is of a beauty, which might be admired in Europe, and I spared nothing to adorn it. You have been able to see by the details that I have given in my letter to my nephew, that in the depths of these forests, and among these Savage nations, the divine Service is performed with much propriety and dignity. It is to this I am very attentive, not only while the Savages reside in the village, but yet all the time that they are obliged to inhabit the seashore, where they go twice each year to find there something to live on. Our savages have so fully despoiled their country of beasts, that for ten years they have no longer found there either moose or deer. Bears and beavers have become very rare there, they have scarcely anything to live on except corn, beans, and pumpkins. They crush the corn between two stones to reduce it to flour, then they make a broth of it which they sometimes season with grease or with dry fish. When the corn fails they search in the tilled fields for potatoes or acorns, which they esteem as much as corn. After having dried it, they cook it in a kettle with ashes, to remove the bitterness from it. For myself, I eat it dry, and it holds for me the place of bread.

"At a certain time, they repair to a river a short distance off, where during a month the fish ascend the river in so great quantity, that one could fill fifty thousand barrels of them in a day, if one could have sufficient strength for the work. They are a kind of great herring very agreeable to the taste when they are fresh; they press forward one upon another a foot in thickness, and they dip them out like water. The savages dry them during eight or ten days, and they live upon them during all the time they sow their lands.

"It is only in the spring that they sow their corn, and they only give it the last hoeing towards Corpus Christi Day. After which they deliberate as to what place on the sea they shall go to seek something to live upon till the harvest, which is not ordinarily made until a little after the Assumption. After having deliberated they send to pray me to repair to their assembly. As soon as I have arrived there, one of them speaks to me thus in the name of all the others. 'Our father, what I say to thee, is what all of those whom thou seest here would say to thee, thou knowest us, thou knowest that we want food; scarcely have we been able to give the last hoeing to our fields, and we have no other resource until the harvest, but to go and seek food on the shore of the sea. It will be hard for us to abandon our prayer; that is why we hope that thou wilt accompany us, so that in seeking something to live upon we shall not interrupt our prayer. Such and such persons will embark thee, and that which thou wilt have to carry will be dispersed among the other canoes. That is what I have to say to thee.' I have no sooner replied to them *Kekikberba* (this is a savage term which means, I hear you, my children, I agree to what you demand), than all cry together *ouriourie*, which is an expression of thanks. Immediately after they leave the village.

"As soon as they arrive at the place where they should pass the night, they plant poles at intervals in the form of a chapel, they surround them with a large tent of ticking, and it is open only in front. All is finished in a quarter of an hour. I always carry with me a fair cedar board four feet in length with what should support it; it is this which serves for an altar, above which is placed a very appropriate canopy. I adorn the interior of the chapel with very fine silk stuff; a mat of reeds dyed and well wrought, while a great bearskin serves for a carpet. They carry this all prepared, and they have only to place it when the chapel is arranged. At night I take my rest on a carpet. They sleep in the air in an open field if it does not rain; if it rains or snows they cover themselves with bark which they carry with them, and which is rolled up like cloth. If the excursion is made in the winter, they remove the snow from the space which the chapel should occupy and they arrange it as usual. Then they make each day the evening and the morning prayer, and I offer the holy sacrifice of the mass.

"When the savages have reached their destination, on the next day they occupy themselves in erecting a church, which they cover with their bark. I carry with me my chapel, and all that is necessary to adorn the choir, which I hang with silk stuffs and fair calicoes. The divine service is performed as in the village and indeed, they form a kind of village of all their cabins made of bark, which they set up in less than an hour. After the Assumption, they quit the sea and return to the village to make their harvest. They fare then very poorly until after All Saints, when they return a second time to the sea. It is in this season that they make good cheer. Besides large fish, shell fish, and fruits, they find bustards, ducks, and all sorts of game, with which the sea is all covered in the place where they encamp, which is divided by a great number of little islands. The hunters who go out in the morning to hunt ducks, and other kinds of game sometimes kill a score at a single shot. Towards the Purification, or later toward Ash Wednesday they return to the village, it is only the hunters who scatter themselves abroad to go in pursuit of the bears, of the moose, of the deer and of the beavers.

"These good savages have often given me proofs of the most sincere attachment for me, above all on two occasions, when, finding myself with them on the shores of the sea, they took lively alarm on my account. One day when they were occupied with their hunting, a rumor was suddenly spread that an English party had made an irruption into my quarters, and had carried me away. In that very hour they assembled, and the result of their deliberation was that they should pursue the party until they had overtaken it, and had snatched me from their hands, should it cost them life. They set off at the same instant toward my quarter, rather far into the night. When they entered into my cabin, I was occupied in composing the life of a saint in the savage language. 'Ah, our father,' they cried, 'how glad we are to see thee.' 'I am eagerly rejoiced to see you, but what is it brings you here at so frightful a time?' 'It is mainly that we are come, they had assured us that the English had carried thee off; we came to observe their tracks and our warriors could hardly wait to come and pursue them, and to attack their forts, where, if the news had been true, the English would have without doubt have imprisoned you.' 'You see, my children,' I replied to them, that your fears are unfounded; but the friendship my children show me fills my heart with joy; because it is a proof of their attachment to the prayer. To-morrow, you shall depart immediately after mass at the earliest hour to our brave warriors, and deliver them from all uneasiness.'

"Another alarm equally false threw me into great embarrassment, and exposed me to perish with hunger and misery. Two savages came in haste to my quarters to inform me that they had seen the English within a half day's journey. 'Our father,' said they to me, 'there is no time to lose, it is necessary that thou shouldest retire, thou wilt risk too much to remain here; for us we will await them, and perhaps we will go in advance of them. The runners depart at this moment to observe them; but for thee it is necessary that thou shouldest go to the village with these men whom we bring to conduct thee there. When we shall know thee in a place of safety, we shall be easy.' I set out at break of day with ten savages who served me for guides; but after some days march, we found ourselves at the end of our small provisions. My conductors killed the dog which followed them, and ate it; they soon came to their wolf bags which they likewise ate. This is what it was not possible for me to taste, nevertheless I lived on a kind of wood which they boiled, and which, being cooked, is as tender as radishes half cooked, except the heart which is very hard and which they throw away; this wood had not a bad taste, but I had extreme difficulty in swallowing it. Sometimes they found attached to the trees those excrescences of wood which are white like large mushrooms; they cook them and reduce them to a kind of pulp, but it is quite necessary to acquire a taste for them. At other times they dried in the fire the bark of the green oak, they pounded it immediately, and made it into a pulp or else they dried the leaves which grew in the clefts of the rocks and which they called *tripes de roche;* when they are cooked, they make a pulp very black and disagreeable. I ate of all this, because there is nothing that hunger does not devour.

"With such food, we could make only very short journeys. We arrived in the meantime at a lake which began to thaw, and there was already four inches of water on the ice. It was necessary to cross it with our snow shoes; but as these snow shoes are made of strips of skin, as soon as they were wet, they became very heavy, and rendered our march much more difficult. Although one of our men marched at our head to sound the way, I sank suddenly as far as to the knees; another who marched beside me sank presently up to the waist, crying out; 'My father, I am dead.' As I approached him to offer him my hand, I sank myself still deeper. At last, it was not without much hardship that we extricated ourselves from this danger, through the incumbrance which our snow shoes caused us, of which we could not rid ourselves. Nevertheless, I ran still less risk from drowning, than from dying from cold in the midst of this half frozen lake.

"But new dangers awaited us the next day, in the passage of a river which it was necessary we should cross on the floating ice. We extricated ourselves from it happily, and at last arrived at the village. I at first dug up a little Indian corn, which I had left in my house, and I ate of it, all raw as it was to appease my first hunger, while these poor savages made all sorts of efforts in order to regale me. And in effect the repast that they brought me, although frugal and but little appetizing, as it might appear to you, was, in their eyes, a veritable feast. They served me at first a plate of mush made of Indian corn. Now for the second course, they gave me a small morsel of bear, with acorns and a little cake of Indian corn cooked under the ashes. When I asked them why they had prepared for me such good cheer; 'How now, our father,' they replied to me, 'it is two days that thou hast eaten nothing; could we do less; would to God that we could very often regale thee in this way.' While I was thinking to recover from my fatigue, one of the Indians who were encamped on the sea shore, and who was ignorant of my return to the village caused a new alarm. Having come to my quarters, and not finding me there, nor yet those who were encamped with me, they did not doubt that we had been carriew away by a party of English; and while on his way to give warning to those in his quarters, he reached the bank of the river. There, he tore the bark from a tree upon which he drew with charcoal the English about me, and one of them cutting off my head. This is all the writing of the savages, and they understand as well among themselves, by these kinds of figures, as we understand each other by our letters. He then placed this sort of letter around a stick which he planted on the bank of the river, in order to instruct the passers by what had happened to me. A short time after, some savages who passed there in six canoes to go to the village, discovered this bark. 'There is a writing,' said they; 'let us see what it tells. 'Alas,' they cried on reading it, 'the English have killed those of the quarter of our father; as for him, they have cut off his head.' They immediately plucked off the lock of hair which they leave negligently flowing over their shoulders and seated themselves around the stick until the next day, without saying a single word. This ceremony among them is the mark of the greatest affliction. The next day they continued their route to within a half league of the village where they stopped; then they sent one of them into the woods quite near to the village, in order to see if the English had not come to burn the fort and the cabins. I was reciting my breviary while walking along by the fort on the river, when this savage arrived opposite me on the other side. As soon as he perceived me 'Ah, my father,' cried he, 'how glad I am to see thee. My heart was dead, and it revived on seeing thee, we have seen the writing which said the English had cut off thy head. How glad I am that it has lied.' When I proposed to him to send him a canoe to cross the river. 'No,' replied he, 'it is enough that I have seen thee; I return upon my steps to carry this pleasant news to those who await me, and we shall come very soon to rejoin thee.' Indeed they arrived there the same day.

"I believe, my very dear brother, to have fulfilled that which you desired of me, by the summary which I undertake to make you of the nature of this country, of the character of our savages, of my occupations, of my labors, and of the danger to which I am exposed. You judge without doubt that it is on the part of my gentlemen, the English of our neighborhood, that I have the most to fear. It is true that for a long time they have sworn my destruction; but neither their ill-will for me, nor the death with which they threaten me, shall ever be able to separate me from my old flock; I recommend it to your holy prayers, and am, with most tender attachment, etc."
The winter following Harmon's failure, another ex-

pedition was attempted against Norridgewock by Capt. Moulton.¹ After an arduous march through thick forests and frozen swamps, which lay between him and his elusive foe, Moulton reached the vicinity of the village, as he supposed undiscovered, and cautiously approaching, thought to surprise it. To his chagrin it was deserted. Ralè and his neophytes had been apprised of danger, and fled to the woods.

---

¹ This Jeremiah Moulton was a native of York, and brother-in-law to Johnson Harmon, to whom he held a subordinate position in the attack on Norridgewock, but the credit of success on that occasion was by popular acclaim awarded to him, although he received no public recognition for his services. In 1735, he was elected a member of the Provincial Council, and represented York in the General Court for several years. He was also county treasurer of Yorkshire, and judge of the Court of Common Pleas. He was lieutenant-colonel of militia, and in 1761 was judge of Probate. Williamson says of him that "though he was unassuming in his disposition and manners, and never a restless aspirant for office, few men of this age and this Province, had a greater share of public confidence, or were called to fill so many places of official trust and responsibility," and that "the prudence, skill and bravery which marked his conduct, gave him rank among the military characters of distinction. He was a member of the Council Board seventeen years in succession — a man of sound judgment, possessing a character of uncommon excellence."

Though greatly annoyed at this lame conclusion of his labors, Moulton, with commendable magnanimity, forbade his men from doing any injury to the church or dwellings of the savages, and they were therefore left unscathed. Ralé told his converts that this wise and generous act was the result of cowardice, and that their church was spared because he had threatened the English, that if they destroyed it, he would destroy all their churches. Such is the spirit of prejudice that it blinds men to what is praiseworthy in their adversaries.

Ralé was urged by his friends to withdraw into Canada, but underestimating the steady perseverance of the English, and regarding the danger of capture to be light, he sternly refused.

If we had stood on the morning of August 19th, or 8th, old style, 1724, upon the glacis in front of Fort Richmond, we should have witnessed an interesting scene of activity. Along the leafy banks of the Kennebec lay seventeen large boats, such as were then used by whalers, which, one by one, were soon filled with men, arms and provisions, and having been formed into a long line were rowed rapidly away. It was an expedition of two hundred and eleven men, three being Mohawk savages, friendly to the English, under the leadership of Harmon and Moulton, going against Norridgewock; this time in summer, the season that Ralé had told his savages that the English were too cowardly to approach their village, even with a force seven or eight times greater than their own.

Reaching the present site of Winslow, on the 20th, the party disembarked, at the foot of Ticonic falls, where they encamped for the night, and the next morning leaving their boats guarded by forty men, Harmon and Moulton, with the rest of their command, proceeded on their way to Norridgewock. As the shades of evening fell about them, they were still threading their devious way along the river bank, when suddenly they surprised an Indian and two Indian women, who fled at their approach. The success of the expedition depended upon surprising the elusive foe, and if these Indians escaped and carried the alarm to Norridgewock, the campaign would terminate as on former occasions, in failure, if not in disaster. There was but one thing to do under the circumstances and they fired upon the fugitives as they strove to escape by the river. The man and one of the women fell, the other woman surrendered. The savages whom they had slain proved to be Bomazeen, one of their most treacherous enemies, and his daughter; the prisoner being his wife. On the 23d, about midday, they were near the doomed village, and the force was divided,[1] Harmon filing off with a part of the men toward the cornfields of the savages, to surprise any who might be there, while Moulton proceeded toward the village.

It was about three o'clock when Moulton saw from the leafy covert which concealed him and his little band of eighty men, the cabins of the savages almost within reach; but not a human being was in sight. The place seemed deserted as they had found it on other occasions, and but for certain unmistakable signs of occupation, the anxious leaguers would have believed it to be so. Suddenly from one of the cabins a solitary savage emerged to perform some necessary duty, when looking around, his quick eye discovered the presence of a foe. Instantly his shrill war cry aroused the lazy warriors,

---

[1] Johnson Harmon, born about 1680, married Mary, the daughter of Jeremiah Moulton, Senior, of York. He achieved a wide fame for his skill in Indian warfare, and for his services at Norridgewock was rewarded by promotion to the rank of colonel. He represented York in the General Court in 1727, and shortly after removed to Merriconeag Neck with his son-in-law, Richard Jaques. He died April 17, 1751.

and they sprung to their arms ready for the fray. Moulton, with a coolness born of constant exposure to danger, sharply commanded his men on pain of death to reserve their fire, and the savages discharged their guns in the faces of their implacable foemen, overshooting them in their wild excitement. The English without breaking their ranks steadily returned the fire, and the savage warriors quickly reloaded, while the rest of the inhabitants fled in dismay to the river; but although Ralé has extolled the bravery and hardihood of his neophytes now, as upon all other occasions when matched with civilized man, they failed in true heroism, and discharging their guns a second time without execution, they broke and fled, although their force was nearly two-thirds as large as that opposed to them, and they stood on familiar ground, a matter of considerable importance in warfare. A wild rush of men, women, and children was made for the river, which was but about sixty feet wide, and at its lowest stage; so that the taller men could ford it. Some attempted escape in their canoes, but had no paddles, while the greater part of the savages were obliged to trust to their natatory skill. Of course, the women and children in the wild confusion which surrounded them suffered most.

The English had but one duty to perform. Here was the very source of that pernicious power, which had spread ruin, desolation, and death, accompanied by unparalleled horror and suffering, through New England. Its complete destruction was not only a necessary but a beneficent act, if any act of warfare which cuts off human life to prevent its greater destruction may be properly so called.

It was an affair of but a few moments. Some of the English seizing paddles, which they found, sprung into canoes, while others waded into the river and fired upon those who had not already found shelter on the opposite bank, killing some and driving even those who were attempting to escape in their canoes to seek safety by plunging into the water. Those who escaped were soon beyond the reach of pursuit, and the English, who had followed them to the river, quickly returned to the village where occasional firing could still be heard. This firing was from two cabins; in one was Mogg with his wife and two children, and in the other Ralé with an English boy, about fourteen years of age, captured some months before, and now in the keeping of the priest.[1] A shot from Mogg struck and killed one

---

[1] This boy was the son of William Mitchell of Scarborough, and with his brother was captured on

of the Mohawks, which so exasperated his brother
that he rushed upon the cabin, broke down the door
and shot Mogg dead, and in the mad excitement his
wife and two children were likewise slain. Moulton
had given strict orders to spare Ralé, intending to
make him a prisoner, and to deliver him into the
hands of the authorities at Boston, but his design
was frustrated by Lieutenant Richard Jaques,[1] his

---

the 17th of the preceding April, at which time his
father was killed.

[1] Richard Jaques, son of Daniel and Mary Williams Jaques, was born at Newbury, Mass., where descendants of the family still reside, on Feb. 2, 1696, and married Mary, born Mar. 23, 1704–5, the daughter of Johnson Harmon, the commander-in-chief of the Norridgewock expedition. As with so many others, whose campaigning led them along the winding shores of the Kennebec and Androscoggin, Jaques was enamored with the beauty and fertility of the region, and in 1727, in company with his father-in-law, Col. Johnson Harmon, he removed to Merriconeag Neck in the town of Harpswell, where he settled upon a tract of land belonging to the Pejepscot proprietors, and for several years led the peaceful life of a farmer; but, when the call came in 1745 for troops to strike a blow at Louisbourg, the stronghold of French power, which the English frontiersman so hated, his military ardor was reawakened, and he joined the enthusiastic volunteers with a company of his townsmen, and participated in the glorious success which the English achieved in reducing "the Gibraltar of

nephew, and the son-in-law of Harmon, the commander-in-chief of the expedition, who breaking in the door of the cabin from which Ralé was firing, saw him in the act of dropping a bullet into his gun. Hastily demanding if he would surrender, or, in the parlance of the time, would "take quarter," he was answered in a spirited manner by the priest, that he would not, whereupon, without further parley, he shot him dead. In the cabin was found Mitchell, the captive boy, shot through the thigh and stabbed

---

America." After his return from Louisbourg we have but little that is definite concerning him. There is a tradition in the family, unsupported by any record, however, that he commanded a company of soldiers sent to Bagaduce not long after the fall of Louisbourg, to hold the savages in check, and while on this service was ordered by the officer commanding the expedition to lead his company across an exposed point to reconnoitre for savages. His long experience in savage methods of warfare rendered him prudent, and he expressed to his commander the opinion, that to cross the point in question might expose him and his men to the danger of an ambush. Angry at having his order questioned, the hasty officer taunted him with cowardice, which stung him so keenly that Jaques replied that "he would not turn on his heel to save his life," and proceeded to carry the imprudent order into effect. He had proceeded but a short distance when a savage, who had been concealed behind a tree, fired upon and wounded

in the body, who declared that this was done by Ralé.[1]

Moulton was angry with Jaques for his disobedience of orders, and reprimanded him for it; refusing to accept his excuse that Ralé was reloading his gun, and refused to give or take quarter. The victors

---

him severely. He was carried home to Harpswell, where he died a few months after from his wounds. Parkman calls the slayer of Ralé Benjamin Jaques, being probably misled by an article in the Brunswick Historical Magazine of 1864. Benjamin was the son of Richard, and was living many years after the death of his father. An island near the former place of residence of Richard Jaques still preserves his name, sometimes strangely transformed into Jaquinth and Jaqueth Island. The children of Richard and Mary Jaques were Marianna, b. June, 1725; Susanna, b. June, 1728, and Benjamin, b. Oct. 17, 1731.

[1] This statement, though its veracity has been doubted, notably by Dr. Harris, who says, "We search in vain for the evidence of this revengeful deed" (Mass. Hist. Col., 4th series, vol. 8, p. 257), has never been disproved, which is strange, as there must have been several persons conversant with the particulars of the affair who lived for years after it happened. Moulton was a man with a nice sense of honor, and was present when the body was found, yet he never appears to have questioned the story. In spite, however, of this, it is too revolting for credence, and we ought not to accept it without further evidence.

encamped in the village for the night, being joined after the fray by Harmon, and the next morning took up their march homeward, carrying with them what little spoil they could find. Of course, a little corn, a few guns, kettles, blankets and a small store of powder would constitute the worldly wealth of such a savage community; but whatever found was doubtless taken away by the poor soldiers.

Moulton, who was a humane and prudent man, left the village unharmed, as on a former occasion; but after reaching Ticonic Falls, where the boats had been left, Christian, one of the two surviving Mohawks, returned to Norridgewock and set fire to the place, destroying everything. According to the account of De la Chasse, after the English had left the ruined village some of the savages returned and buried the body of Ralé. If they did so, they were soon hurrying to join their brethren in Canada, where they arrived in a destitute condition, and were taken under the protection of Vaudreuil, who supplied their needs, and hastened to apply to the king for an increase of the allowance granted for the support of the families of those engaged in war with the English, which was promptly granted. Among the things found by Moulton was a book which Ralé probably prized above all his worldly belongings,

Busenbaum's Medulla Theologiæ Moralis, which embodied the concentrated wisdom of the order to which he belonged. It is strange that no writer on Ralé has taken the trouble to critically examine this book, which was, without doubt, as it is inscribed, his *vade mecum*. It was studied by him day by day in the solitude of the forest, and he regarded it as embodying the holiest truths, the foundation stones, so to speak, of his thoughts and acts. The logic of this book was his logic, and gave form to his reasonings, hence should it not reveal to us some of the mental lineaments of the man? Any unprejudiced mind will be satisfied of this who gives it a careful examination.[1] Besides this book, was found an un-

---

[1] It has been taken for granted that this book was found in the chest captured by Westbrook in the winter of 1721–22, but this does not appear to me to be the fact. The book, known as the Abnaki dictionary, was undoubtedly found in the box, but there is nothing whatever to indicate that this book, which, it is reasonable to suppose, was carried always about his person, was not taken from him when he was killed. The following is the title of the book, "*MEDULLA THEOLOGIÆ MORALIS Facite ac Perspicua. Methodo resolvens. Casus Conscientiae, exvariis prabistisque Authoribus connata. AR. P. HERM. BUSENBAUM, è Societate Jesu, S. S. Theologiæ Licentiato. Poenitentibus aequè ac Con-*

fessariis perqumutiles. Editio Novissima. Recognita ab unoè Societate & à multis mendis repurgata, que in præcendentibus irrepferant. LUGDUNI, sumptibus. Francisci Comba in vieo Mercatorio ad insgne trium Virtutum. M. DC. LXXV, Cum Privilegio Regis."

On the fly leaf is inscribed the following:

" 'This book did belong to Monsr. Rallé the Jesuit and Missionary from France among the Eastern Indians who was kill'd at Neridgawock when it was surpris'd and destroy'd by Coll. Harman, Maj^r. Moulton & Comp^a. in ye year 1724. This was ye Jesuit's *vade mecum*. It was given by Major Josua Moodey of Casco Bay to Wm Welsteed."

In Mr. Willis' handwriting is the following: "Mr. Welsted was a clergyman, he graduated at H. C. 1716, was a classmate of Joseph Moody, was a tutor at Cambridge from 1720 to 1728. Mr Welsted visited Falm° in July or Aug. 1726 & preached for Mr. Smith. Moody then lived here & probably presented this book to his classmate. W. W."

This book has been of the highest authority among the Jesuits for centuries, as is evinced by the fact that it has been through more than fifty editions, the last having been printed at Rome not long ago, under the authority of the *Propaganda Fide*. Space will permit but the following brief quotations:

Whether one may use equivocation in an oath.

Answer. It is no sin to swear with equivocation when there is just reason for it and equivocation is allowed; because where there is the privilege of concealing the truth and it is concealed without lying, no irreverence is done to the oath. But if it be done without just reason, it will not even then be perjury since he swears truly, according to *some* sense of the words or mental reservation. Yet from its very nature it will be a deadly sin against religion, since it is an act of grave irreverence to use an oath for the purpose of deceiving another in a matter of great weight.

He commits a grievous sin who uses equivocation when he takes oath not being asked, but of his own accord; because then he is held to use words according to their common signification, inasmuch as he has no reason for using equivocation.

He also sins grievously who uses equivocation when an oath is justly demanded, as by a judge or a superior in a weighty matter.

It is lawful to take equivocation if an oath is unjustly demanded, *e. g.*, if any one exact an oath who has not the right, as an incompetent judge, or if he does not preserve the order or form of law. Also if the oath is exacted through force, injury or fear, *e. g.*, if a husband exact an oath from his wife in regard to hidden adultery, or if robbers demand ransom under oath. *Vide* p. 111.

What is allowed a judge in regard to bribes? (*Q.* 4, *p.* 360.)

Ans. 1. Although he who receives bribes may sometimes sin either by reason of scandal or the danger of subverting justice, he yet acquires the right of ownership of the things received, in the eyes of the natural law.

Ans. 2. Although the positive law forbids the acceptance of bribes, still the receiver is not held to restitution before the sentence of the judge, unless the law expressly says so, because the acceptance was not only illegal but also invalid.

CONFESSION. (Pages 516 et seq.)

Besides completeness (*integritas*) these three conditions are necessary to confession.

1st. That it be *by word of mouth* (*vocalis*) &c.

2d. That it be *secret*, that is, made to the priest alone — not necessary indeed but according to the usage of the church. Moreover, public confession, as in time of shipwreck, or battle or in a hospital where many are near, or confession made through an interpreter, is not binding (at least as regards hidden sins) upon one who, at the point of death, is in doubt concerning his contrition. Even then it is enough to confess those things which occasion less disgrace (*infamiam*).

3d. That it be *true*, &c.

It is not a mortal sin nor does it render the Sacrament (Confession) void:

1st. If in the confession you lie mildly (*mentiaris levited*) about things not pertinent or not necessary to the Sacrament, for instance, if you tell a false story or deny a venial or mortal sin which you are not held to confess.

2d. If you falsely accuse yourself of a venial sin; yet this will become a grave mortal sin if you do this without giving some instance, since you thus render the form void and also the Sacrament; unless you do it from scrupulousness or confusion.

May one sometimes deny the true faith or profess a false one? (Chap. 3, page 45.)

Ans. In no case is it allowed whether it be done with voice or other sign since Christ says, "Whosoever shall deny me before men, &c." In the meantime, however, "although it is not lawful to lie or pretend what is not; yet it is lawful to conceal what is or to cover up the truth with words or other ambiguous signs," &c. Shades of the Martyrs!

It has been authoritatively denied that the Jesuits hold or have held that the end justifies the means; yet here we have it in the following words: "*Cum finis est licitus, etiam media sunt licita: When the end is lawful the means also are lawful.* This single quotation would solve every difficulty we have met with in trying to reconcile with contemporary history many erroneous statements of Ralé, De la Chasse and Charlevoix; indeed, if we could know that Ralé accepted this as absolutely true in letter and spirit, and by his oath he was bound to so accept it, we could not be blamed for believing the wildest stories, which were circulated about him by our Puritan ancestors, but which we have avoided repeating in these pages, because they are not accompanied by proofs. It is more reasonable and certainly more agreeable to believe, that Ralé was an earnest, self-sacrificing man, whose whole heart was moved to establish the kingdom of Christ in the world, but whose mind was so involved in the meshes of a false system of religious philosophy, as to be incapable of just judgment. In conclusion it is but just to say, that Busenbaum's Medulla contains very many acceptable truths, as well as many unacceptable ones.

finished letter, which Ralé was writing to De la Chasse, as follows:

"NORRIDGWALK, 23^d *Aug^t*. N. S., 12 O. S.[1]
"MY REVEREND FATHER,

"My people are returned from their last Expedition, wherein one of their Bravest Champions was killed. Believing there were above two hundred English divided in three Parties or Bands to drive them out of their Camp, And expecting a further number to Enforce them in order to ruin all the Corn in the Fields without doubt —— But I said to them, how Could that be, Seeing we are daily Surrounding & making Inroads upon them everywhere in the midst of their Land, and they not coming out of their Fort, which they have upon your own Land, Besides in all the War you have had with them, did you ever see them Come to Attack you in the Spring, Summer or in the fall; when they knew you were in your habitations. You know it, You Say Your selves that they never did, but when they knew you were not, but when you were in the Woods. For if

---

[1] This is a contemporary translation. The letter may be found in the Office of the Public Records, London, where it was copied by the author, *verbatim et literatim.*

they knew there were but fifteen or twelve Men men in your dwellings they dare not Approach you with One hundred. We told you after the fall fight of Ke-Ke-penagliesek that the English would come with the Nation of Iroquois to Revenge themselves. You Opposed it and said they should not, and yet they did, you see now whether You are in the right."

"I had Reason to Believe it Founded on the Kings word; who could ever think that he should forge such a falsehood & how should I then Answer a Right. And it was to make good their false Designs that they came here to show themselves as Master of your Land (contrary to my Expectation) where they would not have a Romish Priest to dwell. And if they did not burn the Church, it is that I did send them Word in your behalf, that if they should burn it, you should burn all their Temples. Therefore there was an Order to the officer not to burn anything. They hearken to all my Reasons aforegoing, but follow their own. They Design to quit the Village for a fortnight, and to go five or Six Leagues up the River, they proposed it to me, and I have Given my Consent. When I spoke to them on such an Occasion I Declared my thought, without Obliging them to follow the same; But Declared to them that I was ready to follow their own. It is but a few days since we came to the Village and the last are arrived this morning.

"The day before yesterday arrived a party of the Becancourians being nine in number, but I have no dependence on them. But my Dependence is upon Kounaouons, the former being favourers of the English. Yesterday 12 or 15 Pannaouanskeians four Hurons with One wounded arrived here almost Starved — Therefore they must be Supplied tho the Corn is not Ripe. They must take it as it is, for we are almost reduced to a Famine Provisions being so Scarce. As for my self thro the Grace of God I have gathered in the most part of my Field and Husked the same, which is now a drying; for I can expect none or little from the Savages.

"Three Hurones are this morning to depart, and go into the War with Becancouriens; The Pannaouanskeians Desired the Hurones to carry away their wounded. Say they, 'You seek nothing but Scalps, there is five which we give you.' They have had some likewise in this Village, & are to depart to morrow Morning. My own People are also to depart and are now Deliberately Consulting whether they shall Joyn with the Becancouriens Ratio Dubitando Est. That the Ouarinakiens have not Acted against the English Save one of them, that the English should have no Occasion to Complain of them; for Kounaouans who is of this Village has all along been with them. The Ouarinakiens said when my People came to War that they Joyn with the Norridgwalks who follow the English very close by frequent discharge of their peeces when the others keep at a distance. And when they return they would take all the honour of the War to themselves, which is very displeasing to my people, who are Deserving of the true Honour Therefore they Conclude to go by themselves in different Parties as I had advised them.

"It is therefore for the same Reason that they did let the Hurones go by themselves. At their Arrival here, there was a Party ready to Embark; And I advised my People that two of them should go as a Guard to the Hurones Ousauniones and Mathiru are to Joyn them. But my People Come and tell me that the Hurones being in Company with them before used to say in Canada That the Norridgwalks were but women in the War &c. I am sure said I that is a Calumny that the Hurones Cast upon them, they have no reason to say any such thing. They have seen you in the Action and you have Given them several scalps &c. But they know the way & tell us every Spot, however let them go by themselves.

"I just now received a Letter from Father Loverjat with Four Codd fish out of Eight he sent me. The Bears[1] have Eat four by the way, and said it was a Case of necessity being for want of Provisions. Tho their Village is full of Codd fish out of 15 or 16 Vessels they have taken. The Father sent me Word that by a suitable Opportunity he shall send me more And hath sent me word that they have newly taken three Vessels & killed ten Men, some on the Spot and others by reason they revolted from those who had spared their lives &c. They have Attempted to burn the Fort of St. George by two fire Shipps or Vessels, but for want of Wind they miscarried. The fire began to take the Wood part of the Fort, whereupon they heard the English make a great Cry & Lamentation some of them coming out of the Fort to Attempt to Extinguish the fire, which the Indians Could not kill by reason of their being posted on the Contrary side, they not foreseeing that the English Could Come out of the Fort on that side. The fire of one of the Vessels went out soon of itself and the English had it.

---

[1] Bearers.

"After that nine of the Indians went off in a Vessel, where they were Attacked by two English Vessels, they Engaged for some time; And the Indians having no more powder Attempted to Board one of them, but they Shunned it. Wherefore the Indians were Obliged to retire Eleven other Indians went in a Vessel and espied two English Vessels in the Road, & went to plunder them, but seeing they were full of People and themselves not able to stand them, did save themselves by swimming a shoar & leaving their vessel. Says the Father I attribute the Bad Success to their Ungratefulness to God and their Disobedience to me. A Vessel said he which comes from Mines for to bring us Provision said that an English Man Assured him that they had a very great Inclination for Peace at Boston; And he doubted not but it would be Concluded next fall, which appears very Probable because a Vessel which went from here to Boston to bring a Ransom for the Prisoners that are here is not returned, notwithstanding the time is a great deal Expired, And I have Answered them that did not agree with the Council D'Orange that were Resolute to keep their Land I further said That I would never permit my People to receive a Ransom for those they take, for there is not one but would Ransom himself, and if we should harken to it, the English would never think to return the Land for the loss of their People, that they would easily buy &c.

"The Father Loyard wrote to him that his People with the Mickemacks have been in two Parties to make an Attempt upon the English at Port Royal; one of those Parties Attackt the Fort it self, where they did kill Six Men & burnt two Houses after they had plundered them, the other party is not yet returned back.

"My People are Absolutely willing to Return to those Forts where one of our Brave Champions was killed in the last Party.

"I am very glad that Mr. Lieutenant hath Accepted my present. They have brought me my Chocolate. The two Bills that James was to have brought with him are Cast away by over setting a Canno. I am well stock'd with Chocolate for a long time, which I came easily by, & it shall not be presently Carried away for it is very weighty. As for the Remaining part you keep for me it may be it troubles you as much, as it would trouble me if I had it. The Father Dupy had a Warehouse where I put all the woolen linen Shot & powder as well as the Blanketting & gun you got for me since the Canno of the Hurones was here I added those things to his Merchandize for him to make the best profit. As for me I am Contented & I think well paid. The Wine shall be put into the Cellar to be mixt wth that of the House. If the Tobacco were here it should be put into ye Magazine.

"I am very much Obliged to you my Rev. Father for the Care you take of me, You are willing I should live as a Chanoine till the Spring by the plentiful supply that you have sent me by Pauscawen. I have yet considerable for my self for the Winter, since they sent me some Wine I take a glass after my Mass but I dont find it keeps me so well as a Dram of Brandy I want nothing but Spanish Wine for the Mass. I have enough for myself for above 12 months. Therefore I pray the 3d. time to send me no more Wine. I shall send for more when I want it."[1]

The French account of the affair at Norridgewock differs materially from the English account, which was carefully compiled by Hutchinson from the personal testimony of the chief actors in the drama. That the French account is a tissue of errors is seen by a brief examination of its details; indeed it could

---

[1] This letter is marked "Not finished," and bears the following attestation: Examined from the Translation in the Secretary's Office, per J. Willard, Sec'y."

not be otherwise, when we consider its source. Not a single European witnessed the affair except the English; hence the dramatic recital of de la Chasse, adopted by Charlevoix, was based upon the stories of savages half crazed with excitement, and always notoriously unreliable in their statements, as Ralé himself regarded them. It may be well to notice some of these accuracies. Charlevoix gives the number of Harmon and Moulton's men as eleven hundred. This is no typographical error, as his editor has suggested,[1] for it is not in figures, but plainly, "*ouze cens hommes.*"[2] As a matter of fact, there were in both Harmon and Moulton's commands but one hundred and seventy-one men, forty of the two hundred and eleven who marched from Fort Richmond having been left to guard the boats, and in the attacking party there could not have been over a hundred. De la Chasse speaks of the English force as "*une petite armie d'Anglois & de Sauvages,*"[3] while Charlevoix says that it was composed of "part English and part Indians,"[4] and that more than

---

[1] *Vide* note in Shea's Charlevoix.
[2] *Vide* Lettres Edifiantes et Curieuses, letter of de la Chasse, where it is so given.
[3] Ibid.
[4] Shea's Charlevoix.

two thousand shots, "*De plus de deux mille coups de fusil*," were fired upon the savages. We know that there were but three savages in the expedition, and as the fight was speedily over, thesta tement of the number of shots fired must have been grossly exaggerated.

We are also told that Ralé went fearlessly to meet the assailants, in the hope of drawing all their attention upon himself, and thus saving his flock at the peril of his own life ; that he was immediately fired upon by the English, and that seven Indians who accompanied him in order to shield him with their bodies, were slain beside him. Shea, the Roman Catholic historian, a careful and conscientious writer, realized the incorrectness of this statement, and in a note to his translation of Charlevoix, alluding to the English statement that Ralé was killed in the cabin he was defending, and to several doubtful stories concluding with that of Jaques, that he refused quarter, he says, " Moulton doubted the last statement, and we may well doubt the rest, *beyond the fact that he was killed in a cabin from which a vigorous defense was made.*"

Shea appreciated the importance of the fact, that Lieut. Jaques would not have acknowledged the slaying of Ralé, especially against his superior's orders, unless he had really slain him. The excuse which the lieutenant offered in palliation of his act, when his commander arraigned him for killing Ralé in a cabin, when he ought to have taken him prisoner, to the effect that the priest refused to give or take quarter, Moulton, angry at having an order disobeyed, would not accept; but he never doubted that Jaques committed the act, and in spite of the blame attached to him for it, Jaques never denied it, but went to his grave the self-acknowledged slayer of Ralé. Hence none can reasonably doubt that Ralé was slain by Jaques, nor that he was slain in a cabin which was being defended.[1] Had de la Chasse's story, told him, as before remarked, by some excited savage, been true, that he was fired upon by a general discharge of guns, especially directed against

---

[1] A piece of independent evidence is furnished by the statement of Benjamin Larrabee of Scarborough, who was in Moulton's command. Some time before, a band of the Norridgewock tribe, on one of their murderous raids, had sought his home and killed his father and brother. While the savages were flying from the village, young Larrabee rushed into a cabin, where he saw Ralé, but as he was eager to avenge himself upon the savages for the loss of his relatives, he left the priest unmolested and followed the rapidly disappearing enemy. Returning somewhat later, he found Ralé lying dead in the cabin where he had seen him a short time before.

him by the English, there would not have been men wanting to refute Jaques's story, nor would there have been occasion for Moulton to doubt that Ralé refused to give or take quarter. De la Chasse's statement that Ralé's body was mutilated is doubtless true; for if he was shot through the head and scalped, this would have been mutilation sufficient to account for the appearance of the body, and we need not for a moment entertain the shocking suggestion that it was maliciously mutilated after death.

The French report of the number of savages who lost their lives at Norridgewock, namely, seven men, seven women and fourteen children, is doubtless correct. Some of the latter were probably drowned in the confusion of crossing the river. If but seven men in all were killed, then none were killed by all the firing but de la Chasse's seven mythical heroes, who shielded Ralé with their own bodies.[1] De la Chasse's statement, that the English, after the victory, fled as if smitten by a panic, is in harmony

---

[1] These seven included Bomazeen, who was killed before the party reached Norridgewock. Penhallow supposes the number of savages who were killed and drowned at Norridgewock to have been eighty, and writers generally have accepted this opinion. The savages, however, from whom the French accounts came, would not have been likely to understate their

with his other statements, and partakes of the over-
wrought credulity of an age in which men of all

loss, and were in a better position to know their number than the English.

The following is from the Massachusetts Archives:

At a Council held at the Council Chamber in Boston, on Saturday, August 22, 1724.

Captain Johnson Harman being arrived from the Eastward with twenty-seven Indian scalps, together with the scalp of Sebastian Ralle the Jesuit and Missionary among the Norridgewock Indians, and the Standard of ye s^d Tribe of Indians, was directed to attend in Council. And there gave a short Narrative of his March to Norridgewock (with four companies of Soldiers under his command) & of his Action at the s^d Place the twelfth instant, where he destroyed a great number of the enemy, many of whom being slain or drown'd in the River, he could not recover their bodies.

His Honour the Lieut^t Governour in consideration of the extraordinary Service of the s^d Captain Harman, presented him with a Commission for Lieut^t Colonel of His Majesty's Forces Eastward under the Command of Coll^o Thomas Westbrook.

Coll. Johnson Harman made solemn oath that the Twenty seven scalps above ment'd (which were produced in Council) were the Scalps of Rebel or Enemy Indians slain by him and the Forces under his Command, and that they had taken Four Indians Prisoners.

Coll^o Johnson Harman likewise made oath that the other Scalp was the Scalp of Sebastian Ralle a Jesuit who appeared at the Head of the Indians and creeds saw in every event a miraculous interposition of Providence in their own behalf.

Shea admits that it is not easy to form an opinion in Ralé's case, and that he "apparently advised the

---

obstinately resisted the Forces, wounding sev^{el} of the English & resolutely refusing to give or take Quarter.

Then follows a recital of the vote of the General Assembly to encourage the bringing Sebastian Ralle, passed July 13, 1720.

"This Court being credibly informed that Monsr Ralle the Jesuit, residing among the Eastern Indians has not only on several occasions of late affronted His Majestys Government of this Province but has also been the Incendiary that has instigated and stirred up those Indians to treat His Majestys subjects settling there in the abusive insolent hostile manner that they have done, Resolved that a Premium of One Hundred pounds be allowed and paid out of the Public Treasury to any person that shall apprehend the s^d Jesuit within any part of this Province & bring him to Boston & render him to Justice."

A Warrant was made for the Treasurer to pay the s^d sum of 100 pounds to Johnson Harman for his service in the destruction of s^d Sebastian Ralle. Vol. 8, Council Records, pages 71 and 72.

Col. Westbrook in his report to Governor Dummer gives the same number of scalps and says: "Capt. Harman and the officers Judge that by the modestest Computation, besides the Scalps and Captives they brought in, what they kill'd and drownded, there would not be less than thirty or forty." Mass. Arch. 52: 34.

Indians that war was just." Any one who carefully studies the subject, will inevitably reach the latter conclusion, and however much he may admire Ralé's devotion and faithfulness to his calling, and his readiness to sacrifice his life in the performance of what he believed to be his duty, he must finally regard him as an agent of the French Government, exciting the savages against the English settlers, and an agent rendered doubly active by his abhorrence of the Englishman's heresy. This is amply proved by his letters, which partake of the character of much contemporary writing. Crimination and recrimination were common between partisans then, as now. The French condemned the English people because a few rascally traders sold fire water to the savages; yet, the French minister at Versailles did not hesitate to tell Vaudreuil, when the latter advised the king that it was necessary to fortify Niagara, because the English, backed by the Iroquois, were too powerful for him, that he could at least craze the savages by dosing them with brandy;[1] and yet, Vaudreuil, according to his epitaph in the Cathedral of Quebec, was "le haut et puissant Seigneur & Grand Croix del' order militaire de St. Louis, Governeur et Lieutenant General de toute la Nouvelle France." The English,

---

[1] *Vide* Collection de Manuscrits, etc.

too, were arraigned for their barbarity in placing a bounty on savage scalps, when so brisk at one time had become the traffic in scalps, English and Iroquois alike, in New France, that the French began to doubt if all the European scalps presented for bounty were really English, as it was impossible to distinguish an English from a French scalp, and it was shrewdly suspected at Montreal, that their savage friends, finding it more convenient, were surreptitiously despoiling Frenchmen of their chevelures.[1]

Such is weak human nature, and we must not wonder to find zealous partisans, especially of a century or two ago, exaggerating or even suppressing facts, as we find Charlevoix among others doing, when we study the sources from which he drew his material.

In conclusion, Ralé cannot be properly denominated a martyr, nor the English murderers. There can be no doubt that he was killed in the excitement of battle, while in a building from which a defense was being made, and against the intentions of the English commander. Yet there has been a great deal of sentimental writing on the subject, based on

---

[1] *Vide* Relation de Jesuits.

the account of de la Chasse,[1] while the unwarrantable killing of Dummer, Rolfe, and Willard,[2] three English divines, who were quietly pursuing their peaceful labors, has hardly been noticed by our writers, in spite of Gov. Dummer's manly letter to Vaudreuil in response to his accusation of murder against the English for Ralé's death.

---

[1] Although there is but a single original French account of the attack on Norridgewock and slaying of Ralé, this of de la Chasse, it has served as a basis for many accounts among which the student may profitably consult, Nouvelles des Missions; Missions de l'Amerique; Die Katholisches Kuche in dem Vereinigten Staten; Les Jesuits Martyrs de Canada Bibliogr. Patrignani Menologie, 23 agosto, p. 190, Cassani Varones, ilustres. t. I. pp. 677, 679. Annales de la Propagation de la foi. t. I. p. 177. Brasseur de Bourbourg, Hist du Canada. Penhallow and Hutchinson who base their account of the affair upon the statements of Moulton and Harmon, furnish the basis for the English accounts.

[2] Rev. Shubael Dummer was a graduate of Harvard College and was fifty-six years of age when slain. His wife, a delicate and refined woman, was taken prisoner with their son; but was given her freedom by the savages. Turning back she begged piteously for the release of her son which was refused and she was sent away. Again she returned urged by grief and fears to pray for her son's release, and was told that since she desired captivity she should be gratified. The hardships of savage captivity soon put an

With a reticence respecting the cruel killing, some years before, of his reverend uncle, which shows more than words could show his weariness of such hypercriticism, he limited himself to a simple statement of fact, and told the Frenchmen, "that had Rallé Confined himself unto the professed Duty of his function, viz, to Instruct the Indians in the Christian Religion," and had not instigated them "to War and Rapine, there might have been some ground of complaint; But when instead of preaching Peace, Love and Friendship Agreeable to the Doctrines of the Christian Religion he had been a constant and Notorious Fermentor & Incendiary to the Indians to kill, burn and Destroy" as appeared by "many Original Letters and Manuscripts," which he had before him, had often "appeared at the head of a great number of Indians in a hostile manner, threatening and Insulting, publicly assaulting" the English, and if, after all this, "such an Incendiary" had "happened

---

end to her suffering. Rev. Benjamin Rolfe was also a graduate of Harvard and had been settled at Haverhill fourteen years when he was killed. The Rev. Joseph Willard was a graduate of Yale, and had but a short time before been ordained at Rutland. He was surprised near the village and having a gun defended himself, but was overpowered and slain and his scalp carried to Quebec.

to be slain in the heat of action" among the "open
and Declared Enemies" of the English, no one could
"be blamed therefor but himself." Moreover, he
said to the disingenuous Frenchman, "I think I have
much greater cause to Complain, that Mr. Willard
the minister of Rutland (who never had been guilty
of the facts charged upon Mr. Ralé[1] & applied himself solely to the preaching of the Gospel), was by
the Indians you sent to Attack that Town, Assaulted,

---

[1] It will be seen that Gov. Dummer places an accent on the final e in Ralé's name. In English correspondence it appears as Ralley, and in the Jesuit priest's book found at Norridgewock the name is written Rallé, which shows that it was so pronounced by the English, while in French correspondence of the time the accent appears. The writer has therefore adopted the spelling used by Ralé himself, with the accent, although the accent does not appear in his autograph as printed. The original of this autograph is, unfortunately, lost; but if Ralé even, and not the copyist, omitted the accent, it would not prove the incorrectness of its use to one familiar with the carelessness of the best writers of a century or more ago. To show, however, how common it is, even in our own time to omit the accent, the case of Pierre Soulé, M. C., from Louisiana, may be cited. Although he always pronounced his name as if spelt *Sulay*, many of his associates in Congress persisted in pronouncing it as if spelt *Sole*, and the newspapers almost invariably printed it as if so spelt; indeed, he is commonly referred to now as Mr. Soule.

slain & scalpt & his scalp Carried in Triumph to Quebec." A misdirected spirit of charity, springing perhaps out of a desire to show the world that we disavow participation in the prejudices of our forefathers, has caused a too copious gush of sympathy for the subjects of their animosity, without, perhaps, a sufficiently careful consideration of the causes of that sentiment.

But to reverse our point of view; suppose Dummer, Rolfe or Willard, or perhaps, better, Mather, for he was better known, and better represented the extreme type of the New England divine; suppose Cotton Mather had accompanied bands of savage Iroquois, who were neighbors and inimical to the French, to attack their settlements in a time of peace between his country and theirs; had not only encouraged them in their bloody designs, but had, after the destruction of their homes and the slaying of their friends, conducted his hated services before the eyes of the suffering Catholic prisoners; nay more, had as Ralé says he himself did, displayed himself to the French, who with their wives and little ones were shut up in their block houses, while their homes were blazing around them, merely "to pleasure them," and increase their fury against him; and, if at some time, he had been slain among his savages, no matter under what circumstances, how would the case have then stood? Would Mather have been considered a martyr? Suppose, too, that the French commander, a man who had proved himself to be prudent and humane as Moulton had, after all this provocation, had expressed regret that Mather was killed, and blamed his subordinate, who averred that the act was done in self-defense, should we have signalized him as a murderer?

Some doubt has been thrown upon the burial of the body of Ralé the next day after he was killed. That the savages were demoralized and fled precipitately from the scene of ruin is shown by Vaudreuil's report to the king of their arrival in Canada. This fact coupled with an expression in a letter from the king to Vaudreuil, that he loved Ralé too much to leave him longer without being *covered*, and, in a subsequent letter two years later, that he was glad to learn that his orders to *cover* the body of Ralé had been executed, naturally raises the question whether the savages returned immediately and buried the body as described by de la Chasse. A careful consideration of the subject leads to the opinion that some of the savages returned to their ruined village after the departure of the English, and secured by burial the body of their priest, and that subsequently, de la Chasse may have gone to Norridgewock with a company of his converts to conduct there such ceremonial services as he deemed appropriate. The whole question rests upon the exact meaning of the word *couvrir* as used by the king.[1]

---

[101] These expressions are as follows : " Sa Majesté a été fâchée de la mort du Père Raslé, missionairé des Abénagnis de Narantsouak qui a éte tué pas les Anglois. Elle l'affectionoit trop pour le laisser plus longtemps sans être couvert, et son intention est que le Sieur Marquis de Vaudreuil prenne les mesures necessaires pour le faire couvrir, et pour cet effet qu'il invoie des collieres aux villages Abinakis de St. François, de Bécaucourt, Panaouamské et Medoctek avec 15 couvertes et 40 livres de tabac pour chacun de ces villages, que le Sieur de Chazel fera délivrer des magazines. Le Sieur de Vaudreuil chargera de cette expedition quelques officiérs voyageurs et fera le tout de concert avec Le Superieur des jesuites à Québec," and "Sa Majesté a appris avec plaisir que les ordres qu 'Elle avoit donnés pour couvrir le corps du Peré Raslé aient été exécutés et que le Peré de la Chasse s' en soit chargé." Memoire du Roi aux Sieurs Marquis de Vaudreuil et Chazel, and aux Sieurs Marquis de Beauharnois et Dupuy. A Versailles, le 15 Mai, 1725, and le 29 Avril, 1727. These extracts have been submitted by me to scholars of the highest attainments, among whom were noted men of Ralé's own order, and their opinions of the exact meaning of the words solicited. Two quite opposite opinions were given and firmly adhered to by both parties, after each knew that an opposite opinion had been given. One opinion was that

As before remarked, we cannot regard Ralé as a martyr; indeed it is hard to understand how men even of his own order can to-day so regard him.

Yet he is so regarded in his native country, where the anniversary of his death is still religiously observed. It is, however, quite as difficult for us to understand how our forefathers could have complacently regarded the exhibition of his scalp in the streets of Boston. We can only wonder at so low a condition of public sentiment; but it was a sentiment not peculiar to New England; it belonged as well to New France; aye, to Old France and Old England; to the age in which it found expression, " *Tempora mutantur et nos mutamur in illis.*"

---

reference was made to the covering of the savages' grief by presents, according to a custom among them of making gifts to the friends of a dead person, to make them forget or mentally cover the image of the deceased. The other opinion was that the king referred to the burial of the body of Ralé, and would not be likely to employ a figurative term, limited only to savage comprehension, when addressing his ministers. Among the men holding this opinion was, perhaps, the most noted writer on the customs and languages of the savages of America at present living. I am satisfied, however, after a most careful study of the customs referred to in the first opinion, that the word *couvrir* is used figuratively in this instance, and that it was not meant to indicate the interment of the body.

RALÉ'S MONUMENT AND SITE OF THE INDIAN VILLAGE AT NORRIDGEWOCK.

APPENDIX.

COLLATERAL DOCUMENTS.

INCLUDING, WITH OTHER PAPERS OF THE PERIOD, THE FOLLOWING, EXCEPT DUPLICATES AND SUCH LETTERS AS ARE PRINTED IN THE BODY OF THE WORK, NAMELY:

"*Thirty-one Papers produced by Mr. Dummer, in Proof of the Right of the Crown of Great Britain to the Lands between New England and Nova Scotia, and of Several Depredations Committed by the French and Indians, between 1720 and June, 1725.*"

1st. Extract of the French Kings Patent to Charles de Menour K^t Lord d'Aunay.

2. Massachusets assistance to the Goverm^t of New York in 1690.

3. Conference of the Indians with Col: Walton and Major Moody &c 1720.

4. Letter from Several Tribes of Indians to the Governor of N: England in 1721.

5. Translation of the foregoing letter to a Jesuit in 1721.

6. Copy of Mr Begon a French Intend^{ts} letter to a Jesuit in 1721.

7. Monsr Vaudreuils letter to Seb: Rallé a French Jesuit in 1721.

8. Paper taken from the Church Door at Norridgewock in Octo^r, 1722.

9. Monsr. Vaudreuil the French Gov^{rs} letter to the Govr of New England, 1723.

10. Answer from the Lt Govr of New England to the foregoing 1723.

11. Lannerjats Letter to Monsr Rallé Jesuit concerning the English killed at Winslow.

12. A Copy of a letter from Seb: Rallé a French Jesuit to another Priest giving a detail of the Depredations committed by the Indians on the English in North America Aug: 1724.

13. Letter from the Lieu^t Govr of Massachusets to the Govr of Rhode Island in 1724.

14. Translation of Monsr Vaudreuil Govr of Canada's letter to the Lt Govr of ye Massachusets about the French Jesuits &c. dated Octr 29th 1724.

15. Duplicate of the Same.

16. Instructions given by the Governm^t of New England to their Commiss^{rs} Sent to Canada to demand the English Captives &c in Novr 1724.

17. Journal of the said Commissioners.

18. Letter from the Lt Govr of the Massachusets to the Lt Govr of N. Hampshire Decr 1st. 1724.

19. D^o to Govr Cranston of Rhode Island dated Decr 1st 1724 & to Govr Talcot of Connecticut.

20. D^o to Govr Burnet of N: York Decr 1st 1724.

21. Vote of the Govr and Council of N: York of 16 Decr 1724.

22. NB. this is Annexed to No. 19.

23. Govr Talcot of Connecticut's letter to the Lt Govr of the Massachusets Dated Decr 1724.

24. Narrative of the Indians Managem^t and of several Treaties with them 1724.

Appendix. 277

25. Letter from the Lt Govr of the Massachusets to the Govr of Canada 1724-5.
26. Cap: Jordans Declaration in May 1728 of his usage by a French Fryer.
27. David Golds Testimony of Depredations committed by the Indians in 1725.
28. The like of Saml Harris 1725.
29. Declaration of the New England Com^{rs} to Canada made to the Govern^t of New York.
30. The said Commiss^{rs} demand to ye Govr of Canada.
31. French Receipts of Mony for ye Ransom of English Prisoners 1725.
B. T. New England, Bundle Y, Vol. 17
Rec^d }
Read } Sept. 30, 1725.

[*Paper 1.*]

EXTRACT FROM THE FRENCH KING'S PATENT TO CHARLES DE MENOU, K^T. LORD D'AULNAY.

"Louis, By the Grace of God, King of France and Navarre, To all present and to come . . . do appoint and establish . . . Charles de Menou, Chevalier Sieur d'Aulnay Charnizay . . . Governor of New France and Our Lieutenant General of the Country and Coast of Acadia . . . *from the Great River St. Lawrence . . . as far as Virginia* . . . We will that the said Sr. d'Aulnay de Charnizay may cause to be built and constructed, Towns, Forts, Ports, Harbors and other places as he shall see useful . . . and to establish there such officers and garrisons as shall be needed. And do generally for the conquest, peopleing, settlement and preservation of the said country, lands and coasts of Acadia *from the said River St. Lawrence as far as Virginia*, their appurtenances and dependencies, under our Name and Authority, all that we might be able to do if We were there in Person."

[*Paper 2.*]

MASSACHUSETTS ASSISTANCE TO THE GOVERNOR OF N. YORK.

At the Adjournment of the General Court in Boston. May 14th, 1690.

PURSUANT to the Agreement of William Stoughton & Samuel Sewell Esq[rs] Commissioners from the Colony with the Commissioners from the other Governments met at New York the first of May instant Ordered that One hundred and Sixty Soldiers be Detach[d] out of the Several Regiments within this Colony in proportion following That is to Say, Out of Hampshire Regiment Forty, Middlesex lower Regiment Twenty, Upper Regiment Ten; Essex Upper Regiment Ten, Middle Regiment Twenty; South Regiment Twenty; South Suffolk Regiment two & Twenty, Boston Regiment Eighteen, to be Improved for the Strengthening of Albany and prosecution of the Common Enemy, French & Indians.

A True Copy as of Record.
Attest: J. Willard Secry.

The Deposition of Lewis Bane of York Esqr.

This Depon^t Testifyeth and Saith That he being Imployed by the Government As Commander of a Small Detachment of Men the last Sumer was at the Eastward New Settlements, where there were some threatning Speeches and unfriendly Actions of the Indians, when this Depon^t was Among them; & he asked them why they Acted After such a Manner with the English, who were their very good Friends; And he understood by them that One Chief Cause was, That the French Fryar Sebastian Raylée stirred them up so to do, telling them that if they suffered the English to go on in setling those parts in two years they would be so strong that they would not be able to remove them And also that then the English would take away Neridgawalk from them.

SUFFOLK ss : — Boston, 2^d. December 1719.
Lewis Bane personally Appeared before us the subscribers two of his Majesties Justices of the peace in s^d County and made oath to the truth of this above writen Testimony taken perpetuam Rei : Memoriam — —
        Samuel Lynde
        Habijah Savage

Lewis Bane Justice of the peace Quoram unus.

B. T. New England, Vol. 15, W. 81, Office of the Public Records, London.

The Deposition of John Minot late of George Towne in Arowsick but now of Boston Merch^t.

That he being the last Spring sent by the Governm^t to Narantswalk on a message to the Indians there, did then heare Sebastian Rale the Popish Preist or Jessuit who resides with those Indians say —

That the King of France had given the Govern^r of Canada orders to assist the Indians against the English, if they proceeded to settle the Eastern parts of the County of York, and that the Govern^r of Canada had promist to assist the Indians against the English.

And when the Regents health was offerd to him the said Jessuit he refused to pledge it, saying the Regent was a Protestant, speaking refleckting words of him.

And the Indians of Narantswalk at the same time told him the said Minot, that the said Jessuit was continually inciting the Indians against the English, and that it was their best way, to beat and fight the English And to disturb them in their settlements.

And that the said Jessuit had wrote to the English Govern^r in their names, Otherwayes then they intended, and things they did not Consent to.

And at other times, the said Indians being Instructed by the said Jessuit had said to him the said Minot, that King George was not the right King that he came in at the back door, and that there was Another who was the right heir to the Crown.

The above mentioned or words to the same purpose have bin spoken in my hearing

John Minot

SUFFOLK *ss:* — Boston 27th November 1719.

John Minot personally Appeared before us the Subscribers two of his Majesties Justices of the peace

Appendix. 281

in s[d] County and made oath to the truth of the above writen testimony

    Samuel Lynd (Justice peace
    Habijah Savage (Quoram unnus
taken in perpetuam
Rei Memoriam
 End;) Massachusetts Bay
 Depositions of Lewis Bane, Esq[r] & John Minot, Merch[t], taken at Boston, in Nov[r] & Dec[r] 1719, in relation to a French Fryar, Sebastian Rayleés, stirring up the Kennebeck Indians to revolt from His Majesty, & disturb the Neighbouring English Settlements.

    Rec[d] with M[r] Dūmer's Memorial

[*Paper 3.*]

CONFERENCE WITH THE KENNEBECK INDIANS.

At a Conference with the Chiefs and some others of the Kennebeck Indians at George Town November the 25th, 1720.

 Present

  Shadrach Walton Esq[r] ⎫ Commission-
  Sam[ll] Moody Esq[r]   ⎬ ers on behalf
  Capt. Johnson Harman ⎪ of the Gov-
  Capt. John Wainwright ⎭ ernment.

Were also present of the Indians

> Warrawenset alias Mogg
> Wowurna alias Capt Joseph
> Obomaukawk
> John Hegon
> Tuddebawhunjerit
> Ketterremuggus alias Moses

Interpreters
Lieu^t Joseph Bean } being sworn
Mr Saml Jordan

Commiss^{rs} — Tell the Sachems and other Indians here present That we four Gentlemen are Authorized and Impowered by a Commission from our Great Governor, Pursuant to a Vote of the Great Court and Assembly that are now sitting at Boston to Manage a Treaty with you at this time and according to appointment here at Arrowsick.

Indians — We are very well Satisfied that you are so Authorized and Impowered.

Commiss^{rs} — We presume that you are also Authorized and sent by your Tribe and that you represent them; and we Suppose it to be the same thing as if your whole Tribe were here present to act.

Indians — We Desire that the People may be removed from Merry Meeting.

Commiss^{rs} — That's no answer to what we proposed, that matter may be Discoursed in the proper place & Season Tell us whether you represent your Tribe, and how we shall know that you are sent to act on their Behalf We Insist upon your Answer because we would leave no room for any of your People to make Objections Against your proceedings afterwards.

Indians — Mogg (holding a Belt of Wampum over his Head) Replied We are all upon a Hill in View of all the Indians, who see and know that we are here to act for them, and this Belt is a Token of it. This is our Letter and Comission.

Commiss^rs — If that be your Letter and Comission, and a Token of your being Impowered we are satisfied: We shall then proceed.

Indians — We desire that we may go on with our talk, first that the People that are upon Our Land at Merry meeting may be removed.

Commiss^rs — We'll not be Interrupted, but will proceed with what we are about to offer, and you may have the Liberty Afterward to say what you please referring to that matter You cant but Remember that Several Gentlemen were sent down the last Winter to Casco Bay where they had a Conference with several of the Chiefs of your Tribe and at that time acquainted you with the Ill Carriage of your People towards the English Inhabiting those parts of the Country in killing their Creatures, Threatning and Insulting their Persons and unjustly disturbing their Settlements and Demanded Satisfaction for the wrong done us, which you then firmly Promised to make in the Spring, as soon as you Could Assemble your whole Tribe to Consult the matter But Instead of Complying with those Promises and Engagements, you have on the Contrary repeated your Insults and Barbarous Carriages of that kind which we are now to acquaint you that the Government will bear no longer And we are Directed by His Majesties Government to demand the reason of your Non Complyance with your Promises so Solemnly made to those Commissioners, and have made no restitution for the wrongs done us either the last year or the summer past, We Expect your Answer to those things forthwith.

Indians — We did not sit in Council about that matter till lately.

Commiss^{rs} — Tell us why you did not when you so solemnly Promised, and what is the Result of your late Council.

Indians — The Reason why we did not meet sooner was because there were so many Reports of Mischief Done and so much noise that we Could not Assemble to Consult.

Commiss^{rs} — Who did any mischief but yourselves? What Occasioned all that Noise but your Insolent Carriage towards the English and your base Treatment of the Inhabitants in these parts, as we have already hinted to you.

Indians — We are sensible that our Young Men were the Occasion of the Disturbance that has happened and we have Striven to hinder them as much as in us lyes.

Commiss^{rs} — Then you ought to Govern your Young Men and Punish them for their Insolence, and if you Cant restrain them you should have informed us of it, and have Delivered them to us in Order to their being brought to better manners; And you have Obliged your selves by all former Treaties not to Disturb us in our Settlements And yet have suffered your Young men to persist in their Insolent Behaviour towards our Inhabitants to their great Discouragement and Damage.

Indians — We desire to go on with our talk; If all those People were removed from Merry Meeting Bay, all other differences between us would be easily Composed.

Comiss^{rs} — Yee will still break in upon us to Evade

that matter which we are firmly resolved to Insist on. Tell us what you Determined at your late Council.

Indians — We are Come here to Desire Peace and long Life, and as a Token of our sincerity We offer these two Belts of Wampum. Three of our Towns have held a Great Council : We are Incapacitated to make restitution for the damage done this fall ; but we will Endeavor to do it by next June or July ; let us know what we are to pay?

Comiss^{rs} — You Promised before that you'd pay this fall, but have not Complyed. Abomazen when at Piscataqua Desired that the Indians might be allowed till the time of their fall hunting to pay for the damage done us & now you would put it off till next June or July; but we shall give you no further time.

Indians — Did Abomazen Give any Letter or lay down any Wampum for the Binding of his Promise?

Commiss^{rs}—You threw down Wampum at the Great Treaty on Arowsick with His Excellency Governour Shute ; yet that was far from being Binding to you ; for you have since been Guilty several times of a Manifest Breach of the Articles you then Signed & Sealed in the presence of God and many Witnesses.

Indians — But this hath been a stronger Council, and we are now Resolved to be as good as our words.

Comiss^{rs} — Was your late Council stronger than what you formerly met at His Excellency Governor Dudley at Casco, when all the Tribes were assembled, and there Called the Great God to Witness of the sincerity of your Hearts & made the most Solemn Protestations Imaginable in the Light of the Sun (which you then Declared was a Witness to that Days Transaction) that you would live quietly & peaceably and no more Molest and Disturb the English in their Settlements. Was your Council stronger than what you met his Excellency Our present Governor at this place; which we have already hinted to you when you laid yourselves under as Strong Bonds as was possible by Belt of Wampum you then offered? All which (besides many other solemn Promises and Covenants lately made with us) you have Perfidiously broken as you Cannot but acknowledge. What reason have you to think we can give any Credit to what you now Say? what security will you Give us that you will make us satisfaction in the Spring for the Injuries done us, for we will take your words no longer — here they paused for some time & made no answer.

Indians — It's our young men that don't Attend our Prayers that have done you g^t damage; your men have also Injured us but we are loth to Complain.

Comiss^{rs} — If you have any Complaints to offer we are willing to hear them; but you are Coming off from the Business we are upon We demand security of you for the payment of what is due for the damage done.

Indians — How many Skins are we to pay, give us a Letter or account of it?

Comiss^{rs} — Capt. Giles had an Acco^t this Summer, which he was ordered to Communicate to you.

Indians — Only one of us viz., John Hegon, heard it.

Comiss^{rs} — He ought to have told the rest.

Indians — It is Customary when any one of us hear of such a thing to Inform the rest, but he did not do it.

Commiss^{rs} — We have Reason to think you have been fully Informed of it, for several of your Indians told our People that they were going to hunt for Skins to make paym^t for the English were sick for want of their skins, and they should be Sick also if the People were not removed from Merry Meeting. But indeed the half of what is our due was not Inserted in the acco^t and we can Name the Men that have done us the wrong, and accordingly several Persons were mentioned.

Indians — These were our Young Men that don't pray.

Comiss^{rs} — It is not only your Young Men, for here is Nathl present who is one of your Old men, and hath been Notoriously Guilty of Insulting our People, and you shall Punish him, or we will Cause him to be well Scouraged. There is Captain Joseph also that was present, when some of your People killed a hogg belonging to one Stockbridge ; for which he hath received no Satisfaction so that the old men are Guilty. You are the Heads of your Tribes, and must answer for what they do. But to make Short of the matter we demand 200 Skins of you, which is but a Small matter in Comparison of the injuries you have done us ; and tho you were ordered at a Conference some of us had with you the last month, to warn your Young Men of their Ill Carriage, they have persisted in it, and some of your People have within a few days past, broken a Lock and robbed a Sloop at Casco Bay, which is death by our Law.

Indians — We did faithfully warn our Young Men, but they are a Vagabond sort of men, that will not take warning.

Comiss^{rs} — If you Cant restrain those Insolent Young Men you will force us to take our own Satisfaction. The Government has always Treated you fairly, and is very Tender of Shedding any blood. But if you will not Reform, but will constrain them to use any Violent proceedings against you, you must thank your selves for any mischiefs that may Ensue; and here we must further Observe to you how wickedly the Jesuit has Imposed on you, more Especially by Informing you of a War between Great Britain & France Whereas the two Nations are in a Strict League of Friendship and have a Prospect to Continue so for a long time (so that upon your own knowledge & Observation of these matters) you may be satisfied of his falsness and Deceit, and may make it very Evident to you, that the false Insinuations of your Father Rallé (that in Case of a Breach between the English and you the French will afford you their Aid & Assistance Can have no other Tendency but your utter Ruin & Destruction.

To which they made no Reply.

Comis^{rs} — We shall leave these things to your Consideration and adjourn till the afternoon.

Afternoon at 4 o'Clock met again.

Comiss^{rs} — Have you Considered what we last proposed to you? We must have Satisfaction & good Security for your Behaviour.

Indians — We have Considered of it, and will leave one of our Old Men Terreamuggus that is here present as a pledge for the Compliance with our Promises & Engagements.

Comiss^{rs} — He is an Old Man & one that you have Rejected & turned out of your Council, & we don't think him a sufficient security.

Indians — He was of our Council, and we don't know that he has been Excluded.

Comiss^rs — We have been Informed that he was shut out by your Jesuit, but whether that be true or false, we do not see Cause to accept of him, tho' we suppose him to be as honest a man as any of you; Yet we neither think it to be reasonable or Honourable for us to Comply with you in that Regard. We must have better Security.

Indians — He is one of our Principal Men, & we still Insist upon having him as a pledge.

Comiss^rs — We will have three more of your Principal Young Men and you shall pay the Charge of their subsistence, for we will not bring any Charge upon the Government.

Indians — We Desire to withdraw for some time to Consult among Our selves.

Comiss^rs — Make all the Dispatch you Can we will give you half an hour.

They withdrew accordingly & returned in half an hour.

Comiss^rs — We are now ready to hear what you have determined.

Indians — We will leave three of our Chiefs. We are sending two to Penobscot, two to Narridgewalk, & two to Pigwackit, & we have no more here that we Can spare

Comiss^rs — We must take a little time to Consider this matter and will give you our final Determination to-morrow morning. We shall Order you a little Provision & something to Drink this Evening; and we Strictly Charge you that you don't abuse your selves by drinking too much. Some of your People were Drunk last night, and one of them drew a knife upon one of our Inhabitants, which was an Insufferable Abuse. You may Assure yourselves that we are in Earnest with you and we are Resolved not to take such base Treatment at your Hands; therefore we advise you to be very Cautious.

Indians — We desire one word more; we like what you have offered, Only you are pleased to tell us that you Cant assure us of the Governments bearing the Charge of Our Mens subsistence.

*Comiss*ʳˢ — You shall bear the Charge that may arise for the subsistence of your Hostages, unless the Government should see Cause to favour you in that matter.

Saturday November the 28ᵗʰ, met about 9 o'clock in yᵉ Morning

*Comiss*ʳˢ — We have well Considered of what you proposed yesterday of leaving only three of your Chiefs with us, and can by no means Consent to it. You shall be obliged to bring the 200 skins within 25 Days, & at the same time shall deliver Four of your Chiefs into our hands there to remain during the pleasure of the Governmᵗ & any greater number that the Governmᵗ shall Demand as security (not only for payment of those Skins in Case you fail of performing your obligation) but for your good Behaviour towards the English for the future.

Indians — We approve of what you say, & we hope within six days to Inform our whole Tribe of what we have done.

*Comiss*ʳˢ — Do you really Consent to what we propose?

Indians — We do Consent to it, and will Comply with your demand.

*Comiss*ʳˢ — Tell us what you will leave for we will not be Imposed upon, or accept of any but your principal Men; and we Doubt not but the Government will Allow of Your Exchanging them, for the like number of as good Men in Convenient time.

Indians — We have Determined to Deliver into your hands Jnº Hegon, Terremuggus, Obomohauk,

Currebooset, & in Case of his failing Inddebawhunsewit his Brother shall supply his place. These are the four.

Comiss^{rs}— It is well we have drawn up something for you to sign as an Obligation for the true performance of what you now Promise & Engage ; And after you have signed this Instrument you shall have ye Liberty to go on with what you were about to propose to us Concerning your Land, & the Inhabitants of Merry meeting Bay, or any other matter, which you have to offer.

The Obligation is as follows viz —

The Obligation —

At a Conference held at George Town with the Commissioners Authorized and Impowered by the Governor & Great Council of Boston to treat with the Indians of Kenebeck River November 1720.

We the Subscribers Delegates of the Tribe of Norridgewack in Kenebeck, being Convicted and made deeply sensible of the repeated Wrongs & Injuries done by our Tribe to the English residing in these parts for several years past, in killing their Creatures and Disturbing their Settlements Contrary to former Treaty's Covenants and Promises Do by these presents for our selves & in behalf of the Tribes whom we represent firmly promise and Engage to Pay to the said Comissioners viz Col Shadrach Walton Esqr Capt Samuel Moodey Esqr Capt Johnson Harmon Capt John Wainwright or their order at the Town of Falmouth in Casco Bay, Two hundred good large Beaver skins or other Furs or ffeathers Equivalent to said Skins within twenty five days after the date of these presents; And at the day prefixt to deliver up four of our Chiefs viz Lackwadawmeck Alias John Hegon, Obomawhawk Ketteramuggus Curreboosett as Hostages not only for the security of said Payment of 200 skins (in Case of our Default) but said Hostages still to Remain in the Hands of the Government, to be subsisted and Maintained at our Cost and Charge And we do further Covenant and Promise that the aboves[d] Hostages or any greater number that the Government shall demand after S[d] Payment is well and truly made shall then be Delivered into the Hands of the English to remain and Abide as Pledges and Security for our good Behaviour for the time to come.

In witness whereof we have hereunto set Our hands & Seals the twenty sixth day of November In the Seventh year of His Majesties Reign Annoque Domini 1720.

Signed Sealed and Delivered.

in presence of			
Isaac Taylor	Mark of Mogg		(Seal)
Rob[t] Temple	Mark of Wowurnapa		(Seal)
Joseph Bean			
Sam[ll] Jordan	Mark of Tuddebaw	hunsewit	(Seal)
Alex[r] Forsyth			
John Parker	Mark of Kettera	Muggus	(Seal)
Thos. Newman			
Eben[r] Allen	Mark of John Marke Obomaw	Hegon of hawk	(Seal) (Seal)

Appendix.

The aforesaid Instrument was several times Distinctly and Faithfully Interpreted to them, which they Declared that they rightly Understood, and accordingly signed sealed and Delivered the same in the presence of the afors^d Witnesses.

Comiss^{rs} — Have you now any thing to offer us.

Indians — We have no more to say at present.

Comiss^{rs} — You offered something yesterday about your Lands and removing the Inhabitants from Merry meeting.

Indians — We have said all that we were ordered to say.

Comis^{rs} — You declared that you did not Approve of our People settling there, and you have now the Liberty to proceed But Inasmuch as you Decline it, we have something to offer to you upon that Head. We are directed by the Governm^t to tell you that the English have no Design to take your Country or any of your Lands from you, or to deprive you of any of your Just rights or Priviledges. The Claims of the English to those Lands in Kenebeck River have been Examined and we are fully Satisfied that the English have a good Title thereunto as appears by their Deeds and Conveyances from Indians above 70 years since. And the Government is Resolved to Defend the Proprietors in those their just rights. It's therefore in Vain for you to Expect that even those Inhabitants will be removed. The Government is very loth to draw the sword, which you have Given them just Provocation to do. But you may depend upon it that the Forces which have been raised at a vast Expence for the Curbing of your Insolencies will not be Disbanded till you have Complied with the Obligation you have now laid your selves under; And if you will Constrain us by your repeated Insults to any violent proceedings, we have force enough, and will pursue you to your Head Quarters (which we are well acquainted with, and can easily take possession of) and will not leave you till we have Cut you off Root and Branch from the Face of the Earth. It will be your Interest to Consider these things, and you may Believe that we are in Earnest, and this is the last warning we shall give you. And if you Imagine you can make your terms more easy with the Government you may have Liberty to go to Boston, as soon as you please.

Indians — We are well satisfied, and will Comply with all that you have Offered.

Thus Ended the Conference which we hope will be Acceptable to Your Excellency and the Government as attested by us.

Sha^d. Walton.
Sam^{ll}. Moodey.

Copy Examined
℔ J. Willard, Secry.

Paper No. 4, entitled " LETTERS FROM SEVERAL TRIBES OF INDIANS TO THE GOVERNOR OF N: ENGLAND IN 1721," may be found at page 111.

[*Paper 5.*]

CONTEMPORARY TRANSLATION.

MONS^r BEGON TO FATHER RALLÉ.

I have received my Reverend Father the Letter that you did me the Honour to write me the 18th last month Monsr De Vaudreuil being at Montreal at the arrival of the Indians you sent here. I engaged four of them to go to him & Carry the Letter you wrote him, which was Accompanied with one I wrote to him to Comunicate to him the Sentiments of Father de la Chase & my own upon what we think Convenient to be done till the Counsel of Navy Explain themselves, if it be the Kings Intention, that the French joyns the Indians to support them openly against the English; or if we shall content ourselves to furnish them with Amunition of War as the Counsel has advised Monsr De Vaudreuil might do in case the English makes any Enterprize against them; I send you the Copy of my Letter to the end you may furnish me with your thoughts which appears to you to be best.

Monsr De Vaudreuil is Come down here with the Indians & pass'd St. Francois & Besancour to Invite the Indians to those Missions to send Deputies from their Villages to advise whats to be done.

He had a Design to Write to the English Gov[r] but since his return has Changed his Sentiment & Contents himself to follow the principal Articles of the Memorial you sent him, which are to keep themselves on their Lands, & in the Religion they have embraced & to have no longer different sentiments amongst them, But to unite to speak to the English with Resolution. He thought it likewise more Convenient that the Revd Father de la Chase should accompany the Indians of St. François & De Besancour than Monsr de Croisil Lieu[t] whom he brought with him with a design to send him with those Indians, because that the journey of the R. F. De la Chase is of no Consequence in respect of the English, seeing the Treaty of Peace does not forbid one Missionary to Visit another in His Mission; whereas if a French officer were sent, they might Complain we send ffrench Men into a Countrey they pretend to belong to them to Excite the Indians to make War on them, on which we are of Opinion it's Convenient to await the orders of the Court for them, to the end not to Exceed Seeing you Cant abandon Your Mission to come Your self to Comunicate your thoughts on this subject and that it's Difficult to Explain them amply enough by a Letter & Consequently Instruct us in what you may know of the Rules we must Limit our selves by, We thought the journey of the Revd Father De La Chase very Convenient at this present Conjuncture that he may thorowly Acquaint you with Methods that we think we are Obliged to use towards the English that we might Exceed and that he may Comunicate to us at his return all the reflection you make on the disposition of your Indians, & those of your two other Missions.

Monsr De Vaudreuil has read to your Indians & to them that Accompanied them the Memorial he sends you Containing his speech, that they may no longer say that it is that of their Missionary: we believe you'l find it in the sense you proposed it.

I Caused to be given a Blanket, a shirt, a pair Mittons, Tobacco, powder, and shot to Each of the five Indians you sent and I believe they return Contented & with good Intentions; as you are always too reserved in what regards Your self I have desired the Revd Father de la Chase to know of you in Amity what I can send you, that will be most Agreeable. I pray youd make use of it without Compliment; nothing is better approved of, than what you said to the Indians upon the news of the English Governor your great Enemy being turned out; I wish that he that fills up his place proves more Reasonable, & that he letts you & your Indians live in quiet: This is to be wished for till we are well Instructed. If it be the Kings Intention that openly we joyn with the Indians against them, if they attack them wrongfully. Because in the Interim we Cant assist but by amunition which we shall give them & they may depend that we wont let them want.

In respect to Taxus, I find you had great Reason to use him as you did, & you Could not be less Steady than you were, it being necessary to have no Regard for those that appear more attached to the English than to us.

I am with all my Heart & with all possible attchm^t
My Revd Father
Your humble & Obedient Servant
Signed   Begon.

Quebec the 14th June 1721.

Since my Letters being wrote the Indians of St. Francois & of Besancour having desired of M^r De Vaudreuil that Monsr De Croisil go with them to be Witness of their good Dispositions, he Consented, & is Joyned with the Revd Father de la Chase

Copy   Examined
℔ J. Willard Secry.

Rec^d wth Col^o Shutes Lre of 13th March, 1721.
Rec^d } May 15th {
Read } Do 25th { 1722.

[Am. & W. I., Vol. 5.]
(Copy.)
Govr Shute to the Canadian Governor.
Letter to the Governour of Canada from His Excellency Gouvernour Shute.

Sir

Being Informed That Your Excellency has Orders sent you Immediately to release the English Captives that are in your hands, I do my Self the Honour to write to you on this Affair; I need not Observe to you, how Agreeable it is to the Law of Nations and the Strict Allyance between the two Crowns (which God long Continue) That the Remnant of the Captivity of this Governm^t should at length be returned; and I perswade myself you will be glad of this Occasion of shewing Your Justice and Humanity in this matter; I would acquaint you That this Government has lately been Insulted by our Eastern Indians without any Provocation and Contrary to their own repeated and Solemn stipulations & Treaties, a number of two hundred of them Entring in a Hostile manner into an English Town under French Colours, & Treating the English Inhabitants after a very Insolent manner. This is such a Breach upon His Majesties Government to which these Indians have subjected themselves, as we shall by no means Endure, & are Determined to have satisfaction for. I the rather Acquaint Your Excellency with this Affair because the Indians were Headed by two French officers, one of them said to be from Canada (his name I have lost) and two Jesuits. This last Circumstance, I look upon as an Infraction of the Treaty of Peace and Friendship between the two Crowns Concluded at Utrecht, unto which I assure my self, you will most Strictly Conform; And therefore I doe very Earnestly Desire you would Enquire after this Officer and proceed with him according to his Deserts; And also that you will do your part to recall Monsr Rallé & the other Jesuit from residing in any part of the Territory belonging to the Crown of Great Britain so Contrary to the Treaty aforesaid, His Majesties Laws at Home, and the Laws of this Province.

And in Case any of our Eastern Indians should make their Application to Your Excellency you will use your Influence and Advise them to behave Loyally and peaceably toward His Majesties Government wherein they be, That so the English People on the Frontiers may live in Peace and not be troubled and abused by the Savages; And in Case the present rupture with the Eastern Indians should Come to a Warr, I shall then Notify Your Excellency of it, & Expect Your Friendship and Assistance therein.

I am

Boston July 21
1721

Your Excellencies
Humble servant
Sam^{ll} Shute.

Examined ℔ J. Willard Secry.

Paper No. 6 is the original French of the foregoing.

[*Paper 7.*]

CONTEMPORARY TRANSLATION.*

GOVERNOUR VAUDREUIL TO FATHER RALLÉ.

Quebec Le 25th September 1721.

I received my Reverend Father your Letters of the 4th August 10th and 14th this month, I have a great

---
*For the French of this paper, see New England B. T. Bundle X, vol. 16, office of the Public Records, London. A verbatim copy is in the possession of the author.

deal of Satisfaction in your having found means in Concert with the Rev. Father Superior to reunite all the Indians in the same Sentiments, & to Inspire them with that Resolution, with which they Treated the English in their Interview with them; I'm also very well Satisfied with the Message they sent the Governour of Boston I'm perswaded it will Embarrass him, and that he will Elude as much as he can an Answer; But it's for your Indians to see what they have to do, if after the Remonstrance they Gave him he do not Satisfy their Demands.

I'm of the sentiment, if they have taken for me, a sincere Resolution not to suffer the English on their Land, that they ought not to suspend Chasing them out, as soon as possible, and by all sorts of means, seeing they dont prepare to retire on their own accord. Your people ought not to fear the want of Ammunition, since I send them a sufficiency, as you may see in the Memorandum Inclosed, And that I'll continue with other succours they shall want, having Orders not to lett them want, and even to sustain them if the English attack them wrongfully. I am charmed that Owrené has thus distinguished himself in this Treaty, and that he has laboured as he has done, that the speech of the Nation was such to the English, he'll receive for his son Marks of the Satisfacon I have for him, or his services, for I have sent all you Desired for Him.

It is not the Malaowins that are a setling the Isle of St. Johns, that Island, and that of Magerlaine and others that are in the Gulph St. Lawrence having been given by the King to M^r Le Compte de St. Pierre who causes it to be Inhabited for the Cod fishery, Seales & Sea Cows so that your Abenakis cant Expect any thing from that place.

I will consult with the Reverend Father Superior after what manner I shall receive those of your Village that were attached to the English, They are on the way, and may be here about All Saints; But you may depend I will make the Degraded sensible how much I am Discontent with their Conduct. I am perfectly my Reverend Father your Most Humble and Obedient servant   Signed
                                    Vaudreuil

You may promise a great Medal of the King reigning to him that shall be chosen for Chief in the place of him Degraded
                     ⸺   ℔ J. Willard Secry.

COLONEL SHUTE TO THE LORDS COMMISSIONERS FOR
          TRADE AND PLANTATIONS.
    [The notes in the margin are the remarks of the Lords Commissioners.]
My Lords

The last Letter I had the honour to receive from Your Lordships bears date the 23^d of August last; And I could not Slip the first Oppor- He has received the Boards Letter of 23d August, 1721. tunity to return the R^t Honble Board my gratefull Acknowledgements for the kind Representation your Lords^{ps} promise to make to His Majesty in relation to my Administration.

I hope my last Letter to Your Lords^{ps} which bore date Septemb^r 8th last is arrived.

The affairs of this Province remain in the same posture as when I last wrote to your Lords^{ps}, for which Letter I acquainted You of the Affairs of the province same as when he wrote last. Rebellion of the Indians occasioned by the French governor and Jesuits. Rebellious behaviour of the Indians: and find it was chiefly occasioned by Monsr Vaudreuil, who is the Governour of Canada, Permitting (or I rather fear encouraging) Father Le Chasse who is a Jesuit residing with him, and also Monsr Croizeen a ffrench Officer, to come down into His Majestys Government, and there joyn with another French Jesuit, whose name is Raillée, who constantly resides among the Indians, that are in His Majestys Territories, who all combined together as Incendiarys to perswade the Indians to Commit this Insult. These Proceedings keep our Eastern Settlements constantly Alarmed and obliges me to keep Troops upon the ffrontiers to the great Expence of this Province which puts them under many Difficulties. I earnestly beg of your Lords^{ps} to take this Matter into Your wise Consideration and more Especially since these Proceedings of the French are directly Contrary to the Treaties that have been made between the Crown of Great Britain & France.

<small>He desires the same may be taken into consideration as being contrary to Treaties.</small>

     I am with great regard
      My Lords
       Your Lordships
        most humble Servant
         Samuel Shute.

Boston December 13th 1721
To the R^t Honble the Lords of Trade &c.
   Recd. Janry 31st } 172$\frac{1}{2}$
   Read 6th Feb^{ry}
X. 43. B. T. New England, Vol. 16.

Col^o Shute to the Lords Commissioners for Trade and Plantations.

  Boston New England March 13th 1721.
My Lords
 In my Letter of the 13th of December last to the R^t Honble Board I took the liberty to hint to your

Lordships that I had good reason to suspect that Monsr Vaudreuil the Governour of Canada did Underhand stir up my Neighbouring Indians to Maletreat His Majestys liege Subjects. *He suspects Mr. Vaudreuil stirs up the Indians against his Majtys subjects.*

The Inclosed Letters will give plain Demonstration that my Suspicions were well Grounded. I have only sent your Lordships well attested Copys, not daring to send the Originals and run the risque of the Sea without direct Orders from home so to do. *His suspicions well grounded. Sends copies of Letters.*

I shall take the liberty to remarke to Your Lordships, that these Letters were found in Monsr Ralés House a ffrench Jesuite who constantly resides among my Neighbouring Indians & is Useing his Utmost Indeavours to Engage them in a War against the English. *These Letters found in Mr. Ralés House. Stirs them up against the English.*

Your Lordsp^s will observe that the ffrench Government (in the Inclosed Letters) Advise the Indians to drive the English off from their Lands; from which I must remarke to Your Lordships that those Lands which the ffrench Government call the Indians Land, are Lands which the English have long Since purchased of the Indians, and have good Deeds to produce for the Same, & have also Erected some fforts thereupon; and that the said Lands have been at Several Gen^{ll} Meetings of the Indians and English Confirmed to them, and once Since my being Governour of these Provinces, as will Appear by the Inclosed Treaty of the 19th August 1717. *French advise Indians to drive English off their Lands.*

I also take the Liberty to Acquaint Your Lordshp^s that full Credence ought to be given to Monsr Vaudreuils Letters, I being well Acquainted with his hand, having re- *Mr. Vaudreuil's Lres Authentick.*

ceived Several letters from him since my residing in these Parts, and have compared the Originals I have by me, with those, I had formerly received from him; and find them to Agree Exactly.

As for Monsr Begon the Intendants Letter I cannot Speak so plumply to it because I never had any Correspondence with him, but am well Informed the Original is of his writing.

<small>Belives Mr. Begons are so too.</small>

I further Judge it necessary to Acquaint your Lordships that in a piece of a letter where the name and date were cutt out there is Mention made of one Charlevoix who comes from the Court of ffrance in the quality of an Inspector to make Memoirs on Acady & Missisipi & the other Countrys thereabouts.

<small>Charlevoix made Inspector of Accady & Missisipi.</small>

The Indians have lately killed some of our Cattle & threaten our Eastern Settlements, So that I am Under some Apprehension that a War will break out this Summer (which I will Indeavour if possible to prevent) Except Some Measures be taken to Oblige the ffrench Government at Canada to Act Strictly up to the Stipulations Agreed to, betwixt the Crowns of Great Brittain & France.

<small>Fears an Indian War.</small>

      I am
      My Lords
       Your Lordships
        most hum^{ble} Servant
         Samll Shute.

To the R^t Honble the Lords of Trade &c.
B. T. New England vol. 16 Bundle 6.

A Letter from His Excellency the Governour to the Marquess de Vaudreuil Governour of Canada.

(Copy)

Sir

Since the finishing of my Letter of the 14th of March last past I have the honour to receive one of yours dated at Quebec the 22^d day of December last, Consisting of several Articles to which I shall Endeavour to give a particular answer. And first, As to the Order of the Regent of France for the Return of the English Captives I have Inclosed you a Faithful Translation of the Original, by which you will Judge whether I have been under any Mistake in that matter, and notwithstanding what you are pleased to say of the Liberty that was given to the Prisoners to return, yet I am well Informed there was such pains taken & Arts used to dissuade them that they could not be said to act at full liberty.

In my other Letter, I have given you a large Account of the Insult of the Indians at Arowsick and, yet from some passages in your Letter I am Obliged to act something further in this ; You are pleased to call Arowsick (where the Indians made their Hostile appearance) a place of the Indians own Land ; I persuade myself, if you knew the Circumstances of that part of this Province, you would not be of that opinion: Arowsick is a small Island at the Mouth of one of our Chief Rivers, purchased by good Deeds from the Natives near Seventy years agone, and settled with a good English Village above fifty years since ; Besides a Patent of Confirmation from the Crown of Great Britain to the Purchasers ; since my arrival in this Government the Inhabitants of that place have sent a Burgess to represent them in the

General Assembly of this Province, and yet you are pleased to call this Town a place of the Indians own Lands.

That the Indians will deny their own Deeds tho never so Solemnly Ratified and justly Obtained, I am very apt to Believe, but in the meantime that does not destroy the Title to such Lands; neither can I be of your opinion, as to their Treaties, That they are Null, because the Body of their Nation shall please afterwards to Disavow it; I am sure it is otherwise by the Law of Nations and usage of all Civillized Governments in the World; all Treaties, Stipulations, and Transactions that are Managed and Concluded by Plenipotentiaries or Delegates being Obligatory to the Nation or Government that Imploy them; Now it is Notorious, That at all times when this Government Accepted the submission of, or Treated with those Eastern Indians, their Delegates, or some of their Chiefs were present, and produced their Powers or Credentials from the Tribe; And it is very wrong and unjust in them to Insinuate, That they were ever menaced or forced into any of their Deeds, Treaties or Submissions.

They have also misinformed you in Saying, That I had appointed to meet them the last year; for on the Contrary I sent them word by an Express, That some of the Principal Gentlemen of this Government would see and treat with them at Arowsick, who accordingly went thither, but finding no Indians returned.

As to their Insolent Letter, I shall say no more of it in this, having taken particular notice of it in my other.

I am obliged to you for your Grave Advice against a War with those Salvages, and am very sensible of the hazzards, mischiefs and Expence of it, And I assure you, I have no design at present to Enter into a War with them, unless they force the Government upon it.

All that I design at present, and which I am firmly Resolved in is, to Defend and Protect the English Inhabitants of this Governm^t in their just rights, and Possessions from the Injuries and Insults of the Indians, and I hope for the Divine Assistance and Blessing in so doing, Having my Great Masters positive Orders to Maintain all the English Garrisons and settlements in those parts of the province.

You are pleased to say that the Abanakis Nation are under the Protection of the Crown of France, If you Intend the Indians at Norridgewack, It is the first time I have heard the French pretend to any such thing, much less can I conceive upon what Foundation it subsists. If they chuse the Allyance and Protection of the French, In Gods Name, let them move into the Confines of the Government of Canada; I am very sure the place of their residence at present Viz^t Norridgewack is within the Territory of Great Britain, and accordingly they have Actually by many Solemn Treaties upon Record in this Government, Put themselves under His Majesty's Protection, and received Marks of his Royal Favour; As you may depend upon it, I shall never Concern myself with any of the Indian Tribes that live within the bounds of Canada, or any French Government; so I Expect to be Treated on your part.

You are very particular in Your account of Monsr Bellisle, who it seems was not with the Indians; But then you are very silent as to Monsr Croissel, who was a French Office and under your Command, and yet at the Head of the Indians at Arowsick. This even by your own Letter, was not Agreeable to the Treaty of Peace & Friendship between the Two Crowns.

As to Monsr Casteen, before the receiving of your Letter, I had by the Consent of the General Assembly of this Province, Given Orders for his Discharge and return; But then it was upon his humble submission & Parole of good Behaviour for the future towards this Government, as to himself personally, so also very much with respect to the Indian Tribe at Penobscot; And tho you seem to be of Opinion, That the sending for him was so very wrong and unjustifyable, yet he himself was sensible of the Contrary, and has acknowledged by a Memorial under his hand, That by his appearance with the Indians at Arowsick he had given just occasion to this Government to call him to an account.

As to Monsr Rallé's Mission among the Indians, I shall be Glad, if by his preaching he has brought those poor Salvages any thing nearer to the Kingdom of Heaven, than they were before he went thither; But that which I have to say to him, and to you upon his Account is, That Norridgewack the seat of his Mission, is within the Territory of His Majesty King George, and that it is Contrary to an Act of Parliament of Great Britain, and a Law of this Province for a Jesuit or Romish Priest to Preach or even reside in any part of the British Dominions.

I have now, I think, Given you a particular answer to everything you were pleased to Observe to me; I should have been much better pleased our Correspondence might have turned on a Subject more Agreeable and Pleasant; I shall be very Glad, while I have the Honour to be in this Government, to live in perfect Peace with our Eastern Indians and nothing shall be wanting on my part; At the same time, I must Intreat you to use all your Interest and Influence (which I believe to be very Considerable) for the Same good purpose: This is what you have once and again, in your former Letters Given me an assurance of.

     I am, Sir,
    Your very Humble & Obedient
    Servant
        Sam^{ll} Shute.

Boston April 23^{d}
1722
Examined ℔ J Willard Secry.

JOURNAL OF THE HOUSE OF REPRESENTATIVES.

At a Great and General Court or Assembly of His Majesty's Province of the Massachusetts Bay in New England. Begun and Held at Boston on the 30th day of May, 1722, &c.

     June 29 1722.

* * * * * * * * * * * * * * *

p. 51. Ordered, That an Officer with Two or Three Soldiers in the Service be sent forthwith to Norridgewock in the Name of this Government to demand the Liberty and Restitution of His Majesty's good Subjects lately surprized and carried away by the Indians.

That His Excellency the Governour be desired to send a proper Remonstrance to that Tribe of Indians upon their late Insults and Hostilities in Kennebeck-River, and at Damaras-Cove, demanding as well their Reasons, as a Satisfaction for the Injuries and Damages done by them. To observe to them that their Indians now with us were delivered as Hostages with their free consent, not only for the Payment of Two Hundred Beaver Skins, but also for the good Behaviour of the Norridgewock Tribe towards the English, That they have not paid the said Bever Skins, much less have they behaved themselves well towards this Government. That though this Government ordered a March up to their Head Quarters last Winter yet no Violence or Damage was done to the Persons or Goods of the Indians, Whereas on the other side the Indians Against all Justice, and in a barbarous manner have lately burnt and destroyed Houses, Mills, and a Number of Cattle, with little or no Advantage to themselves, leaving the Carcasses of the Creatures to rot on the ground; besides taking a great deal of Plunder. In case they do not return the Persons so taken by the Messengers, Then to propose their Appearing before Commissioners at Time and Place to be appointed by this Government, bringing with them the English People taken as aforesaid: Then and there to make or propose some suitable Satisfaction for the Damages done by them; which if refused, to assure them that this Government will take effectual Methods to compel them thereto; That a suitable Messenger be sent to the Penobscot Tribe to enquire whether they were any ways concern'd in or did assist the Kennebeck Tribe in their late Insults and Hostilities aforesaid?

Sent down for Concurrence.

J. Willard, Secr.

* * * * * * * * * * * * * * *

July 6. 1722.

P. 60. * * * * * * * * * * * *

Voted, that two meet Persons with a skilful Interpreter be immediately dispatched to Noridgawack or elsewhere, where the Heads of the Tribes of the Eastern Indians may be found, under a Flagg of Truce, with a written Message from this Government to them demanding the Reasons for their late Insults and Acts of Hostilities in surprizing so many of His Majesty's good Subjects and destroying their Substance directly contrary to the Articles of Peace formerly stipulated with this Government, That the Messengers propose to the Indians, that they or their delegates Meet with the Commissioners appointed by this Government at Arrowsick some time in this Month, where they may be assured to see our Commissioners, and upon their Surrender and Delivery of all His Majesty's good Subjects there, which they have lately seiz'd and surpriz'd as aforesaid, the Commissioners will deliver up the Hostages, and will also be fully impowered by this Government to Treat and Conferr with them on any just Article of Grievance between this Government and them, and that Col. Turner Esq; Major John Quincey and Mr John Dyer be a Committee for the Ends aforesaid, and that His Excellency be desired to give Orders that the said Commissioners (with the Hostages) immediately proceed to Arowsick aforesaid, (with agreeable Instructions). Sent up for Concurrence.

* * * * * * * * * * * * * *

B. T., New England, Vol. 16.

Govr Shute to the Lords Commissioners for Trade and Plantations

My Lords

Since I had the honour to write to Your Lordships which was in March last, I Received a Letter from Monsr Vaudreuil the Governour of Canada, which was in Answer to two Letters I Sent him, in which he openly Declares, that he has and will assist the Indians, and that he has Orders from the Court of France so to do.

All the Indians that Border upon the Sea Coast, by the Instigations of the French have lately Robbed & Plundered our Sloops & fallen upon our ffishing Vessells, and killed two of His Majestys Subjects; at the Same time our Eastern Indians Notwithstanding their Repeated Submissions to His Majestys Crown and Government have fallen upon our Eastern Settlements & killed and wounded some of the Inhabitants, burnt their houses & Destroyed their Cattle, which has Obliged me with the Advice of His Majestys Council to Issue forth the Inclosed Declaration.

I hope your Lordships will speedily lay that Affair before His Majesty in order to obtain some Redress for this Province will not be long able to support the war which is now begun I am with great respect

My Lords
Your Lordships most hum^ble Servant
Boston New   Samll Shute.
England July 27th 1722

To the R^t Honble The Lords of Trade & Plantations.

Recd Septem^r 10th }
Read   do   12th } 1722.

B. T. New England. Vol. 16, Bundle X, 89.

Appendix. 313

DECLARATION OF GOV' SHUTE.
[inclosed in Letter of 27th July 1722]

By His Excellency,
Samuel Shute, Esq;
Captain General and Governour in Chief, in and over His Majesty's Province of the *Massachusetts-Bay*, in *New England*, &c.

A DECLARATION
against the *Eastern-Indians*.

WHEREAS, the Indians Inhabiting the Eastern Parts of this Province, notwithstanding their Repeated Submissions to His Majesty's Crown and Government, their Publick and Solemn Treaties and Engagements Entered into with the Government here Established to Demean themselves Peaceably and amicably towards His Majesty's good Subjects of this Province; and notwithstanding the Kind and good Treatment they have Received from this Government; Have for some years last past appeared in Considerable Numbers, and in an Hostile Manner, and given Disturbance to His Majesty's Subjects in the Eastern Parts of this Province, Killing their Cattle, and Threatning Destruction to their Persons and Estates; and in abuse of the Lenity and Forbearance of the Government, have lately with the utmost Injustice and Treachery, proceeded to Plunder, Despoil, and take Captive many of his Majesty's good Subjects, to Assault, Take, Burn and Destroy Vessels upon the Sea Coast, and Houses and Mills upon the Land, to Wound some, and in the most Barbarous and Cruel Manner to Murder others of the Inhabitants of this Province, and in a Way of Open Rebellion and Hostility to make an Audacious and Furious Assault upon One of His Majesty's Forts, where the King's Colours were Flying:

I Do Therefore, by and with the Advice of His Majesty's Council, hereby Declare and proclaim the said Eastern Indians, with their Confederates, to be Rebels, Traitors and Enemies to His Majesty King George, His Crown and Dignity, and that they be henceforth proceeded against as such; Willing and Requiring all His Majestys good subjects, as they shall have opportunity, to do and Execute all Acts of hostility upon them; hereby also forbidding all his Majesty's Subjects to hold any Correspondence with the said Indians, or to give Aid, Comfort, Succour, or Relief unto them; on Penalty of the Laws in their Case made and provided.

And whereas there may be some of the said *Indians* who have not been Concerned in the Perfidious and Barbarous Facts before mentioned, and may be Desirous to put themselves under the Protection of this Government.

To the Intent that the utmost Clemency may be shown to such

I do hereby Grant and Allow them to come in, and render themselves to the Commanding officer of the Forces, or to the respective officer of any Party or Parties in the Service; provided it be within Forty Days from this time.

AND to the Intent that none of Our Friend-*Indians* may be Exposed, or any Enemy or Rebel *Indians* Escape on pretence of being Friends;

I do hereby also strictly forbid any of the said Friend-Indians to move out of their respective Plantations, or such other Places whereto they shall be assigned; or to come into any English Town, or District within the late Colony of the Massachusetts-Bay, or the County of York, without special Order in Writing from My Self (or being Attended with such English Man as I shall appoint to Oversee them) at their Peril, and as they tender their own Safety.

And further, I forbid all the Friend-Indians to hold Communication with, Harbour, or Conceal any of the said Rebel or Enemy Indians; requiring them to seize, and secure all such that may Come among them, and to Deliver them up to Justice..

And all Military Commission Officers are hereby Authorized and Commanded to put this Declaration and Order in Execution.

> Given at the Council Chamber in *Boston*, the Twenty-fifth Day of *July*, in the Eighth Year of the Reign of our Sovereign Lord GEORGE, by the Grace of GOD of *Great Britain, France* and *Ireland*, KING, Defender of the Faith, *&c Annoque Domini*, 1722.

S. Shute.

By Order of His Excellency
  the Governour, by and
  with the Advice of the
  Council,
      Josiah Willard, Secr.
      GOD SAVE THE KING.

IN THE HOUSE OF REPRESENTATIVES — AUGUST 8th 1722.

May it please your Excellency,

Your Excellency having at the Opening of this Session Acquainted the Court that by and with the

Advice of His Majesty's Council, You have Issued out a Declaration against the Indians as Rebels and Traitors to His Majesty's Government, for breaking through their Repeated Solemn Treaties and Engagements and frequent Submissions to His Majesty, by their many ways destroying the Eastern Settlements, and Cruelly Murdering some of His Majesty's Liege Subjects Inhabiting there. This House having had due Consideration thereof do hereby Declare and Manifest that Your Excellency and Council had Just and Sufficient Reasons to Resent the many Repeated Insults and Outrages done and perpetrated by those Indian Salvages on the People Inhabiting those Parts, by declaring them to be Rebels and Traitors as aforesaid: And we deem it our indispensable Duty and Interest at this Juncture to pursue those Indians in a most Vigorous War (agreeable to Your Excellency's Sentiments thereon) that so by the Blessing of God on our Just Endeavours they may be never able more to rise up against this People, and Your Excellency may depend upon all Chearful and necessary Assistance from this House to pursue that Matter.

* * * * * * * * * * * * *

Voted, That a Message be sent to His Excellency the Governour desiring there may be laid before this House an Account of the Number of Forces in the Service on the Frontiers, how they are Posted, and what Instructions are given to the Commanding Officer, for their Prosecuting the War against the Eastern Rebels.

Penn Townsend Esq, brought down the Number and Disposition of the Soldiers in the Publick Service, viz.

Appendix.

- 412 Men in the East Part of the Province of Maine.
- 60 Men gone on the Coast of Cape Sables to recover the Fishing Vessels taken by the Indians. Upon their Return to be added to the Forces in the Province of Maine.
- 20 Men gone with Capt. Westbrook to S^t. George's River.
- 15 Men, a Scout from Dracut to Lancaster.
- 20 A Scout, at Rutland.
- 20 At Brookfield.
- 10 At Sunderland.
- 20 At Deerfield.
- 14 Added to the Garrison at Northfield.
- 30 A Scout for York, Berwick and Wells.
- 15 A Scout at Haverhill.

636

And further, That their Orders were only to cover the Frontiers, and secure their Harvests. And that there had been no Order sent to the Officers since the Declaration of War.

* * * * * * * * * * * * * * *

ALEXANDER HAMILTON'S JOURNAL.

Half way House June 14th 1722.
on Kennebec River.

This night at ten a clock Alexander Hamilton was besett at his Dwelling house by a great Number of Indians, with divers Canno's, who took said Hamilton out of his Bed, and tyed him and fell a plundering his Shop & Warehouse until they left nothing;

And when they had finished their Plundering One Captain John an Indian Conducting said Hamilton to his Canno, was Stopt by two Indians, one called Captain Nathaniel, and the other Sabia son to said Nathaniel, who Challenged the said Hamilton as their Prisoner, in Regard that Sabia had first laid Hands on said Hamilton. This Dispute held a Quarter of an hour; at last the said Captain John Protested, if Hamilton were not allowed to be his Prisoner he would Immediately kill him; so drawing a Stroak with an ax on said Hamilton's head; said Nathaniel and son held his Arm & told the said Captain John, rather than Hamilton should be killed they would allow it. After the Dispute Hamilton was ledd to Captn Johns Canno, and so proceeded to Norridgewack & Stopt at the Chapps of Merry meeting Bay, where were a great number of Captives in the House of Captn Robert Temple, They having Robb'd sundry Houses that night, and brought the Owners and Families Captives. Next morning being the fifteenth, the Indians Chose five Persons of the said Captives Viz^t Zachariah Trescott Alexander Hamilton Henry Edgar Robert Love & William Handsord, and having Stript the rest let them go. And suddenly the whole Body of Indians being forty two in number all Arm'd & Painted for Warr Attended with Nineteen Canno's Were ordered by Wewarena, an Indian who was their Commander to Embarque for Norridgewack, and setting fire to Capt Robert Temples House went off, and landed presently after at Abagadasset point, where there was dispatcht a number of Indians to rob a House belonging to Mr John Jeffries. After the performance of which said Indians returned greatly Loaden, and threw that Plunder along with the rest, which they had Landed in one heap, and so Divided the spoil, and then Imbarqued again, and proceeded up to Swan Island House, where appeared a number of Soldiers. The Indians ordered Hamilton to hale the English and Desire them to come to the Shore, two of which Immediately came, and talked awhile and so went off: As also the Indians without doing any damage, Save killing one Dogg and Cutting a hole or two in a Whale Boat, and the same in a Canno that lay there, so proceeded further and got to Richmond Fort, whom the said Hamilton hailed and begged they would not fire upon us, and presently after landed: And some of the Soldiers came out to us on the Parole of the Indians, and talked a while. The Indians told them they need not be afraid, for they would kill none; but the Governour of Canada had given them Orders to take Captives in lieu of theirs whom the English wrongfully detained in Boston. Our Conference being ended we went off, and so arrived at a place called Browns Farm where we slept that night, and two days after being the Seventeenth got to Norridewack where we were received with great Joy by a number of Squaws Papooses and the Jesuit.

Norridgewack June the 21st 1722.

Two Indians were dispatcht away to Canada with an Account of the Indians taking of five Captives as also burning one House and robbing of Several Families, & killing of many Creatures.

July 22d 1722

The two Indians Returned and reported They were kindly received by Governour Vaudreuile & shewing the presents he had Given them, for carrying the Agreeable News of this Action being a blue laced coat and a silver Meddal which was sent to another Indian Named Caraboussett, as also Commissioning him Captain for his Distinguishing Activity in that Expedition.

The twenty ninth day arrived here Captn Moses Moxus or King at Norrincowook from Canada, and brought great quantities of Tobacco, and told us, he was sent from Quebec with great honour, and had the respect of having the Guns firing & Trumpets sounding upon his Departure.

September the 3^d

This day arrived several Cannos from Canada bringing French Mowhawks who live within three miles of Quebec at a place called Lorret They Joyned more of their Nation who had been here before, who made in all thirty five & brought three Casks of Powder & a great quantity of Tobacco. On their arrival, at one of their Dances Alexander Hamilton one of the Captives was made a present of to them as a Slave forever, as a Reward of their Fatigue in Coming to Assist in the War.

The Seventeenth day.

The above Indians took their Departure with their above Slave Hamilton bound for Canada, & at several carrying places the s^d Hamilton observed them raise out of the ground sundry Quantities of meal, pork and Tobacco, which they had been supplyed with from the Governour of Canada for that Expedition.

The 28th day.

The Indians & Hamilton arrived at Canada, and went by the Town of Quebec without calling, but great hooping and hallowing of the Indians, and the Captain of them had a Scalp in the Nature of a Jack

Appendix. 321

in the head of his Canno, which was got at the Onsett at Arowsick.

The 29th day

The Indians and Hamilton Marched into the Town of Quebec, having assembled the whole Indians belonging to that Tribe living at Lorett as afores^d and moving procession like with that Scalp on one End of a long Stick, Hamilton the Captive marched after all the Indians who went one after another making great hooping & hallowing, which gathered all the Mobb & People in the Town and with an Infinite number of Spectators were Conducted to the Governor who received the Indians very cheerfully, & Congratulated them, and Immediately sent for an Interpreter, who related their Success and for their reward in Assisting their Brethren the Eastern Indians, they the said Eastern Indians had made a present of that Captive as a slave shewing the said Hamilton to Governour Vaudreuil, which they further added not only Contented them but also made an Atonement to s^d Eastern Indians for a Hostage called Brasaway who dyed in Boston, And also Declared their further Intention that they would dispose of said Hamilton to an Indian Squaw seventy five Leagues distant from Quebec in Order to be her Slave she having lost her Husband in the former War with the English. All which was related before Governour Vaudreuil who gave his Concurrence and wrote a Note by the Indians to the Kings Bakehouse, Ordering every Indian there present a loaf of Bread and a Considerable Quantity of Tobacco, & so dismist them. After the receipt of which, the Indians, and said Hamilton marched after the Usual Order to their Town and were received there with much Indian Ceremony. The said Hamilton continuing there in a very Melancholly Condition for about fourteen days and then got liberty to go to Quebec, in order to beg for as much money as would buy them shoes And happened to meet with a Lady who took Compassion on him, and sent for an Interpreter whom she desired to ask if s^d Hamilton would live with her if she should get him released from the Indians. It being so Agreeable an Offer was soon Embraced by s^d Hamilton. And in some short time after the Lady made Interest among the Jesuits & the Governour who suddenly got him released from the Indians, and Entertained him the whole Winter.

October.

All the Numerous Families of Eastern Indians withdrew from Norridgewack and Wintered at the Town of Wewenack and St. Francis, the former being thirty leagues distant from Quebec up the River, and the latter forty two, At their arrival were presented with five hundred bushels of Indian Corn and four Oxen.

Quebec, February the 4th day.

Arrived here Abomazeen Wewarana Westaminut Capt. John and several other Indians from Wewanuck who were Conducted to the Governour by one of the Jesuits that headed the Numerous Army of Indians at Arowsick in the year 1721. They were received very kindly and Entertained while in Town plentifully, and sent off with a quantity of Blankets, new Guns, their Old repaired and a Considerable deal of Amunition, together with presents of a laced Capp to Weewarena, and sundry presents to the rest. Some of them as they said were bound to the great pond distant from Quebec SSE about One hundred and fifty miles where they and several others and the Jesuit Winter'd.

March the 5th day.

Arrived here from Norridgewack Wesememis also Cap Job Abagahansetts son and sundry other Indians who were Conducted by the Jesuit, and received with all marks of Favour by the Governour & while they stayed in Town Entertained plentifully and had sundry Presents, and were fitted out with quantities of Ammunition all their Guns repaired, and some new ones given them, and so departed.

March the 15th day.

Departed hence twelve of the aforementioned Mohawks known here by the Names of Lorett Indians, directly bound for Norridgewack who were fitted out with all necessaries for War.

The 20th day.

The said Hamilton being Desirous to go to Mount Royall in Order to get home as soon as the Lake was clear of the Ice, acquainted the Governour who said he should not go until he heard from New England which hindred his Intended Journey.

April 19th 1723 N. S.

A Son of Coll° John Schuyler of Albany arrived here, who made Inquiry for the English Captives, who was Informed there was two of them in Town, namely Hamilton & Handsord, upon his finding them out he told them he would take them home if the Governour would admit them They desired him to take the trouble to Speak to the Governour in their Favour, who readily undertook it, and prevailed for Hamilton to go directly home, but for Handsord, the

Governour said, he Could not Answer that to the Indians for letting their Prisoner go, for the s^d Handsord was only left in Trust with a French Gent^n in Town, s^d Gent^n was lyable to produce him ; But the Governour added to shew his willingness to oblige Mr Schuyler, That he in his way to Mount Royal where he was suddenly bound was to meet with a great number of Indians at a Town called Troi River, and there he would speak in favour of said Handsord to the Indians, & Endeavour to get him returned; and desired s^d Schuyler to take s^d Handsord, in his Canno along with s^d Hamilton that length; and if he the s^d Governor Could not prevail with the Indians he the s^d Handsord must expect to return to Quebec again. Some few days after Mr Schuyler Handsord and Hamilton left Quebec in Company with the Governour bound for Mount Royal, and got up some days after to Troi River, where was a great Quantity of Indians Assembled & several Jesuits, All whom held a great Council, the Governor making his request in favor of Handsord had it readily granted by the Indians, and some of the Head Indians Attended the Governour to Mr Schuylers Lodging, the Governour told him that he had prevailed for said Handsord, the Indians taking the said Handsord by the hand, Delivered him to the Governour as a Present. The Governour presently after Embarqued and next day s^d Handsord & Hamilton proceeded after him to Mount Royal, and when arrived there the s^d Mr Schuyler placed s^d Hamilton & Handsord in a lodging, & told them he should not go in fourteen days, but Contrary to Expectation the s^d Schuyler was order^d out of the Country the next morning, and was told by s^d Governour he should not take the Captives along with him. The s^d Hamilton and Handsord meeting with a Gentleman named Deautell who could speak English, made known their Condition to him who answered he had formerly received great Friendship in New England; And in return he would let them want nothing; and accordingly took lodgings for the said Handsord & Hamilton & got them Cloaths.

St. Francis May 22^d 1721

A Great Council was held there by the Eastern Indians who Concluded to bury their Ax, & accordingly *did so;* and at said Council to shew their willingness to come into a Peace with the English, Concluded to send three of their English Captives home, Namely Hamilton Handsord & Trescot, in order to which they brought s^d Trescott on the 29th of May to Mount Royal, distant from St. Francis up the River South Eighteen Leagues. The next day being the thirtyeth they held a great Council in the Governours hall where were present the three Governours Viz^t De Vaudreuil, Deramsey and Languile several Jesuits and Gent^n before whom they discovered their intention with respect to sending home the English Captives, which was presently Discountenanced by the s^d Governours Especially Governour Vaudreuil, who told them they had senty forty or fifty Captives home to the English when first the War began, & desired them to declare how many of their Captives they had rece^d in return of the above number (the Indians answered none) Therefore says Governour Vaudreuil I think it a piece of Inadvertency of you to Trust the English Generosity by sending these Captives to them unless you first have yours Delivered here which Speach took with the Indians & stopt the Delivery of s^d Captives & Trescott was ordered down to S^t ffrancis to his wigwam; Handsord & Hamilton acquainting the s^d Trescott with their good Friend & Benefactor whom they had met with Viz^t Deautell, and how he not only supplyed them with every thing, but promised if any of the Captives Could purchase themselves from the Indians he would Disburse the Money agreed on said Trescott went to Monsr Dotell & related his Melancholly Circumstances unto him. The said Dotell made the like offer to Mr Trescott as he had done to Hamilton and Handsord and told him he would write him a paper in ffrench, which he Desired him to Deliver the Governour and Conceal the Author. The said Deautell wrote the paper being a Petition from Trescott wherein it set forth That he was a Subject of King George and Inasmuch as there was so good an understanding between the two Crowns, he hoped his Excellency would get him clear of that Indian Bondage that he then Laboured under; The Governour gave but little Encouragem^t. The s^d Mr Dotell meeting with a Gentleman who was very Intimate with the Governour told him, That he admired That the Governour suffered King Georges Subjects to be tossed about Canada by the Indians after so Barbarous a manner; And also said, It was not Consistent with the Peace of Utrecht, and that it would be Ill lookt on at home were it known. The Gentleman after the Conference Ended went directly to the Governours, and Discovered what had passed between him and Mr Dotell. The Governour Immediately sends for Mr Dotell & orders him to Depart the Town & go to Quebec. Some few days after the s^d Dotell was obliged to go, as Commanded. The thirtyeth day of May the Indians & Trescott went from Mount Royall bound for St Francis, and before his Departure, Declared to the

English Captives, That they would do any thing to send them home but could not for the Governour of Canada.

June the 2ᵈ Day.

Two Indians Named Abraham & Abagahamak were dispatched to Albany.

June the 10th Day.

Eleven of the Lorett Indians returned to Mount Royall and declared they lost one of their Number, but brought in seven English Scalps, being Indians which were fitted out from Quebec the 15th of February.

The fifteenth Day.

Twenty Indians arrived here from Lorett, and were fitted out with all necessaries for War, and in two days took their Departure for the Eastward of New England, in Order to revenge the Blood of the Man they had lost at North Yarmouth the last Spring. Four Canno's with Eight Indians arrived here from New England, and brought three Scalps & presently departed, having first received some presents.

Mount Royall July the 8th 1723.

Abagahamak one of the two Indians, which was Dispatched to Albany returned here & was immediately hastened away by the Governour to Cahnawagaw or Town of Mohawk Indians distant from Mount Royall four Leagues up the River. And at his return Informed the Captives, That he had a Message from the Governour desiring the aforesᵈ Indians to Aid the Eastern Indians; for the English had engaged the five Nations of Mohawks against them; And likewise said the Indians Intirely Declined it, and was Resolved to stand Neuter.

The ninth day of July.

Hamilton having a former promise of the Governor of Canada, That upon the first News he had from New England he would let him go home. That upon the return of a Message from Albany said Hamilton took an Opportunity of waiting on him; Being asked his Business, Answered his Excellency, he understood he had heard from New England, And that pursuant to his promise he Expected he would let him go home. The Governour Answered it was unreasonable of him to Expect he should let him go, Considering the English had Engaged the five Nations of Mohawks to Come and kill his Abnakees als Eastern Indians. And in a great Passion very much blamed the English for their Extravagancy in Giving One hundred Pounds Beaver for One Scalp, and Sixty pounds for a Prisoner. Then the said Hamilton told his Excellency he hoped his Excellency would not resent the steps the English took to Justify themselves on him, in regard he had been the Main Instrument of getting him clear from the Indians, And that he would not detain him any longer in the Countrey, to make him miserable. To which he got no Answer which made him urge further, That he hoped his Excellency would let him take a passage from Quebec to Europe, he Answered he should not. Upon which said Hamilton told his Excellency he had spent a great deal of Money in the Countrey, & that he had run so much upon Credit already that he could have no more help from his Benefactor, he Answered his Maintenance was none of his Business & so went away.

July the 10th day 1723

Mr Dotell arrived here from Quebec having no time limited for his stay there, and went to pay his respects to his Excellency, who upon his appearance Ordered him directly to Goal, and gave a Strict charge to the Goaler to let none of his English Captives have any Communications with him.

July the 30th day 1723

Governour Vaudreuil sent for Hamilton the Captive, and ordered him to get ready to go down to Quebec with him by two a Clock which he Observed & Embarqued with the Governour, Attended by his Secretary, his Life Guard and an Interpreter.

On the 15th arrived at St Francis where was a great number of Indians together with a Jesuit drawn up on the shore Expressing their joy by a Dance for his Excellencies safe arrival; presently after they held a Council, and as soon as it was finished, said Hamilton was ordered to Come before them, and Desired by his Excellency to Give Attention to what the Indians said, and relate it to his Governour and Council when he should go hence. The said Hamilton made Answer he Chose to take in Writing by reason it would be too Burthensome to his Memory The Governour Desired him to go next day and take the Interpreter along with him to the Indian Town where the Jesuit lived, and he would repeat the whole sentiments of the Indians which they told to him, as also his willingness to assist in making a Peace for the English. Said Hamilton Enquired of His Excellency, if there should be a Cessation of Arms until he got home to Inform his Government of what was proposed by the Indians, and his Excellency turned to the Jesuit whose opinion he wanted, who Immediately shew his Dislike, and Instantly answered to Hamilton the War must go on.

Wanagungus the 16th day.

This morning the Interpreter and said Hamilton got here, and with much difficulty obtained the Indians Speech to be Translated into English, but the Jesuit would have it after his manner of broken English, least he should add more than the Intent of the matter mentioned, and was so Exact, that he took the copy of what was drawn up by s^d Hamilton. The same Evening Captain Nathaniel an Eastern Indian and Hamilton happened to discourse on several Passages, Nathaniel told s^d Hamilton That he in some few sleeps would Visit the Western parts of New England with the Army that he saw the day before at the Council, which consisted of between fifty and sixty men. The said Hamilton Declares That the Ammunition and Bisket (as he has Reason to believe) were brought into the Canno from Mount Royall for to fit out the said Indians for that Expedition, as also a fat Cow Ordered them at St Francis for the same purpose.

This 18th July.

Sett out for Albany in Company with three Indians and arrived the 17th July at Fort Chambly, and the said Hamilton shewed his passport to the Comander there, and so proceeded towards the Lake. The 19th July we were met with four Indians with four Indian Cannos Laden with Beaver bound for Albany, and about tew a Clock at night were Questioned by a large Canno Manned with eight Soldiers, who Imagined we had been laden with Beaver bound to Albana, which Trade by the Law of Canada is prohibited, and Demanded a Passport which was produced and perused by them and the s^d Hamilton & Comp^a was dismist.

The twenty first day of July the s^d Hamilton observed one of the Indians perusing a paper which was Wrote in Indian, and Hamilton demanded of the s^d Indian, what it was he was reading. The Indian made answer it was a speech from the Governour of Canada and the Indian Council which was lately held at St Francis, which speech he was to Deliver to the Mohawks, and that his order from the Governour & Jesuits was first to go to the Mohawks Countrey and then to proceed to Albany with the said Hamilton.

On the 22^d July 1723.

We met on the Lake two Cannos with several Indians on board having a great quantity of Barque for Canno's, one of which Indians told the said Hamilton in English, That all the old Indians were for Peace, but the Young Men were for War, as also the Governour of Canada as the Depon^t understood.

On the 23^d we arrived at the Head of the Lake Superiour where were several Eastern Indians with whom we had a long Conference, who persuaded our Indians to go first to Albany and after to proceed to the Mohawks assuring them and the s^d Hamilton That the Road they were taking would be more Fatiguing of the two. Upon which they agreed to the Advice, and so proceeded to Albany where we arrived the 17th O S. and were received kindly by Coll^o Schuyler, who Informed Hamilton that several Commissioners from Boston had lately been there, and that they had a promise from a great number of Sachems belonging to the five Nations That they would meet in Boston in Sixty days together with the Eastern Indians in Order to make a Peace. The said Hamilton Assured Coll. Schuyler That he was

Certain none of the Eastern Indians would Attend there, Giving them his Reasons and Informing him, That the Indians speech with the Governor of Canada to Our Government was quite the Reverse.

That by Coll° Schuyler and Mr Jacob Wendell of Boston Merch^t their advice, the Comissioners for managing the Eastern affair at Albany were made acquainted with the premises; And the s^d Hamilton Informed the Comissioners, That one of those Indians which Conducted them from Canada had a speech from the Governour of Canada, Jesuits and Eastern Indians, and that he was of the opinion, if Care were not taken, would oversett what the Comissioners of Boston had transacted with the Mohawks. Whereupon the s^d Indian was Questioned closely Concerning the same; who at first denyed it, but soon after Confessed the Fact Upon which the Commissioners Resolved to send an Interpreter with the said Indian to hear the speech and to hinder the Mohawks from breaking their Word to the Boston Commissioners, which after three days they dispatcht with the said Indian, and Hamelton was advised, by Coll° Schuyler & Mr Wendell to wait until news of the reception & return of the s^d Indian, which they judged was highly Convenient to be brought to the Governour at Boston, and accordingly the s^d Hamilton waited Eighteen days for the answer, which was that the Indians had brought two peices of Wampom, which he presented to the Mohawks, and begun a speech which was put to an End by the Interpreter of one Hendrick a Head Sachem of the Mohawks, who bid the s^d Indian to return, and if he had any thing to say to come to Boston and there they would hear him, and upon failure they would take him by the hair.

Appendix. 333

August the fifth.

The said Hamilton took his departure from Albany for Boston, attended by an Indian sent pr Collo John Schuyler, as also a horse as far as Westfield, and arrived there, and applyed himself to Capt Ashley of the s^d place who procured a Man & two horses to Conduct the s^d Hamilton to Boston, where he arrived the twelfth day of August. And the next morning waited on his Honour the Commander in Chief & Delivered the Indians speech & the Governour of Canadas, & also Informed the Honourable House of Representatives then sitting of the Conference that had been between the s^d Hamilton & Capt Nathaniel, an Eastern Indian at parting, wch was on the 16th of August N. S.

Boston Septr 1723.

The said Alexander Hamilton likewise Testifys That Monsr La Longue Informed him that Mr de Ramsey told Mr Philip Schuyler at his Departure, That had not Monsr De Vaudreuil been then present in Mount Royall, That he the s^d De Ramsey would have sent him to Goal As also the s^d Le Langue Attended the s^d Mr Schuyler, as the Depon^t Imagined after he had got his discharge to leave the Countrey in the Nature of a Guard until he took his departure from Mount Royall; Immediately after which he the said la Longue posted to the House of Monsr De Vaudreuil & Informed his Excellency that Schuyler was gone.

And he the said Alexander Hamilton further Declares That the aforegoing is a true Journal as far as he could learn and find out by Interpreters Fellow Captives & Indians, & being himself also an Eye witness to most of the Transactions & he has many strong Circumstances to Convince him of the truth of what he has related of those things which he did not see.

Alexander Hamilton.

Province of the Massachusetts Bay
Sworn before the Honble the Lieutenant Governor & Council this Seventh day of December 1723.

    Attest. J Willard Secry.
    A true Copy
        Examd ⅏
            J. Willard Secry.

R^d in March 172$\frac{3}{4}$.

Paper No. 8, entitled "PAPER TAKEN FROM THE CHURCH DOOR AT NORRIDGEWOCK IN OCT^R, 1722, may be found at page 122.

[*Paper 9.*]

GOVERNOR VAUDREUIL TO THE GOVERNOR OF BOSTON.

Copy
  S^r.

    I know not what you now think of the War with the Abanakeys which you have drawn upon your selves, in Taking and possessing (against all right) their Land; you may see that it is not so Easy a thing as you thought at first to reduce those Indians, I can likewise assure you, That you will find more difficulty in the pursuit than Ever for that besides their Resolution of Defending their Countrey as long as any of them remain and not to hearken to any Accomodation until you entirely abandon all their Rivers, and that things be set on the same foot, as they were before the Treaty of Utrecht, All the Indians of other Nations to whom they have reported the Evil Treatment which they have received from you, have taken up the hatchet for their help or succour, and are ready to strike the blow on all sides, to revenge the Abanakeys their Countreys & Friends, and to Deliver them from the Yoke and Oppression which you would reduce them unto; have they not in Effect reason, what new right have you acquired upon the Abanakeys & their Lands; I know not of any; the Treaty of Utrecht do's Conceed to you L'Accadie, Conformable to it's Ancient limits; the Lands of the Abanakeys are they Comprehended? if so wherefore do's the same Treaty add in the 15th article that there shall be named on each part Commissioners for the Regulation of the limits between the two Crowns, and to determine the Indians that are subjects or Friends to either one or the other.

Is it not Evident that your pretensions renders utterly useless this wise Regulation which must fall upon the Abanakes and their Lands, altho there has been no Comissioners named to decide any thing of their residence; you have in Fact put yourselves in possession of these Lands which you did me the honour to Write that the Indian Inhabitants were subjects and Rebells, notwithstanding you ought not to be Ignorant of the Strict Allegiance that has been at all times between us, I leave it to you to Judge, Sir, whether you or I do most Conform our selves to the Rules of the said Treaty, which Contains That the Inhabitants of Canada, or other of His Majesties subjects shall not Molest the five Indian Nations who have submitted themselves to Great Britain, nor the other Nations, Friends to that Crown, likewise that the subjects of Great Britain shall behave themselves Peaceably towards the American subjects or Friends of France. You cannot be Ignorant Sir, That in divers Letters which I had the honour to Write you, That I represented the unhappy Consequences that must Infallibly follow the Evil Treatment you have used in Regard to the Indians Our Allies, for which I Esteem you Responsible; I assure you it is to me a great Chagrine, to see the great Union that is between my King and Yours, may be Changed by the Occasion of a pretended right, by which you have Seized On the Land that from all times belonged to our Allies; for in short I cannot sooner or later hinder my self from Engaging in their Quarrel; were it not better, Sir, in the mean time, until Commissioners be named for this purpose, as is Expressed in the Treaty of Utrecht, whereby to Regulate all things Amicably, to let the Indians Enjoy Peaceably their Land in which they have always been in possession and hereby to reestablish the Peace of these Countries, which we see with pleasure to be in Europe.

The Sieurs La Rond and de la Geste are both Officers of the King & Men of Consideration, will have the honour of rendring my Letter to you, waiting your answer, I have the honour of being perfectly
Your most humble & most
Obedient Servant.
Signed   Vaudreuil.
Quebec the 28th October 1723.
To the Governour Generall of Boston
Examined
℔ J Willard Secry.

Appendix. 337

[*Paper 10.*]
Govr Dummer to Monsr de Vaudreuil.
A Letter to Monsr Vaudreuil, Governor of Canada.

Sir

I received the honour of your Letter ⅌ Messrs Le Ronde & De La Chasse, and am at a great loss to know what part Monsr Vaudreuil would be understood to take between us, & the Indians within this Governm^t. For such are the People with whom we are Engaged in a War. We have often Recognized their Obedience to the Crown of Great Britain, and acknowledged His British Majesties Sovereignty over them, tho at the same time we sufficiently understand the share the French Indians have had in their Depredations, as well as the Encouragement and Assistance both have had from Quebec and Montreal.

At the same time, I shall not have the least difficulty to make it Evident that we have in no respect broken into the Articles of the Treaty of Utrecht mentioned in your Letter. For we have made no Settlements in any Controverted Boundaries, and I must Acquaint you, that the Indians might have enjoyed uninterrupted Quiet to this day had they not been Instigated by Evil Advice from your self & the Priests of your Government to act an Inhumane Barbarous part upon our Quiet & Ancient Settlements. All which I shall fully shew forth at a proper time: But that which most of all surprizes me is to find Monsr Vaudreuil (who speaks so freely of the great Union between the Crowns of Great Britain & France, and of his own Exactness in Observing the Articles of the Treaty of Utrecht) say, that we shall sooner or later Engage in their Quarrel;

which I can Interpret no other ways than that you Intend to make War upon us in favour of those that are Declared Rebels against His British Majesty; Nor can I Conceive that there is any such Power lodged with you to break the Peace so solemnly and firmly Established between the two Crowns by the Treaty of Utrecht.

Upon the whole S^r I assure myself that on due Consideration of this affair you will see Cause to alter your Measures and Instead of Exciting the Indians against us, Advise them to make their Submission to their Rightful Sovereign King George, and thereby Convince me of your sincerity to Cultivate the same good Amity between these Governments that is Established between the English and French Crowns at home, which will be very acceptable to him who is with much respect
      Sir
      Your humble Servant
        Wm Dummer.
December 20th 1723
  Examined
   ℔ J Willard Secry.

[*Paper 11.*]

LANNERJAT'S LETTER TO FATHER RALLÉ.

       Nusalkchunangan
       July 1724.
My Reverend ffather
  P. C. Sixteen Englishmen were killed whilst Joseph was gon to you Two boats were burnt

Appendix. 339

and forty Seven in all were killed and taken prisoners with Eleven Sloops as we Commonly say Sword in hand and that after an obstinate fight on Each side all which will contribute to our gallantry and will increase our Village if it be well preserved.

In spite of all the Indians can say all the Glory is owing to Sagsarrab.
  Examined
    ℔ J Willard Secry.

Paper No. 12, entitled " A COPY OF A LETTER FROM SEB: RALLÉ, A FRENCH JESUIT, TO ANOTHER PRIEST, GIVING A DETAIL OF THE DEPREDATIONS COMMITTED BY THE INDIANS ON THE ENGLISH IN NORTH AMERICA, AUG: 1724, may be found at page 251.

[*Paper 13.*]

THE L^T GOVERNOUR OF MASSACHUSETS BAY TO THE HON^{BLE} SAM^L CRANSTON ESQ^{RE}.

  Letter from the Lieu^t Governour and Council to the Honble Samuel Cranston Esqr Governour of the Colony of Rhode Island (or in his absence to the Deputy Governour) and to the General Assembly of said Colony.

Gentⁿ

The burthen of the Warr growing more Grievous to this Province both on Account of the prodigious Expence in maintaining it, and the many Persons that have been Slain and Captivated by this barbarous Enemy, as well as the lessening of the produce of the Countrey and raising the prices of all necessarys of life; We think it highly reasonable that Our Neighbours the subjects of the same Crown (who feel none of the Calamitys of Warr themselves, but are rather benefited by our Misfortunes in the Great demand & Consumption among us of the Effects of their labour and Traffick) should bear their part of the Expence of this Warr, by furnishing and supporting a proportionable fforce for Our assistance, and therefore we think it proper to make this further application to the General Assembly of Rhode Island, and pray you to lay before them our desires, That they would fully Consider the State of Our Province with respect to this Grievous and Expensive Warr, And Order a number of men to be raised and Joyned with Ours That by a vigorous prosecution of the said Warr, We may by the Blessing of God bring it to a Speedy and happy Conclusion. And We can with the Greater Earnestness press this matter, because We are Conscious of the readiness of this Governm^t (expressed in many Instances) to Assist their Neighbours in Distress; Besides the Governours or Comanders in Chief of this Province are Instructed by His Majesty in case of a Warr to require a Quota of men of the Neighbouring Governours, and likewise to Assist them in the Same manner when their circumstances demand it, We would Further Inform you That the Government of Connecticut have very cheerfully Supplyed a considerable number of Soldiers for the Security of our Western Frontiers; We doubt not but you will Effectually Consider what is proper to be done by you for His Majestys Service in this Affair, and for the Advantage of these Provinces and Colonys, which being united in Interest ought to be so in mutual Affection and kindness as-

Appendix. 341

suring you that nothing shall be wanting on Our part that becomes a good Neighbour of your Government, and that may tend to promote a good understanding with you at all times, Upon which the prosperity of both Governments do's so much depend. What Assistance you shall order, We shall humbly Represent to His Majesty, to whom we doubt not it will be Acceptable.

We have thought fit to Impower Nathaniel Byfield Esqr (One of His Maj^{tys} Council for this Province and a Gentleman of Great Knowledge & long Experience in our Publick affairs) to Appear for Us and to Treat and Conferr with you upon the matters herein Represented, And we desire that you would give him Credence accordingly, and to receive him to such Conferences with you as may be necessary for that End. Thus wishing you the Conduct of Heaven in all your Publick Affairs, We Remain
        Gentⁿ
            Your Affectionate Friends
              and humble Servants.
        In the Name & by Order of the
          Lt Govern^r and Council
                J. Willard Secry.
Boston October 28th 1724.
Copy   Examined ℗ J. Willard, Secry.

[*Paper 15. No. 14 is a duplicate.*]
GOV^R VAUDREUIL TO L^T GOV^R DUMMER.

I am Surprized that you have not Seen the Safe Guard & the Commission I had given to Father Rallé Sooner. The Abanakis Indians your Neighbours with whom you have always been in War having Submitted themselves to France Embrace the Catholick Religion, and Declare War to you every time ffrance and England have had any quarrell together I say all this ought or should have put you in Mind or Convince you it was not without Orders of the Most Christian King that the Jesuits were among the Indians and preach the Gospel to 'em. If you had forgot it the many Letters I had written to your Governour about it Since the last War between you and the Abanakis Indians ought to have put you in mind of it. No Doubt but you are to Answer to the King your Master for the late Murther Committed by your order on the person of that ffrench Missionary whose head I know you set a price on & had no other reason to be so animated against him only because he had done his duty and has been faithfull to his Prince in Teaching those Indians to whom the King of ffrance could not refuse Missionaries and help 'em in all he could, because they have always been true to him and Served him upon every Occasion or Opportunity that hath been made known to you.

You tell me that you took the Opportunity of the Safeguard I had given to ffather Rallé to let me know for the Second time that the Narantsouac & Panouamsque Indians were without Contradiction Subjects to Great Britain & on their Lands; Give me leave to tell you S^r that what you say is not maintainable.

Dont you know that St Georges River was in 1700 by Order of the two Crowns markt as the bounds of the English & ffrench Lands by which bounds it is plainly seen that all the District of Panouamsque was given to us, and Shews the Injustice you have

Committed against the ffrench to Build as you have done & without Leave a ffort on the Land of one Lefevre of which Enterprize if you dont desist you will Infallibly repent Dont you know now that S^d Lefevre had an habitation at Hosanoueskact, that your Sloops and ours did pay a Duty to him as to the proprietor of that Land every time they came to Anchor there. I believe that Mr Capon (Envoy of England when King George came upon the Throne who came here to aske the Panouamsque Indians to Submit themselves to England) has not Imparted to you the Answer those Indians made to him tho they did give him two Copies of it in writing. Their Answer was that they were French from the beginning and in the Interest of France, that they were Surprized they made Such propositions to 'em That they never would Change their Religion, King nor Interest and were offended they would keep such a discourse to 'em when they knew very well their Union with France of which they look upon themselves as Children and Subjects, that Answer (if Said Capon dont lye that was to be sent to the King and Parliament of England) will show plainly Sir the unreasonableness of your Pretension to those Indians. As to those of Narantsouac you fflatter your Selves of Certain particular Deeds by Vertue of which you pretend they made over their Lands to you. But how can we believe you Since the whole Nation Exclaim against those particular Indians (whom they pretend you have Suborned) that had no Authority to give that Deed; For the first Fort built by your Order upon Narantsouac Land, you Said to the Indians that were against it or Opposed to it that you did not pretend to be Masters of said fforts that they were built only against Pirates that might otherwise take away the goods you had a mind to send that way to trade with 'em. After you had by unlawfull means built those fforts you Spake very Imperiously and thought your Selves able to Subdue the said Indians: But it is that it Self that has brought you to the Confusion and trouble you lye under of which you will have much ado to come off. You have in so doing provoked the Narantsouac Indians against you to See you had a mind to use 'em as your Subjects and even as Slaves, whilst they would have no other relation with you but what follows from Trade among nations. You may Judge of the Truth of what I Say by the Letter you took about three years agoe at ffather Rallé's house when you plundered it against the Laws of men. Youl See in that Letter that the Narantsouac Indians used to come every year to me to Complain of your New Attempts: And that you had a mind to make them Turn of your Side whether they would or no which they were Resolved not to Suffer. You had more need to ask my Advice before you Invade their Land (which I shall never advise to) then I to ask your Leave to Answer the first Complaints of the said Indians, That Since they would not Turn of your Side it was their Interest to defend their Land and drive out those that would Invade it.

It would have lookt very unseemly for me, if for to please you I had Occasioned the Said Indians to turn from the ffrench with whom they have and will live lovingly together & Sacrafice to you If I had I should have made a Breach to the last Treaty of peace who Orders us to have a regard for the Soldiers either Friends or Alleys to ffrance & do nothing to molest 'em   KNOW THEREFORE Sir that if I did Order ffather Rallé to tarry among them it was to Conform myself to the Said Treaty. Nothing could Afflict the Said Indians more than to See their ffather or Priest taken away from 'em, whilst of another Side you did Endeavour to take their Lands.

You must blame no Body but your selves for all the Violence and Hostilities those Indians have Committed against your Nation Since you are the Cause of it in Invading their Lands and presume to make your Subjects those People that never would Consent to be your Allies who being united to France have declared themselves against your Nation. I Can't help taking their parts in this, to let you know you are in the wrong to fall out with 'em as you have. You have by that means drawn upon your Selves a great Number of Indians from Every Side whom to Revenge the Injustice done to those do fall and will fall upon you hereafter. If you had Imitated the Governours of Boston your predecessors, Contented your Selves to Trade with the Abenakes Indians and had built no fforts on their Lands all this Continent would have been in peace. Wherefore I think my Self Obliged to represent to you again, that to procure peace among your Selves, and the People you have justly provoked by your unjust Attempts to pull down all the fforts you have Built upon their Lands since the Peace of Utrecht. If So I promise you afterwards to be your Mediator to the Abenakis Indians and those that help them, and Oblige them to lay down the Hatchet, if can be possible to Appease 'em Since the last Cruelty and unjust Attempts Committed of late against them and their Missionary I am not so Scared of your threatenings to See Nations, that are as you said ready to fall upon us to Revenge your Cause than you ought to be your Selves for the fault you have Committed against France in Endeavouring to take their Alleys from 'em.

I will not however refuse my Mediation to you to bring the Abenakis Indians & their Allies to Peace on Condition Exprest in this Letter which are Conformable to the Mind of those Indians whom (between us) have given you no just Cause to Declare war to 'em. As to the Cruelty Committed by your Order on the Person of ffather Rallé I leave to the two Crowns to Decide of the Justice or punishment that is to be made; having been Obliged to give an Accompt of it to the King my Master.

I am Sir
Your most humble &
Most Obd^t Servant
VAUDREUIL.

Quebec 8^{ber} ye 29
1724   9^{ber} ye 10

Directed to the Governour of BOSTON.
Copy   Examined ℔ J. Willard Secry.

[*Paper 16.*]

INSTRUCTIONS TO THE COMMISSIONERS FOR CANADA.

AT a Great and General Court or Assembly for his Majestys province of the Massachusetts Bay in New England — held at Boston upon Wednesday the Eleventh of November 1724.
Nov^{br} 25th 1725.

The following Vote pass'd both Houses respecting a Message to be sent to Monsieur Vaudreuil Govr of Canada — Viz.

RESOLVED that his Hon^r the Lt Governour be desired in the name of this General Court by an express earnestly to move his Excellency Gov[r] Burnet to appoint and order a Suitable Person of his Government to Joyn with any person or persons that may be Appointed here to repair to Mons[r] Vaudreuil Gov[r] of Canada, and there demand all and every of his Majestys Subjects that have been Captivated by the Indian Enemy & carried into & Detained in any part of his Government and likewise demand that the said Governour Vaudreuil withdraw the Countenance & Assistance which in Violation of the Treaty of Utrecht & contrary to the friendship and Alliance between the Two Crowns he has given to the said Indians in the prosecution of their Unjust War against his Majestys Subjects of these Colonys, Otherwise of our Friend Indians who have with difficulty been restrained, should in pursuit of the Enemy Indians Commit like Hostilitys upon the French Familys who dwell promiscuously with them as have been by the French Indians Committed upon the Inhabitants of this province. The Blame will be entirely owing to his own Conduct, and likewise inform him that if the Indians shall still persist in the war against us the several English Governments will find themselves Obliged with their United Forces by the help of God to prosecute and pursue them to the Uttermost And that his Hon[r] the L[t] Govern[r] be also desired in the Name of this Court by the Same Express to move the Hon[ble] Governour Talcot & the Government of Connecticut, that they would Joyn a Commissioner in the Affair above as also the Governments of Rhoad Island & New Hampshire to Joyn a Commissioner from each Government in the Same Affair

Copy

                Examined ℔ J Willard Secry.

Dec^br 25th 1724.

In the House of Representatives.

Voted that his Hon^r the Lieuten^t Governour be desired to send Commissioners on the Message to Canada already agreed on although the Neighbouring Governments do not Joyn them. And that some Suitable person or persons be accordingly Chosen by the Court before they rise, And that Mr Speaker Mr Wainwright & Col° Chandler & Mr Cushing with such as the Honble Board shall Joyn be a Committee to draw some proper heads or Articles of Instructions for the said Commissioners, And to sit forthwith and make report of their Doings.

In Council Read and Concur'd, And that Col° Fitch & Col° Tailer & Col° Thaxter be Joined in the Affair above.

Copy   Examined ℣ J Willard Secry.

Dec^br 23^d 1724.   Voted in both Houses that his Hon^r the Lieutenant Govern^r be Desired to give the following Instructions to the Commissioners to be Chosen and sent to Canada Viz.

That the said Commissioners proceed with all Convenient Dispatch to Albany & from thence to Monsr Vaudreuil Governour of Canada or the Governour for the time being of that Country & deliver to him the several Letters to him Directed.

That they demand all and every of his Majestys Subjects that have been Captivated by the Indian Enemy and Carried into & detained in any part of his Government.

That they Remonstrate to the said French Governour his unjust Treatment of this Government in the Countenance and Assistance which in Violation of the Treaty of Utrecht & contrary to the Friendship and Alliance between the Two Crowns he has given to the said Indians in the prosecution of this present War, And that they peremptorily insist on his withdrawing his Countenance and assistance from the said Indians for the future. Otherwise to observe to him, That if our friend Indians should in pursuit of the Enemy Commit like Hostilities upon the French Families who dwell promiscuously with them, as have been by some of the French Indians Committed upon the Inhabitants of this province the Blame will be entirely owing to his own Conduct.

And if hereupon the French Governour in behalf of the Indians or the said Indians for themselves should make any Overtures for putting an end to the War, the Commissioners give for answer, that although they have neither powers nor Instructions to conclude or enter into any Treaty, Yet if the Indians or a number of their Chiefs full Authorized are desirous to Treat with this Government in order to make an Exchange of all prisoners and Captives on both sides, and a Just, Safe and lasting peace And for this End will repair to Boston or Portsmouth in the province of New Hampshire They shall have safe Conduct thither and back again and the Commissioners shall give passports accordingly.

Examined ₱ J Willard Secry.

[Paper 17.]
JOURNAL OF THE COMMISSIONERS TO CANADA.

Conformable to our Commission and Instructions from the Honorable WILLIAM DUMMER Esqr Lieutenant Governour and Commander in Chief of His Majestys Province of the Massachusetts Bay We departed the Twentieth day of January 1724 and Arrived at Albany on the Twentieighth day of the Said Month And after having Agreed with five Macuas, and five Scatacook Indians, to go with and Assist us on our Journey to Mont Real, and provided all things necessary, We Set out from Saratoga 40 miles above Albany, the Eighth day of February finding Ice in the River, and on Wood Creek so called until we came near the little falls, where that Creek Empties it Self into the drowned Lands; and Concluding the Lake to be open, we lay Still four days, and made three Cano's, and on the Sixteenth day of February we Set out drawing all our Provisions and other things on Sleds on the drowned Lands until we came to the Crown Point which was on the Eighteenth day of S^d month, And we went one small days Travel further and then made a wooden Cannou Still Concluding the Lake was open but Extream Cold weather coming on, and our provisions being almost Spent by the Indians we dismis'd them all but two and left our Cannous behind, and set out by Land on the 22^d of February and after many difficulties and hardships We arrived at Chambly on the 28th day of the said month where having first obtained permission to go to Mont Real We Arrived there the Second day of March, and waited on the Governour General Monsr Vaudreuil (who happened to get there the day before us) and Delivered him our passports and other Letters to him directed, and after they were translated a time being appointed We gave our demands to the Governour in writing (which are herewith Exhibited) And desired an Answer in writing which he utterly refused; we Convinced him as we apprehended of his being the Cause of the War as well by his own as other French Letters; and all he had to object was That the Letters we produced to him were not Originals. We then Appealed to the Copys he kept, but he would not Suffer them to be Read. He often talked to us of the pretended Grievances of the Indians Concerning Land; we convinced him and his Jesuit La Chase of a Gross mistake they had Laboured under of the Distance between St Georges and Saco River, the Land they laid Claim to and they had no other refuge to fly to, but that the Indians had wrongfully Informed them. The Governour as well as the Indians seemed desirous of Peace by sundry expressions in their Discourse at severall times with us but Insisted upon it That the peace must be made or agreed upon in presence of the Governour at Mont Real, to which we made Answer, that we had no power to treat of peace there, but that if they desired Peace, and would go either to Boston or Piscataqua they should be in safety both in going there and returning home; And the Governments there would we doubted not, be willing to make a just and lasting Peace with them; to which they replyed (being first directed what to say by the Jesuit La Chase as we Imagine) That what was done must be in the presence of the Governour and at Canada, We then told them that if they had nothing more to say to us we had nothing further to say to them; And so our discourse broke off with the Indians.

By all the Interviews and Information we had, the Indians are Inclinable to Peace, and the Western Indians as Cagnawaga, Schoandic, Nipesangs &c. are all against the War, and altho' they have been again and again moved by their Jesuits, by Order from the Government to renew their Hostilities, which some of them did the last year and before Commit Yet they could not be prevailed with So to do And when we Expostulated with the Governour on this Head, and offered to bring some of those Indians before his face to prove this Vile and Wicked practice, all he could Say, and that in some wrath was, that the Indians were Lyars, and he would not then see them least (as we apprehend) he should have been Convicted by them And we must needs say, that such Trifling and tricking as we observed and met with, could hardly be Expected from the very worst of mankind, Tho' at the same time we would do Monsr Vaudreuil that Justice as to Say Seperate him from the Jesuit, he is of honour, good Nature and Easey Disposition.

On our demanding the British Subjects that were Captives in the hands of the French, the Governours Answer was That he had no Captives, there being no War between the English & French Nations, but that the French out of Charity and Compassion, had bought some Poor English People, and that they should be returned if the Sums of money they Cost were repaid. This Buying and Selling our people, Seems to us, to be one great Reason or Cause of the Continuance of the War the Indians being Indebted to the ffrench, they fit them out to get Slaves, for so his Majestys good Subjects are made at Canada, and thereby the Indians pay their ffrench Creditors who make a great Advantage to them selves

Appendix. 353

over and above their debts thus paid them, by Selling the poor Captives Dearer than Negro's may be purchased. On this head we were Sufficiently Moved to Say a great deal to the Governour and his Priest for we could Seldom See the one without the other And all the Answer was Charity and least the Salvages should kill them.

We herewith present to your Honours Certificates Signed by the Secretary & others for money received for some of our prisoners, notwithstanding they pretend to hold or have none.

The ffrench Governour Several times got angry Concerning what the Governour of New York had Said to Our Five nations of Building a House on or near Onondaga River. Our Observations herein we reduced to writing and Delivered to the Commissioners at Albany a Copy whereof N° A we humbly refer to.

And we Observing the kind & good Disposition in the French Maquas at Mont Real and their Sachems who came with us, we had a Treaty with them at Albany as ℔ N° B which we also communicated to the said Commissioners.

All which is Humbly Represented by
Your Honours Obedient Servants
Sam¹ Thaxter }
Wᵐ Dudley } Commissioners.

Boston May 26ᵗʰ 1725
In Council May 28.
1725 Read.
Examined ℔ J Willard Secry.

[Paper 18.]

Lt Govr Dummer to Lt Govr Wentworth.

LETTER from His Honour the Lieu^t Governour to the Honble John Wentworth Esqr Lieu^t Governour of the Province of New Hampshire.

Sir.

You have here Inclosed a Vote of the General Assembly of this Province Expressing their desire that a suitable person from this Government, and one from Each of the Neighbouring Governm^{ts}, should be sent on a message to Govern^r Vaudreuil of Canada, for the Reasons therein Expressed.

And there is Great grounds to hope if he were made sensible That in case he continues to Abett & Instigate our Enemys against us, The several English Governments would with their united Force pursue those Indians, And in their pursuits, the Warr should be brought home to his own Doors, he would soon use means to bring them to proper Terms of Peace and Submission.

I have written to the Governours of New York, Connecticutt and Rhode Island, & Expect in a short time to hear from them, and assure myself That you will not be backward to Joyn with us herein as is desired, Inasmuch as none will be likely to reap Greater Advantage than the Province of New Hampshire in case the proposed End be attained.

I request you will send me your Answer as soon as may be with Convenience.

I am
Sir
Y^r very humble Servt
Wm Dummer.

Boston December 1st 1724.
Examined ⅌ J Willard Secry.

Paper No. 19. "L{T}. GOV{R} DUMMER TO GOV{R} CRANSTON OF RHODE ISLAND AND TO GOV{R} TALCOT OF CONNECTICUT," are of similar tenor.

[*Paper 20.*]

L{T} GOV{R} DUMMER TO GOV{R} BURNETT.

LETTER from His Honour the Lieut Governour to His Excellency William Burnett Esqr Govern{r} of New York.

Sir

The Remarkable Evidences of your Friendship to this Province at the late Treaty with the Maquas at Albany have been by our Agents there fully Represented both to me and the General Assembly here, The Remembrance whereof as it Impresses suitable sentiments of Gratitude on our minds, so it Raises not only our hope but Expectation That your further Assistances will not be wanting as Occasion may require.

This Government after having Exercised long Patience towards the Eastern Indians notwithstand{g} the many and Great Outrages &c. &c. &c.*

* * * * * *

     Your Most Obedient
      Humble Servt
       WILLIAM DUMMER

Boston
 December 1st 1724
 Copy Examined
    ℞ J Willard Secry.

---

* The remainder of this letter is a duplicate of a portion of No. 22, which see.

[Paper 21.]

VOTE OF THE GOVERNOUR AND COUNCIL OF NEW YORK.

AT A COUNCIL
HELD AT FORT GEORGE
IN NEW YORK DECEMB^R 16TH 1724.

PRESENT

His Excellency William Burnet Esqr
Capt Waller
Mr Harison
Doct^r Colden
Mr Alexander
Mr Vanhorn

His Excellency laid before the Board Some papers he had received from the Honourable William Dummer Esqr Lieut. Govr of the Massachusetts Bay (Viz^t) the Copy of the Declaration of War against the Eastern Indians, the Copy of an Address of that Government to His Majesty concerning that War with a Letter from the said Governour to his Excellency.

ORDERED, That the said Letter with the other papers be referred to the Consideration of the Gentlemen of this Board or any five of them And that they make Report thereunto to this Board.

POST MERIDIEM

Present as before

The Report of the Gentlemen of the Committee to whose Consideration the papers relating to New England were referred was Read and is as follows

Appendix. 357

At a Committee of the Council held at the Council Chamber in New York Decemb^r 16th 1724.

PRESENT

Capt Walter
Mr Harrison
Doct^r Colden
Mr Alexander
Mr Abrah Vanhorn

May it please your Excellency

IN OBEDIENCE to your Excellency's Order in Council of this day referring to us the Consideration of Some papers sent by the Lieutenant Governour of Massachusetts Bay to wit a Copy of the Declaration of War against the Eastern Indians a Copy of an Address to his Majesty concerning that War to gether with a Letter from the Honourable William Dummer Esqr Lieut. Governour of that Province.

We have considered of the Same, and altho' it be our sentiments that all the Assistance in the power of this province to give to that of the Massachusetts Bay for putting a hapy End to the War with the Indians ought to be given and were it in your Excellency's power, with the help of the Council to make good what is desired by the said Letter to be told Monsr Vaudreuil we should heartily advize it so far as your Excellency may think it Consistent with your Instructions from his Majesty.

But we do humbly Conceive that the Committing of Hostilities within the Territories of the ffrench King would be in Effect Commencing War against him, which your Excellency is forbid to do by your Instructions without his Majestys Special Commands.

We do also humbly Conceive that if your Excellency should threaten War even only against the Eastern Indians, it would be very Derogatory to the Honour of the Province (if the Eastern Indians did continue the War) not to Joyn the War against them and this your Excellency with any help in the power of this Board to give you without the Assembly Joyning to Raise money cannot Effectually do And the Assembly by their Resolves of the fifth of October 1722 communicated about that time to the Province of the Massachusetts Bay have already given their Sentiments concerning that matter to which he Referrs.

Wherefore we are sorry we cannot advise your Excellency to Comply with what is desired in the said Letter.

We are
Your Excellencys most
Obedient Humble
Servants.
By Order of the Committee
Ja Alexander Chairman.

which Report was approved of by this Board.

A true Copy taken from the Minutes of Council

H. Bobingt^n Ck Coun^l.

Copy   Examined ⅌ J Willard Secry.

Vote of the Govern^r and Council of New York
Decr 16. 1724.

[*Paper 22.*]

L︎ᵀ Govʀ Dummer to Govʀ Talcot.

Letter from His Honour the Lᵗ Governour to the Honoᵇˡᵉ Joseph Talcot Esqʳ Governour of the Colony of Connecticutt.

Sir

The Answer of the General Assembly of Connecticutt to the motion lately made to them by Colº John Stoddard in the name of this Government with relation to the carrying on the Warr against our Enemy Indians, has been transmitted to me, which I have communicated to the General Court of this Province now sitting, And Inasmuch as it is therein Intimated that you had not received such full Satisfaction touching the Grounds of the Warr as you desired, I have therefore directed Copys of the Proclamation of Warr and a Memorial to His Majesty wherein the Grounds of the Warr are set forth, to be Inclosed, Upon perusal of which I hope you will be fully sensible That the grounds were sufficient and the Warr unavoidable. And I would give you further to understand That as this Government, (after having Exercised long Patience towards the Eastern Indians, notwithstanding the many and Great Outrages and Depredations comitted by them upon His Majestys Subjects Inhabiting our Frontiers, till at last by killing multitudes of their Cattle inhumanely abusing their persons, Plundering & burning their Houses, carrying several of them away Captives, wounding and killing others, and even in open and hostile manner assaulting for many hours A Fort where His Majᶦᵗʸˢ Colours were flying, as by the Inclosed papers will appear,

Their Insults became intolerable) did at first with much regret enter into a Warr with such a barbarous lurking and almost inaccessible Enemy to the heavy Expense & Calamity of it not only Obliges us to wish it at an End, but do's also Engage us to Exercise our thoughts how to bring it to a speedy and happy Conclusion. And if the Governour of Canada who has all along abetted and Instigated our Enemys, were made sensible, That in case he continued so to do, the several English Governm^{ts} would with their united Forces pursue those Indians, and in their Pursuits, the Warr should be brought home to his own doors, there is great reason to Conclude that he would either by withdrawing his Assistance or by Exerting his Influence soon bring them to proper Terms of Peace and submission, wherefore the General Court now sitting have desired me Earnestly to move you, that you would please to appoint and Order some suitable person of your Government, to Joyn with such persons as shall be sent from hence, and from the Governments of New York Rhode Island and New Hampshire, to repair to Monsr Vaudreuil Governour of Canada and there to demand all and every of His Maj^{tys} Subjects that have been Captivated by the Indian Enemy and carryed into and detained in any Part of his Government, and likewise to demand that the said Governour Vaudreuil withdraw the Countenance and Assistance which in violation of the Treaty of Utrecht & Contrary to the Friendship and alliance between the two Crowns he has given to the s^d Indians in the prosecution of their unjust Warr against His Maj^{tys} Subjects in these Colonys, And otherwise if our Friend Indians who have hitherto been with difficulty restrained should in pursuit of the Enemy Indians comit like Hostilitys upon the French Familys who dwell promiscuously with them as have been Comitted by the French Indians upon the Inhabitants of this Province, That the Blame will be intirely owing to his own Conduct, and that the said Agents likewise Inform him, that if the Indians shall still persist in this Warr against us, The several English Governments will find themselves Obliged with their united Force (by the help of God) to prosecute and pursue them to the uttermost; And if thro' the blessing of God on our Endeavours herein, a lasting Peace should be brought forward, I trust that not only this Province, but the Colony of Connecticutt also, will have abundant Cause to rejoyce in the happy Effects of the proposed Message.

I hope you will Judge it Expedient to joyn with us in this affair, And desire you will send me your Answer as soon as may be with Convenience, whereby you will much Oblige
   Sir
     Yo^r Most Obedient humble serv^t
Boston   WILLIAM DUMMER
  December 1st 1724.

Copy Examined
   ℔ J WILLARD Secry.

[*Paper 23.*]

GOV^R TALCOT TO THE L^T GOVERNOUR DUMMER.

     Hartford Decemb^r 22^d 1724.
Sir
I have Received yours of November 30th with the inclosed Referred to therein and with that a Copy of

your Assembly respecting the Message to Canada had also been inclosed which your Honour can yet Supply.

I have advised with the Gentlemen of the Council that I could at this Season with Convenience Speak with and am not unsensible of the great Difficulty and Charge the Warr with the Eastern Indians hath brought upon the whole province under your Command. I wish this Government were able to Render the Circumstances of your Province in that affair more Easie but as to what your Honour Intimates respecting sending messages to Canada Altho' that project Seemeth likely to make Monsr Vaudreuil sensible that his Conduct cant be justified neither will it well support the ffrench Cause when the Same Methods shall be taken by New England against Canada the Letting loose the Indians as Intimated in yours will doubtless give Conviction when those things proper to Convince Reason fail And therefore 'tis to be hoped at Sight of it at a distance as Represented by messengers may do something with that Governour.

But yet would further propose to Your Honours advisement whether it may not be proper to Close the Message to Monsr Vaudreuil with a Representation that it is very apparent that our Indian Enemy have such a dependance on him to Support them in the War that he can easily reduce them to quietness And that his Exerting himself in so good a work (as Reducing those Indians to Order would be) may hapily prevent many Mischiefs that Seem to Threaten us as well as the People under his Command and also give us a Special Instance of his good Neighbourhood. And if this or anything Else proper to Insert in the Message to the Governour of Canada might gain him to Influence the Indians to peace it would be well but if he should slight the Motion of being an Instrument to gain a Peace for us I think he would still be the Less Excusable and must thank himself when he is Taught by other Means.

But yet after all must let your Honour know that it is not in my power with the Council to Comply with your Desire And if I should Call our Assembly together (who can only Authorize a person to go upon the Errand you Mention) I fear the Same Scruples (as when Col° Stoddard was with us) will still be started which were principally two. First that the Indians had been wronged in their Lands. Secondly that the Hostages received by your Government of the Indians were only to Secure the payment of some Beaver which the Indians say they have Since paid and therefore the War not just on the English Side.

These things our people have had confirmed to them by many persons (and some of distinction) of your Governm^t I would Charitably hope those Reports are wholly Groundless I should be very unwilling to Entertain such things without the Clearest proofs.

Notwithstanding which in Order to Satisfy our Assembly possibly it may be best to Send to me the fullest accounts that may be come at. Our late very Honourable and Excellent Governour Col° Saltonstall some time before his Death received one of your Treaties with the Eastern Indians which now Cant be found doubtless your Treaties and other writings respecting the Eastern Lands if Communicated to our Assembly might be of Service and a Copy of the Entry made when the said Hostages were delivered up (which Entry Certainly doth Include what they were Received for) will Certainly Satisfy our Assembly how the Matter is as to the Hostages.

Your Honour won't think it Strange that there is need to satisfie our Assembly in these things when you consider our people had the Said Reports from among yourselves as is above hinted and that what persons Confess against themselves is Easily believed and in many things these wants no other proof. I have insisted the more largely that if possible I might prevent all difficulties for I would always cultivate that good understanding that Hath been between the Two Governments.

By Order of the Governour &c of the Colony of Connecticutt.
Signed
℘ Her: Wyllys Secretary.

Copy Examined
℘ J Willard Secry.

[*Paper 24.*]

At the Desire of Coll⁰ William Coddington and Major Thomas Freye Esqʳˢ Commissioners from the Government of Rhode Island to Treat and Confer with the Government of the Massachusetts Bay upon the subject of their Furnishing a number of Men to Joyn with our Forces in prosecuting the War against the Indian Enemy; And in Order to Satisfy the Said Commissioners of the Just Grounds and Reasons of the present War with the sᵈ Indians, that so they may be Enabled to give a Satisfactory Account thereof to the Government of Rhode Island.

Appendix. 365

The Committee appointed by the Massachusetts Governm{t} have here made a Narrative of several Treatys had with the said Indians, and of the steps this Government from time to time have taken in order to Continue them in Peace and Amity with his Majesties Subjects of this Province, as well as some short Account of the Repeated Injuries, Outrages Depredations and Murthers Comitted by the said Indians on the Inhabitants of this Province.

Anno 1693. The several Tribes of Eastern Indians did at a Treaty with Sr William Phipps Governor, at Pemaquid Cast themselves upon Their Majesty's Grace & Favour, acknowledge their hearty subjection & obedience to the Crown of England, Covenant to Abandon the French Interest to restore Captives, Agree that the English shall peaceably & quietly enter upon, Improve and forever Enjoy all their Rights of Land and former Settlements and Possessions within the Eastern parts of the said Province without any Pretensions or Claims by them, or any other Tribe of Indians, and be in no ways Molested Interupted or Disturbed therein. That if any Controversy Arise they will not take private Revenge, but apply to the Government for Remedy submitting themselves to be Ruled by their Majesty's Laws, and Desiring to have the Benefit of the same.

Anno 1703. A treaty was held with the Eastern Indians at Casco Bay by Governor Dudley where they Covenanted and Engaged to Continue in Peace and Amity with Her Majesties Subjects of this Government and two heaps of stones Called the two Brothers, which had been Erected Anno 1701 were there by the English and Indians renewed in Perpetual memory of said Covenant, & yet within a few weeks after viz the beginning of August, they in three parties at the same time fell upon her Majesties Subjects in the Eastern Frontier of this Province, Burning Houses, killing & Carrying away many of the Inhabitants at Twenty miles distance.

Anno 1713 July. The several Tribes of Eastern Indians at a Treaty with the afores^d Governor Dudley at Portsmouth in New Hampshire did acknowledge to have made a Breach of their Fidelity & Loyalty to the Crown of Great Britain, and to have made open Rebellion, and did acknowledge themselves to be the Lawful subjects of Queen Anne, and Promise Hearty subjection and Obedience to the Crown of Great Britain and did then engage for the future to Cease All Acts of Hostility towards all the subjects of the said Crown, never to Entertain any Treasonable Conspiracies with any other Nation to their Disturbance. That Her Majesties Subjects shall & may Peaceably Enter upon Improve and forever Enjoy all and singular their Rights of Land, and former settlements properties and possessions within the Eastern parts of said Province & New Hampshire with all Islands Shoars Beaches & Fishery. And if any Controversy happen they will not take private Revenge but Apply to the Government for Remedy. They then Confessed that they had Contrary to all Faith and Justice Broke their Articles with Sr William Phipps Anno 1693 with the Earle of Bellomont Anno 1699 & with Governor Dudley August 1702 & July 1703 notwithstanding they had been well Treated by the Governours & Cast themselves upon Her Majesty's Mercy for Pardon of all their past Rebellous Hostilitys & Violations of their Promises, Praying to be Received into Her Majesty's Grace and Protection.

August Anno 1717 At a Treaty of Governor Shute with the Several Tribes of Eastern Indians at

Arowsick they did Ratify and and Confirm the Treaty made at Portsmouth with Governor Dudley Anno 1713 & every the Articles, which relate to the Restraint & Limitation of Trade & Commerce, which is now otherwise Managed. And whereas some Rash persons among them had molested some of their good Fellow subjects the English in the possession of their Lands, and otherwise Ill Treated them, they did Disapprove and Condemn the same, and freely Consent that their English friends shall possess Enjoy & Improve all the Lands which they have formerly possessed, and all which they have Obtained a right and Title unto, hoping it will prove of Mutual Benefit to the English, and them that they Cohabit with them, which was signed by Twenty Sachems, and Principal Men of the several Tribes.

NOTWITHSTANDING which the Indians making it their frequent Practice to kill the English Cattle, to threaten & Abuse the Persons of the Inhabitants in those parts of the Government of this Province The Government thought proper to appoint four Gentlemen being officers of the Forces in Pay, to Confer with the Chiefs of the said Tribes of Indians upon the Accompt of the Outrages & Depredations they had committed.

November Anno 1720 Shadrach Walton, Esqr Colonel, the Major and two Captains met with the Chief of those Tribes at Arowsick where being Charged with the Spoils, wrongs and Injuries Comitted by the Indians upon the Persons and Estates of the English, and being Convicted thereof they did Oblige themselves to pay two hund^d Skins towards Satisfaction for the same; And to Deliver unto the Government four of their Principal men, not only as Security for payment of the Skins, but also to remain as Hostages and Pledges to the Government for the Indians good behaviour for the time to come, and to deliver a greater number if demanded Signed by six of their Chief Men as Agents for the rest.

August Anno 1721. The said Indians still proceeding and Increasing in their Robberies & Outrages the Government sent down Penn Townsend Esq' with several Gentlemen of the Council & others to Confer with them, & bring them to Reason; But altho they had notice sent them of their being at Arowsick, and that the Indians sent them word they would Come to them; yet they broke their Promise, and never came near them, so they were forced to return without seeing or speaking with them.

From which time forward for the space of a year they grew more bold and Open in their Insults, killing Cattle Burning Houses, Robbing & Burning vessels, killing His Majesties subjects Openly Assaulting His Forts till at last in July 1722 the Government no longer Able to bear with such Insufferable Treatment found it absolutely necessary to Proclaim War against them By all which Narrative it appears that the Indians have broken their solemn Covenants and Engagements Insulted and killed His Majesty's subjects before the War was proclaimed with the Eastern Indians. And for further Information the Comittee for the Massachusetts Bay Do Declare That Several Tribes of the Indians to the Westward within the French Government, without the least Notice or Manifestation of any Disgust, whether by the Instigation of the other Indians, or by the French or by both have in a very Hostile way & manner Invaded the Province in several parts, have Captivated His Maj^{ties} subjects; Others Murthered, Destroyed their Estates & burnt their

Houses particularly in August 1723 killed the Revd Mr Willard at Rutland & Scalped him & two persons more & Captivated three, one of which has been Redeemed out of their hands & is Returned. In June two killed at Hatfield & one taken. The same year three hundred of the Western Indians (among whom was a French Officer Begon by name) Came upon Northfield burnt some houses, killed some Persons & Captivated one Dickeson. In the present year 1724 the said Western Indians killed one Man at Groton and broke into the Mans Garrison, and had destroyed the same with many Lives, if they had not been prevented by the Bravery of one single person. And in August last the said Indians killed Eight Men at Dunstable & Captivated one, who is in their hands so that the War with these Western Indians the Government have been forced into, without the least so much as pretended provocation, and the necessity thereof is a sufficient Reason ; and therefore the Assistance from the Neighbouring Colonys may very Justly be Expected of them.

Upon the whole this Province being Involved and Perplexed with this Bloody War, & His Majesties good subjects put to great and heavy Expence Calls as loud for Assistance as if the two Crowns of Great Britain & France were at Variance, if not more, the Indians being the Common Enemy by Land as Pyrates are by Water ; And altho the Government of Rhode Island was not Advized with on this Head ; yet the War being Unavoidable, they as well as the other Governm^{ts} is fully acquainted with the proceedings of this Government and Carriage of the said Common Indian Enemy ; We doubt not will so far sympathize with the Distressed Case of their Fellow Subjects, as to Joyn all together in the Vigorous prosecution of this War until a happy Safe and Honourable Peace may be Obtained.

In Council December 15th 1724. Read and Ordered That this Report be Accepted, and that the Committee of this Court be Desired to Deliver a Copy thereof to the Commissioners from the Governm^t of Rhode Island.
     Sent down for Concurrence
       J Willard Secry.

In the House of Representatives December 14th 1724.
  Read & Concurred
       Wm Dudley Speaker.
Copy Examined
    ℞ J Willard Secry.

[*Paper 25.*]

Lt Govr Dummer to Govr Vaudreuil.

    Boston N England January 19th 1724.
Sir
 Your Letter dated Quebec October 29th ℞ Henry Edgar one of the English Captives came Safe to me; on perusal thereof I am greatly Surprized at the matters Contained therein, which are so unjustly represented, that I cannot Satisfy my Self to pass them by unanswered. In the first place As to what you say relating to the death of Monsr Rallé the Jesuit, which you set forth as so Inhumane & Barbarous; I readily acknowledge that he was slain, amongst other of our Enemies at Norridgewalk; And if he had Confined

himself unto the professed Duty of his ffunction viz to Instruct the Indians in the Christian Religion, had kept himself within the bounds of the French Dominions, and had not Instigated the Indians to War & Rapine there might then have been some ground of Complaint ; But when instead of Preaching Peace, Love and Friendship Agreeable to the Doctrines of the Christian Religion, he has been a Constant and Notorious Fomenter & Incendiary to the Indians to kill burn & Destroy, as flagrantly appears by many original Letters & manuscripts, I have of his by me, and when in open Violation of an Act of Parliament of Great Britain, and the Laws of this Province strictly forbidding Jesuits to reside or teach within the British Dominions, he has not only resided, but also once & again appeared at the head of great numbers of Indians, in an Hostile manner threatening and Insulting, as also publickly Assaulting the subjects of His British Majesty ; I say, If after all, such an Incendiary has happened to be slain in the heat of Action, among our Open and Declared Enemies, surely none can be blamed therefor but himself, nor can any safeguard from you, or any other Justify him in such proceedings : And I think I have much greater Cause to Complain, that Mr Willard the minister of Rutland (who never had been guilty of the Facts charged upon Mr Rallé & applied himself solely to the preaching of the Gospel) was by the Indians you sent to Attack that Town Assaulted, slain and scalpt, & his scalp Carried in Triumph to Quebec.

As to the next article you mention, That St Georges River was in the year 1700 by order of the Two Crowns Marked as the bounds of the English and French Lands whereby it appeared That Penobscot was given to you, and that one La ffevre had a right to the Land thereabouts, & that all Vessels paid a Duty to him, And that Mr Capon Envoy of England when King George came upon the Throne, went to ask the Penobscot Indians to submit themselves to England, which they refused. I have no difficulty to Answer to each of the afores^d Points; And as to the last relating to Mr Capon you Labour under a very great Mistake to mention him as an Envoy of England, he being far below any such Character, and only an Inferior Officer, Comissary or Victualler to the Garrison of Annapolis, & sometime after that was taken & yielded up to the English, sent by the Lieutenant Govr of that place to visit the French settlements within that District & to require an Oath of Allegiance and Fidelity from them to Queen Anne; but he had no Occasion to Come and Entice the Penobscot Indians to submit themselves to England, for they as well as the Norridgwalk Indians & many other Tribes had done that long before even in the year 1693 at a Treaty of Sr William Phipps Governor of this Province, by which Treaty, I can make it appear, that they not only submitted themselves as subjects to the Crown of England, but also renounced the French Interest & Limited Claim to the Lands bought and possessed by the English; But since King George came to the Throne, Mr Capon has not been in those parts at all, as I am Informed by the People of that Country.

As to St Georges River being the bounds and La ffevres pretended Right it seems very wonderful you should make any mention of those things or lay any weight upon them at this time, when if the Case were formerly as you now represent it, which I do not allow, all such Claim and pretension is wholly superceeded, and at an end; whereof you may soon and easily satisfy your self by Consulting the Treaty of peace at Utrecht Concluded between the two Crowns in the year 1713 by the twelfth Article, whereof it is provided, "That all Nova Scotia or L'Accadie with "it's Ancient Boundaries &c. together with the Do- "minion property & possession of the s^d Islands "Lands & places, and all right to which, the Most "Christian King, the Crown of France, or any the "subjects thereof have hitherto had to the Islands "Lands & places, and the Inhabitants of the same "are Yielded & made over to the Queen of Great "Britain & to her Crown forever. Now by the afore-s^d Resignation, the French King Quitted all Right not only to the Lands, but also the Inhabitants whether ffrench or Indians, or whatsoever they were & transferred the same to the Crown of Great Britain forever, whereby you are Entirely Cutt off from any Claim to the subjection of the said Indians, from thence forward; And we are not Ignorant how far the ffrench King understood the Countrey of L'Accadie to Extend Westward by his Patent Granted to Monsr D'Alney tho you seem to be a stranger to it.

As to the whole Nation of the Indians Exclaiming against some of their Tribe, as pretending they were suborned to give Deeds for their Lands, if it be matter of Fact, that they do so, which is hard to be Conceived, it is a most unjust Imputation, & must Argue a wonderful Deceitfulness & self Contradiction in them, since they have upon all Treatys when the whole Tribes were together Constantly acknowledged and submitted to the English Titles and possessions, which they had by honest and Lawful purchase Acquired.

As to the Building of Forts any where within the British Dominions I suppose you will not scruple to acknowledge that the King of Great Britain has as good a right to Erect Fortresses or places of Defence within His Dominions, as the ffrench King has in his And therefore when you shall please to Give me Instances of the French Kings Applying himself to the Indians for leave to build a Fort or Forts for the Defence of His Subjects I shall then give you a further Answer to that Argument. And in the meantime I must tell you we have always treated the Indians with sincerity, & never thought it proper to make Apologies for Building Forts within our own Jurisdiction (as you Insinuate) but on the Contrary in all Our Treatys with them have Ascerted our undoubted right so to do.

You likewise signify that we must Blame no body but our selves for the Violence and Hostilities Committed against Our nation by the Indians. But syr, If the blame must lye where it ought I must Impute their Outrages, falsness & Ill Conduct towards us, not so much, to their own Inclinations, as to the Instigations of the Jesuit Rallé & others Under your Government, whereof we have had sufficient Information from time to time, as also of your own forcing the Indians against their Wills upon our Frontiers to destroy & Cutt off our People which Cannot be otherwise lookt upon as a direct & Notorious Violation of the Treaty of Peace at Utrecht.

NEVERTHELESS SIR, After all, I have much greater Inclination to live in Amity & good Correspondence with you than otherwise, And therefore I have sent Coll° Samuel Thurber one of His Majesties Council, and Coll° William Dudley one of the House of Representatives who are Commissioned to Confer

with you Pursuant to such Instructions as they have received from me; And I Desire that you will Give CREDENCE to them accordingly.
I am,
Sir,
Your Most Humble &
Most Obed: Servant
WM. DUMMER.
Copy   Examined ℞ J Willard Secry.

[*Paper 26.*]

CAPT. JORDAN'S DECLARATION.

The Declaration of Samuel Jordan Interpreter who went with the Honble Samuel Thaxter & William Dudley Esq^rs Commissioners (appointed by the Lt Governor of this Province) from Boston to Montreal, & other places in the Government of Canada in the year 1725.

The said Jordan saith, That the said Commissioners in their Journey from Albany to Montreal met with two Indians at Shambley River so called, who came down there from their Wigwams to wait on them, and expressed their Joy to see them; They made Inquiry Concerning the Hostages at Boston & signified their Inclination to be at Peace with the English; which the Declarant told them might be

Obtained (if they Expressed their desires to the Governm^t) upon reasonable terms.

Upon their arrival at Montreal the Comissioners Obtained Governor Vaudreuil's Consent, That I might go down to St François & Wenox & other places thereabouts in Order to discourse with the Indians referring to the English Captives, & relating to the War &c. & he sent with me an Interpreter. And in the month of March last I arrived at St Francis, & Tarried at a French House there for M^r De Laune the Interpreter, and asking him why he tarried so long before he came there; he answered that he had been to enquire for Mr Perubres to deliver him a Letter from Govr Vaudreuil, but he was gone to Montreal & that I must tarry where I was till the said Perubres return, which said Perubres was a Fryer; But I being unwilling to tarry unless the Interpreter would forbid any further proceeding under his hand; he with some difficulty allowed me to go to speak with the Indians at St François; where I met with several Indian Women, who told me their Husbands had gone out to War against the English. They frowned upon me at first, and I askt the reason why they lookt so angry, I was told they had several of them lost their Relations in the unjust War with the English (as they Called it) & they could not see an English Man without Indignation I told them that the Indians without Just Cause had made War and the English were Obliged to Defend themselves. To which it was answered, if it was so they were not rightly Informed. They further said, that in time of Peace the English had taken four or five Indian Men, & detained them in Boston as Prisoners; but when I related to them how those Men were sent as Hostages to Boston, and how that matter truly was; and how the Indians began the Hostilities burning the English in Houses &c they seemed to be better Satisfied or Appeased ; And after they had Expressed their Inclinations to Peace with the English, I told them it would be their own fault, if they did not seek it, for the English were well Inclined to live in Peace with them upon their submission. And thereupon they desired that I would do what in me lay to prevail with the Honourable Comissioners then at Montreal, that there might be a Peace.

Afterwards I met with two Indians namely Richard Hegen & John Doane in their Wigwam. They told me they were glad to see me, made Enquiry after the Comissioners and asked several Questions about the War, and told me they were glad to hear the Comissioners were Come to Treat of Peace with the Indians ; I told them I did not understand, they were Come for that End, but to Treat with Governour Vaudreuil referring to his Assisting and Encouraging the Indians in the Management of the War against the English : But yet tho the Indians had made an Unjust War, the English upon their submission and Allegiance to King George were Inclinable upon Just and reasonable terms to Enter into an Alliance of Friendship; and that what the English had hitherto done was to defend themselves from the rage and Cruelty of the Indians : Whereupon one of the Indians viz Hegen said, for his part, he was always of the mind that the Indians began the War, & tho he had many relations killed by the English, yet he Could not blame them since they were killed after the War began ; and wished that some of the Sachems or Chief Men had been there & added that they were gone ahunting, & their return was speedily Expected,

& seemed Concerned that many of the Indians were gone out to War against the English.

One of the Indians said, that the Indians were told by Monsr Ramsie & Mr Laurone (who lately returned home from Boston) That the English said they would never be at Peace with the Indians, for that they Could afford to spare or loose one hundred English men to one Indian I told the Indians that there was no truth in that report And further I observed to the s^d two Indians That Govr Vaudreuil had signified his Inclination to Peace, and that he would send his son to Boston in order to bring it about, One of the Indians said he wished the Governor had been always of that mind. A French Man being present, took Notice to me, That (if he was rightly Informed) the English had wronged the Indians, & taken away their Lands very unjustly. But the Indians said that they were fighting for Land they should never get, but instead thereof the English daily gained ground; & very much lamented the poverty & distress they were brought into by the Calamitous War.

Afterwards I went to Trois river, or three Rivers so called to make Inquiry for English Captives, where one Capt. Chierdau gave me liberty to go & speak with the Indians. I met with Eight or nine Indian Women and two Indian men Coming from the Fort, who told me they were glad to see me; and after they had asked me my Business they told me their Sachem Called France Wex would be glad to see me, And Manifested great Inclinations to Peace with the English, and urged me by all means to go and see their Sachem, who knew me; But having the Governours Letter to Mr Peguncourt (the Lord of the palace as he was Called) I first went and delivered the Letter to him; And he having told me That I might Safely go and see the afores[d] Sachems (only he advised me first to go and pay a civil Complement to the Fryer who kept in the ffort) I accordingly went to the Fort, and sent word to the Fryer, That there was one Come from Boston in order to speak with the Indians for the Liberty of some English Captives, and that he had liberty from Governor Vaudreuil to talk with them; And presently after the Fryer came out to me in an Outragious Violent manner with Outstretched arms says with a loud Voice; What do's this Rogue do here and by what Authority came you here; I told him I came by Governor Vaudreuil's leave, & at the request of several Indians present; he Replied, As for Governour Vaudreuil he has nothing to do here, I am Comander & Chief of this Village; Neither he nor Mons[r] Peguncourt (from whom you Obtained liberty you say also to Come) have any thing to do here; and if I should take you and hang you up this Minute, theres no Body here would dare to say to me why do you so; And had I (said he) but three or four Men here, I would burn you in this place Alive. Be gone Imediately; You are one of them that Murdered our Father (meaning Mr Rallé) and I forbid you to say a word to the Indians; so I was going out from the Fort, but two Indian Men, & some Indian Women met me & told me their Sachem wanted very much to speak with me; I said to them that their Priest or Fryer forbid me to speak with them & threatened to kill me if I did. The Indians answered the Priest has nothing to do here, You are within our Fort, & we are Masters of it; so at their desire I went in to the Sachem; as I entered I saw an English Scalp purposely laid in the way for me to see. And the Sachem (who was blind) hearing me speak asked whether Sam: was there; I then said here I am; he told me he was glad to hear me speak, tho he could not see me; and said that if he had his sight, as he had when he once knew me I should not have had opportunity to come to the Fort, for said he I am a Man, meaning by that Expression (as I took it) that he would have killed me before then. After sundry Questions, he asked me whether I was come to make Peace; I told him we were not come to offer but to receive offers or terms of Peace & told him my Belief that the English would be willing to be at Peace with them, if they sought for it. To which the Sachem replied then you have Changed your mind lately. Immediately thereupon we were Interuped by the afores^d Furious Fryer who came in great Wrath, and spake to the Indians present after this manner "Children I wonder that you "have any thing to say to this Fellow, whom "we know is a Rogue & a Lyar, 'tis the nature "of the English to be lyars from their Cradle, "this is one of them that has killed our Father, "who was such a good Father as you all very well "know; Yea this is one of the Rogues that has done "it; under pretence of Peace at Norridgewalk they "murdered our good Father there; & he's now Come "under the like pretence to Murder you But (quoth "he) you have him in Your hands therefore do what you will with him (or in other words as I took his meaning) knock him in the Head. The English say you may have Peace if you desire it, but let the English beg for peace first, if they would have it, & upon such terms as you will please to give 'em; and let them send home the five Indian Captives they detain at Boston Then I took notice that one of them, had lately had liberty given him to go & visit his ffriends; the Fryer called me a Lyar before them

Appendix. 381

all: And that the truth of what I had said might be Credited by the Indians, I told them what I said relating to the said Indian was as true as that there was a God in Heaven. Then the ffryer in his Passion breaks out, here you see what he is now! As if he knew any thing about a God, a fellow of no Religion, who never Served any body but the Devil; and forbid me speaking any thing further And an Indian who had lost a Cousin in the War standing by, being prompted as I believe by the Fryer Accosted the Indians after this manner Our Father (i. e. the Fryer) is in the right I like his talk very well, he seems now to speak for us, & you may depend upon what he has said; And the Indians by these methods grew surly & Angry; And the Fryer in Indignation again told them I was a Lyar & there was no truth in me, or the Governm^t at Boston The old blind Sachem took hold of my hand, & by the Contenance of the Indians & their Actions there was too much reason to think they intended me Ill, and only wanted more help to put their design in Execution so I left them. And the Fryer at my Departure (which he Endeavoured to delay) told me that if he had but three or four men that he knew of he would either burn me or knock me on the head before I went from the ffort

The next day at the three Rivers some Indians came to my Lodgings, & desired me not to take much notice of what the Fryer had said the day before, for tho he talked so much, yet he was not wholly their Master. And after the Indians had Disclosed their thoughts (that they Believed the Fryer Intended that the Indians should have killed me) The s^d Indians said to me, you tell us we may have Peace if we desire it; we have wrote several

Letters to the Govr at Boston, & never had any answer to them. I told them I did not know of any that had been sent; They said they sent Letters by Messrs Ramsey & Laurow when they came last to Boston signifying their desires of Peace, and that the English refused to Answer them, and put the s^d Laurow & Ramsey into an old Barn & they suffered hunger not being able to bye Victuals for their Money. They further said, the English Declared that they did not want a Peace, for that they Could loose one hundred Men to the Indians one &c I told them that those two Gentlemen were well Treated, and that the Governm^t Expended very Considerably upon them, and that (as I understood) They only brought a Letter to the English Governor, from Governor Vaudreuil, which no ways tended to Peace; but on the Contrary it was reckoned a very Insulting Letter &c, and that they were asked if they had any thing further to offer than what was Contained in their Letter; and they Answered they had not &c A French Gent^n being present at the time when this talk happened between me & the Indians, Observed to me that the s^d Laurow & Ramsey had reported what the s^d Indians had declared to me; And they then said Govr Vaudreuil had not dealt fairly with but deceived them in this matter; And seing it is so (said the Oldest Indian to the rest) I advise you by all means to sue for Peace with the English, since you may Obtain it for asking for, strive for it, and make it your Business to get it; for otherwise instead of getting the Lands you Contend for, the English will kill you all, & much more to the same purpose And the Indians desired me to Intreat the Comissioners at Montreal to stay till some of their Indians could go there to treat with them Concerning a Peace; for that they discovered

More of the Inclinations of the English now than they had before

Further I declare That upon Discourse with the Indians, I understood that they lost several Indians many times when they Attacked our Forces on the Frontiers, & at their Garrisons. And a French Man who lived among them told me, that there was Sixty Indians to his knowledge killed at Norridgewalk; & he believes by the Information received from the Indians they lost near One hundred Indians at that time.

Sam^{el} Jordan.

In Council May 28th 1725 Read.
A true Copy
℔ J Willard Secry.

The above written Samuel Jordan has been sworn as Indian Interpreter to this Governm^t.
J Willard Secry.

[*Paper 27.*]

DANIEL GOOLD'S TESTIMONY.

June the 26th 1725

Daniel Goold of full age Testifyeth & Declareth That he being Master of the Schooner Mary belonging to Marblehead on a ffishing voyage near a place called ffox Island neer Penobscot on the 22th day of June 1724. A number of Indians with one Frenchman who s^d his name was Castein came on board s^d Schooner in Canowes in an hostile manner and Captivated the Deponent & all his Company & killed one of his men & shot & wounded three more, of which said Company they carried four into Penobscot & from thence three of them to Quebeck where the French there received the Indians with manifestations of Great Joy, feasting them two days together.

Also this Deponent Testifyes & saith that he saw the s^d Indians divide a barrel of powder with proportionate ball and flints amongst them which they said was to furnish them to goe against the English.

This Deponent farther declares that he was Informed by an English prisoner at Canada that the Indians burnt at Penobscot an English Captive because he did not doe as they would have him when they went against George's Fort & farther this Deponent saith not.

Daniel Goold.

Jurat & Capt. coram
Nathl Nordon } Just^l Pac^e.
Benj^a Lynde

Essex Marblehead June 26th 1725.

[*Paper 28.*]

Testimony of Samuel Harris.

SAMUEL HARRIS of full age testifieth & Declareth that he being on a ffishing voyage in a Schooner called the Sea-flower Joseph Wallis Master at or near a place called ffox Islands neer Penobscott on the 22th day of June 1724. A number of Indians with two Frenchmen one of which said his name was

Appendix. 385

Castein came on board s^d Schooner in Canowes and in an hostile manner did then & there Kill on board our vessel & other vessels in company with us twenty-two men, & Captivated twenty three (of whom eighteen were wounded) and so we were all carried to Penobscott. And after Eight of us were carried from thence to Quebeck. Where the French received the Indians wth manifestacons of great Joy feasting them for several dayes together.

This Deponent further declares that he was told by the French, & by the Indian Enemy at Canada, That the Indians had burnt an English Captive at Penobscott.

And farther this Deponent saith not.

         The mark of
         Samuel O Harris.

Jurat & Capt. Coram
   Benj^a Lynde } Justⁱⁱ Pac^s.
   John Turner }

Essex ℔ Salem June 28th 1725.

[*Paper 29.*]

DECLARATION OF THE COMMISS^{RS} TO CANADA TO THE GOVERNM^T OF NEW YORK.

WEE the Subscribers having been at Canada on an Errand from the Governments of the Massachusetts Bay and New Hampshire concerning the unjust War the Abernaques or Eastern Indians have with the aforesaid Governments and the Governour of Canada his Asisting and Abetting them therein think proper to Acquaint the Commissioners of the Indian Affairs in Albany and by them the Government of York of Some Transactions in the ffrench Country which may be worthy of Observation.

After we had delivered our Message Monsr Vaudreuill the Governour of Canada told us that our Errand was not as he had Received one from the Government of New York to pray him to Restrain those Indians from Meddling with that Province which he had done upon their Earnest request whereas our Demand was not of that Nature.

MONS^R VAUDREUILL was very angry that the Government of New York should pretend to build any Block-house or ffortification on or near the River Onontaga and told us that he Should look on Such a proceeding as a violation of the Peace made at UTRECHT and would Certainly Demolish any Such Building. And Accordingly at this very Juncture Monsr Longuile who is the Second man in the Government of Canada is gone up into the Onontaga & Senecas country with a Considerable Detachment of French Souldiers his business we do not pretend to Say but we are very apt to think that Such officers and Men's being in that Country can in no wise tend to the Continuing those five Nations in their Allegiance & Dependance on his Majesty King George.

Monsr Vaudreuill told us ffrankly and plainly that he could at any time sett the ffive Nations of Iroquois (Expressly Excepted in the Treaty of Utrecht as Depending on the British Dominion) on the English and Cause them to Kill & Captivate the Subjects of the King.

MONS^R VAUDREUILL has by himself or others So far Instigated the Abenaques to make demands on the Government of the Massachusetts of Thirty Leagues on the Sea Coast all within the Grant of that Province from the Crown of Great Britain and in which has been settled Severall Towns and many hundred Inhabitants and fforts built by Order from home and Some of it possessed upwards of ffour Score years altho the Same has been fairly purchased & possessed as aforesaid.

And our asking those Indians how far their Demands were Eastward their Answer was in the presence of Governour Vaudreuill the whole Country of Lacadie or Nova Scotia Excepting only the ffort of Annapolis Royall notwithstanding the said Country of Lacadie belongs to the British Crown And these unreasonable Indians were countenanced by the said Governour and a numerous Company of ffrench who heard all the Discourse.

The said Indians told us plainly they would have no peace with the said Two Governments unless all the said Land was delivered up the ffort demolished the Church at Norridgewalk rebuilt the plunder there taken returned and their Priest Restored to them who was killed in that action at the head of our Indian Enemy as he had often been before.

We demanded an Answer to our proposal made to the Governour of Canada in writing to prevent any mistake he answered he would not give any Such under his hand tho' at the Same time he said he had not Encouraged the Indians in the War notwithstanding the Contrary was proved by many Letters to the Priest Rallé and other papers and Letters taken by the English at several times.

The Said Governour on our Demand of the Captive answered as for those in the Indians hands he would do nothing As for those in the French hands we should have them paying what they Cost And we could not have them without purchasing of them at

any price their Masters were pleased to Demand And the purchase consideration in many Exceedingly Advanced from the Original or ffirst Cost. By all which it plainly appears what Abuses hardships and intollerable burthen His Majestys Good Subjects lye under being used more like brute Creatures than Men and Christians and calls aloud upon all Men under the Same King to Lend a helping hand to get the aforesaid Governments out of this unjust War.
Sam^{ll} Thaxter
Wm Dudley.

Copy Examined
₧ J Willard Secry.

[*Paper 30.*]

Commissioners Demand of the Governor of Canada.

Your Lordship is sensible of our Errand by the Commission We have delivered to you which Directs us to Demand all the British Subjects which have been taken by the Indians in this present War which they have unjustly made with us And which Prisoners are now Detained in your Lordships Governm^t or any part thereof The Delivery of whom tends to Cultivate the good Harmony and perfect Agreement that there is between the two Princes our Masters and which ought to be followed and put in practice by the Subjects of both Sides.

Your Lordships Government is Large in Extent and no doubt but that there is many Tribes of Indians contained in its Limits And under your

Authority therefore we do Demand all the prisoners that are the British Subjects that are in Such Indians hands that have been taken within this three years past.

We are in the next place to insist on your Lordships with drawing any countenance Aid or Assistance to the Indians that have unjustly entered into this present War And to ffortifie our Demand in this point Your Lordship must remember the great and good Harmomy and Union there is between the Two Crowns and how the Subjects of Each are to live in Peace and Quiet therefore for any Governour to Set on and Instigate any of his princes Subjects to Molest the Subjects of the other Prince is an open Violation of that Quiet And the Peace concluded at Utrecht now that your Lordship has thus done or permitted to be done by the Several Tribes of Indians that do Actually Reside within the Limits of your Government is Notorious. Witness the many poor prisoners and Scalps of Innocent People those Indians now have.

We are further to prove that the Aiding and Assisting and Exciting or Suffering any of the ffrench Kings Subjects to be Aiding Assisting or Abetting the Eastern Indians in their Crueltys and barbarities on King GEORGES Subjects is an open and manifest breach of the good Agreement there is Established between the two Nations now that this has been done by your Lordships Order and direction We do prove by His Letters to our Governour by the Intendants Letter And by Several Letters of the Priest Rallé and which cannot be denyed.

Those Eastern Indians certainly Dwell either in the King of Great Britains Dominions or the Territories of the ffrench King. If in the ffrench Kings

Dominions the Violation of the Peace is very fflagrant they then being his Subjects as his Lordship is pleased to Term them in his Letter of the 29th of Octo 1724, and by a Clause in his Lordships Letter to Monsr Rallé. But and if those Indians have been and now are the Subjects of the Crown of Great Britain and will Reside in his Territories then much more is it a Breach of the Happy Peace to Excite a Rebellion and Mischief amongst his Majesty of Great Britains Subjects. And that those Indians have Submitted witness the many Treatys they have Entered into as that of 1693: 1713: 1717 And many others. And to Evince this Article of their being under the Government of the Crown of Great Britain the 12 Article in the Peace Concluded at Utrecht is most plain the Boundaries of Laccadie being well known to Extend to the English Dominions. And it is Expressly Contrary for any of the ffrench Kings Subjects to have to do with any Lands Islands ffishing or other Matter in those parts. By all which it appears that those Indians cannot be Subjects to his most Christian Majesty Altho' Monsr Vaudreuill is pleased to Term them so in his Letter of the 29th Octo^r 1724. Neither can they be any otherwise Allies or Friends to the ffrench than the other British Subjects are And altho' the Governments have not yet Exceeded their Limits in the Pursuit of these Indians if they dont come to their right minds and Submission we cannot be responsible for any mischiefs that may happen even to the ffrench Kings Subjects if they Reside with, Abett or are found Stiring up the Indians in their unjust proceeding. And we must remark to his Lordship That some of the ffrench Kings Subjects have been at the head of the Indians in their Acts of Hostilety, Wit-

Appendix. 391

ness Mons' Rallés Lett' and by the last Clause in Mons' Begons Letter to the s^d Priest Rallé.
Signed by
SAMUELL THAXTER
Wm DUDLEY.

Copy Examined
℔ J Willard Secry.

[*Paper 31.*]

FRENCH RECEIPTS OF MONEY FOR YE RANSOM OF ENGLISH PRISONERS 1725.

PARDENANT Le No^{re} Royal de l' Isle de Montreal En la Nouvelle France Resident a Villemarie soussigné fut present Joseph Hertel Escuye de present en Cette Ville Lequel a Reconnu Et Confesse auoir Receu Comptant Du Sr Jean delalande Interprette Anglois pour Le Roy ence payes La Somme de deux Cent Liures Monneye de ffrance, que Luy a Eté presentement Comptes Et rcellement Deliureć par La Sr Delalande En Escus Blancs Et autre Bonne Monnoye, au veu Dud No^{re} et Tesmoins, Et ce pour La Rançon de Daniel Goolde Anglois de la Contreé de Maruelet Enla Nouuelle Angleterre qui a Ete presentem^t Remis en mains dud Sr Dela lande par led Sr Hertel Droit &c quittant &c fait et passé Villemarie Etude dud No^{re} Lan Mil Sept Cent Vingt Cinq Le Vingt Neuf Auril Auant Midy En presence des sus

Carle Bonnier Et Nicholas Bourdet Temoine qui ont avec Lesd Hertel, delalande Et nous signe apres Lecture Faite Sur^t Lord^re.

    Jean de La Land Hertel
    Charles Bonnier Nicholas Bourdet

          D<small>AUID</small>
          No^re Royal.

Copy Examined
  ℞ J Willard Secry.

P<small>ARDENANT</small> Le No^re Royal De La Jurisdiction Royalle de Montreal En la Nouuelle france Rendent a Villemarie soussigneé fut present Sr Jean Madelaine dit La Loureur habitant Demeurant a la parroisse de la pointe Claire en Cette Isle de present en cette Ville Lequel a Reconnu Et Confesse auour Receu comptant par Mains de Sr Jean de la Lande Interprette en Langue Anglois pour le Roy en ce payee La Somme de Trois Cent Liures de France, La quelle Somme Luy a Eté presentement Comptee Et Reellement deliureé par le d Sr Delalande au veu dud No^re Et Temoines En-Louis dor de Vingt Liures pices-droit &c. quittant &c. Et ce pour La Rauçon de Nommé

Anglois de Nation du Village de   Lequel Anglois a Ete Remis en Mains dud Sr Delalande auueu &c. fait Et passé And Villemarie Etude du No^re Lan Mil Sept Cent Vingt Cinq Le douzieme jour d'auril apres Midy En presence des Sr Joseph Raimbault et Claude Maurice Temoins Demeurant Aud Villemarie qui ont auec Led Sr Delalande Et

No^re Signé, Led Madelaine ayant Declaré Ne Le Scavoir dud Interpellé apres Lecture faite Suivant Lordonnance.
     Jean De la lande
      Raimbaule.
 Claude Maurice.
       DAUID
       No^re Royal.
Copy Examined ℗ J Willard Secy.

L^T GOVERNOUR DUMMER TO THE LORDS COMMISSIONERS FOR TRADE AND PLANTATIONS.

      Boston 31st March 1725.
MY LORDS

Some few Months after the Departure of His Excellency Govern^r Shute for Great Britain I did my Self the Honour to Write to your LORDSHIPS giving you some account of the Difficulties of this Province with respect to the Indian War, which has been excited by the Governour of Canada, who has Supplied the Salvages with all Stores of War, has Shelter'd them within His Government from our Pursuits & has Reciev'd them in Triumph with the Scalps of His Majestys Subjects Slain by this Barbarous Enemy: which Conduct of the Said French Governour (as I Suggested to Your Lordships in my former Letter) Seems to Me to be a Notorious Violation of the Treaty of UTRECHT and in Some Respects makes the War with the Indians more Difficult than if the French were our Declared Enemies; For by our Successes in the last Eight Months We have driven them from their own

[marginal note: The Govr of Canada supplies the Salvage Enemies wth stores of War protects them receives them in triumph with the Scalps of the English which has prevented his Majestys Subjects good successes over them.]

Settlements in our Neighbourhood to the French Territories from whence they make their Incursions upon us, in Small Skulking Parties and after Mischief done retire thither again, where I am Cautious of Allowing any of our Companies to pursue them, till I can know his Majestys Pleasure in this Respect. And I must further inform Your Lordships That Notwithstanding the Advantages we have lately had over the Enemy and the Distress'd Circumstances We Suppose they are reduced to, the Expense of the War is so Great and Insupportable to this Province that unless it shall please God to put a Speedy End to it, It will Inevitably Ruin Us; Which I humbly offer to Your Lordships Consideration to make such a Representation thereof to His Majesty as You shall think Necessary for his Majestys Service and the Safety & Protection of these his Provinces.

<small>The Expense of the War is insupportable.</small>

I should not Trouble Your Lordships any further, but that the French Governour of Canada has given me to Understand that he shall Address to his Master on the Account of the Death of the Priest who was killed by our Forces in the Fight at Norridgewock of which please to take the following Account.

<small>The ffrench Govr intends to Complain of a Priest being killed in Fight.</small>

<small>An accot how it happened.</small>

In the Action at Norridgewock within this Province which was in August last, our Forces destroyed a Great Number of the Indians and broke up that Settlement among whom was Sebastian Rallé a Jesuit Missionary to that Tribe and the Great Incendiary of this War who was Slain in Fight making actual Resistance to the Forces, at the Same time Attempting to kill an English Captive in his Hands and Refusing to give or take Quarter, To which Account of the Death of the Said Rallé Colº Harman the Com-

mander of the Forces at Norridgewock made Solemn Oath before me in Council, As Appears to your Lordships by the Minutes of Council Transmitted to you by the Secretary of the province. This Jesuit had all along push'd the Indians upon their Rebellion And Marching at the head of Two hundred Armed Salvage through one of the Frontier Towns of this Province before the War was Declared threatned Destruction to them if they did not Speedily Quit the Said Town, of which and more to this purpose His Excellency Govr Shute is well knowing; This I thought proper to hint to Your Lordships in order to Obviate any Complaints that may be made by the French Govern^r whose Conduct in Exciting and Supporting the Indians in this War and drawing down many Remote Tribes with whom We have no Concern, to their Assistance (the Truth of which I have sufficient Testimonies to Support & shall lay them before your Lordships if it be necessary for your Satisfaction) Should rather have put him upon offering an Apology than a Complaint. All which I humbly Submit to Your Lordships And am
   With the Greatest Respect
    Your Lordships
     Most obedient & Most humble
     Servant
      W<small>M</small>. D<small>UMMER</small>.

Recd May yr 7th 1725.
Read Ditto 13th.

LIEUTᵀ GOVᴿ DUMMER TO THE LORD'S COMMISSᴿˢ FOR
TRADE AND PLANTATIONS.

Boston 22d Augᵗ 1726.
My Lords
  Having done myself the honour last Winter of acquainting Your Lordships of the Peace then made with the Delegates of the Eastern Indians which was to be ratify'd in the Spring following by all the Principall men of the Tribes. I am now to acquaint You that after some Delays Occasioned partly by the Severity of the last Winter, in which it was very difficult for the Indians to pass & repass from one Tribe to another the ratification was accomplished at Falmouth in Casco Bay the Sixth of August A Copy whereof & of the Severall Conferences had thereon I now Inclose Your Lordships. The Indians appear to me to be in a very good Disposition at present to perform their Engagements, & it shall be my Care while I have the Honour to receive His Majestys Commands here by all proper means to Cultivate that Disposition in them & the General Court of this Province having granted a Sum of money to be Imployed in Trade with them whereby they will be Constantly supply'd at Easy rates with Every thing they need, I am in hopes they may in a short time be intirely drawne from their dependance on the French & especially if His Majesty shall be pleased of his royal bounty to order a small annuall present to be made them by the Governour of this Province as He has graciously done for the Westerne Indians under the Direction of the Governour of New York which seems the more Needfull here because the Governours of Canada have practised it with these

Indians, which I humbly Submit to Your Lordships Consideration.

There is nothing else of any Consequence to Trouble Your Lordships with but what you will have in the Copys of the Transactions of the Councill & Generall Assembly. Your Lordships will receive with this a printed Copy of the Tryal & Condemnation of diverse pirates lately surprised and brought into these parts, & is all at present from Your Lordship's

Most Obedient
& Most humble
Servant
WM. DUMMER.

Recd Octr 11 } 1726
Read June 8 } 1727.

REV. JOSEPH BAXTER TO PÈRE SEBASTIAN RALÉ.

(For translation, see p. 145.)

Reverende Domine:

Epistolam tuam accepi in Quâ dicis, Mirum fortasse mihi videbitur quòd has ad me miseris Literas, nunc *sincerè* dico Tibi quòd si tibi placeat Amicum commercium mecum habere, Pergratum mihi erit, et Literas ultro citròque Libenter Transmittamus: sed miror equidem quòd Tu (Qui ab aliquibus hominibus existimaris virum eximiae Pietatis & Sanctitatis) Tantâ Iracundiâ scribis, et sine ullâ provocatione ac sine ullâ causâ me accusas Reum esse fraudulentiæ et asseris Te cognoscere, & alios etiam scire me reum esse, & tamen non ostendis mihi & itaque manifestè patet quod non potes ostendere in quo sum dolosus, et nonne mirandum est quod studes me exanimare à Laborando pro beneficio Animarum Immortalium. Quid si opus sit maxime Laboriosum, & Perdifficile, nonne operæ pretium est Perdifficile, et Laboriosissimum opus perficere ut suadeamus homines ad Christum effugere, et in via sanctitatis ambulare & sic accipere vitam æternam: Et Quid si non sunt inter nos magnificentia ornatus, & decoratio Templorum, et nitor, splendor, ac Pulchritudo vestium sacerdotalium attrahere silvestres? neque fuerunt haec in tempore Apostolorum Attrahere Istos Homines ad Quos missi fuerunt Apostoli, et Tamen suaserunt multos credere in Christum, & vitam æternam accipere et nunc plane dicitur Evangelium vel verbum Dei esse Dei Potentiam ad salutem. Rom: 1.16. et Deo Placet homines salvare Insipientiâ Prædicationis. 1 Cor: 1. 21. et quamvis hoc est opus perdifficile perfici apud silvestres tamen Amor Christi et Animarum nos compellit. Quamvis non expectamus merere salutem hoc opus perficiendo: sed Postquam omnia perfecimus quae perficere possumus Inutiles servi sumus. Luc: 17. 10. et totaliter confidimus in meritis Christi, tamen ubi est Amor Christi, ibi est desiderium amplificandi Regnum Christi, et istud Desiderium movet homines Perdifficile & Laboriosissimum opus perficere in suadendo et adducendo homines in Regnum Christi, et Itaque Argumenta Tua Puerilia & Ridiculosa sunt. Tu ais quod cupis respondere pro silvestribus: sed non opus est Tibi istum Laborem accipere. Ego laborabo, ut opportunitatem habebo eos adducere in rectam viam salutis, et dare iis satisfactionem in omnibus. Si ulla spes sit quod pro tuo beneficio erit, qui debes credere & agere, et ambulare secundum verbum Dei Quod Perfecta est Regula Doctrinæ & morum, Libenter Respondebo Tuis Argumentis: sed Tuus nuncius dicit quod cràs festinabit ad te et Itaque nunc opportunitatem non habeo Respondere ad tuam Prolixam Epistolam, valeto Domine.

Reverendo Domino,
Sebastiano Ralé in oppido Nanrantsouak Dicto.

Rev. Joseph Baxter to Père Sebastian Ralé.
(For translation see p. 147.)

Reverende Domine:

Delectaris Procùl dubio Reprehendendo Ideoque ea culpas Quae non sunt Reprehensione digna et in culpando Tuipse crimina admittis. Dicis enim mihi *Tu Anglicè Loqueris utendo verbis Latinis.* In his verbis Domine Tibi ipsi contradicis si Quis enim verbis Latinis utitur, Quamvis non Rhetoricè tamen Latine & non Anglicè Loquitur. Quisquis Anglicè Loquitur verbis Anglicanis utitur. Quid si sincerè sonat Anglicè est verè Latinum.

Dicis *Amicum est substantium nec potest esse Adjectivum* sed non Recte dicis certissime datur Tale Adjectivum Apud Latinos. Amicus Animus est Latina Locutio & vale Lumen Amicum & Humor Pratis Amicus &c.

Ais *Commercium in Hoc est Barbarum Quid*, sed Quis Tuae Dictioni credet absque Probatione. Ipse dixit non valet.

De multis Aliis etiam dicis *non sunt Latina sed Barbara.* At non valet Authoritas Tua certissime Talia verba saepe Inter Latinos Adhibentur.

Dicis *merere est sollescismus. Illud verbum est Deponens, non Activum scribe mereri.* Sed Aiunt Docti Datur mereo merere æque ac mereor mereri.

Merere culpam in infinitivo est Latina Locutio, et merere salutem, &c.

Dicis *mola est Lapis non ædificium:* sed docti aiunt Mola est ædificium Lapis Qui ponitur in molâ, Lapis Molaris est.

Dicis *Domus Habet in Accusativo Plurali Domos non Domus*, sed Quare non habet Domos & Domus.

Multa Alia etiam reprehendis Quae non sunt vituperanda, et si Te Imitarer Possem dicere Tu minister! Tu è societate Iesus et Haec non Intelligis. Dicis verba mea *non sunt Intelligibilia.* Quare non intelligis verba quae saepe Apud Latinos adhibentur: sed exemplum Christi Iesu sequi malo, Qui Conviciis Affectus non vicissim convitiabatur; Quum malis Afficeretur, non minabatur &c., 1 Pet. 2.23. Et Isti Monitioni vel Mandato Auscultabo in Prov. 26.4 Ne Responde stulto secundum stultitiam ejus ne adæqueris ei Tu quoque.

Manifèste patet Te Reprehendere multa Quae non sunt culpanda Tamen concedo errata sunt in scriptione meâ Quam Præpropère scribebam, viz.: existimaris virum pro vir, & movent pro movet &c.

Et in Tuis scriptionibus equidèm multa sunt errata (Quamvis fuisti (ut inquis) Professor Rhetoricæ & Linguæ Græcæ in urbe nemansensi). Ego nunquam fui Professor Rhetoricæ et Tamen errata video. Quot errata tum Posset criticus & vir Perdoctus reperire in Epistolis tuis. Immo in epistola Quam Gloriosissimè scribebas Falsissime me Accusabas dicendo *Tu Te Iactitas Apud Silvestres Te apprime scire Linguam Latinam* nunquam enim Iactavi Inter silvestres non unum verbum Locutus cum silvestribus de Lingua Latina sed Tu maxime Iactabas in secunda Epistolâ & Tamen in eâ scribebas *intelligit & Accurate scribit Latina.* In hac Dictione

Appendix.

Quidem Tu non accurate scribis Latine Nam accusativus casus sequitur verbum scribit. Scripsisse Te oportuit *accurate scribit Linguam Latinam*, vel *accurate scribit Latine*.

Tu etiam scribebas *ut emendatur in scolis* Scolus est mons in Bœotia et oppidum in Macedonia scribere debebas in scholis.

Scribebas etiam *substantium & Adjectium*. At non dantur Talia verba Latina. Scripsisse debuisti *substantivum & Adjectivum*.

Scribebas *nec fideliter citas Locum Pauli dicit Paul virtus enim Dei est in salutem omni credendi*. Si Te imitarer Possem dicere Quid vis Per Haec verba *omni credendi?* Quid significant? non intelligibilia sunt scripseris Potentia siquidem est Dei ad salutem cuivis credenti.

Scribebas *merere est sollescismus*. Quid intendis Per hoc verbum? non datur Tale verbum inter Doctos. Illi scribunt solœcismus. Tuus sollescismus est veró solœcismus.

De multis aliis Loqui Possem & exclamare Tua verba Barbara sunt & non intelligibilia &c. sed Quid valent Tales exclamationes? Te non imitabor video Te Iracundia commoveri & Te Irritare nolim, sed in verbis Apostoli Hortor, Eph: 4. 26–27 sol ne occidat super Exacerbatione tua neque Dato Locum Diabolo, & in ver. 31 omnis Amaritudo & Excandescentia & Ira & Clamor & Maledicentia Tollatur a Te cum omni malitia. Quia scriptum est in Tit. 1. 7. Oportet enim Episcopum Inculpatum esse tanquam Dei Dispensatorem non sibi pertinaciter Placentem non Iracundum &c. et scribitur in Eccles. 7. 9. ne perturbate spiritu tuo Indigneris nam Indignatio in sinu stolidorum conquiescit.

Dicis *Rectène deducitur Haec consequentia Tua? non indicavi Tibi ergo non possum indicare in Quo Dolosus sis.* Respondeo.

Immo Recté deducitur haec consequentia & hoc modo probatur. Si Id ostendere poteras certissime Indicaveris Quia maximé mihi irascebaris & valde optabas ostendere me in crimine fuisse.

Hoc Tibi sumpsisti, viz: Indicare me Dolosum esse hoc modo. 1mo Inquis *manifeste Probavi & Luce clarius ostendi vos non habere nec sequi normam Religionis & nullus inter vos potest probe Respondere Argumentis hoc Procantibus ergo intendens diversam fidei Regulam suadere silvestribus, Tu Infidus Reus fieres Animarum eorum et hoc intendis ut Profundius immergaris in orcum.* Respondeo.

Hoc non probasti nec potest ullus vestrum probare. Quoties Responderunt Reformatæ Religionis Professores ad omnia vestra Argumenta et indicarunt ea vacua esse. Et non Infidus eram Quia omnia mea Documenta consentanea fuerunt sacris scripturis Quae nil docent nisi Rectum nisi verum.

2° *Dicunt silvestres summopere optat Anglus docere ut possit natos nostros Literas & Prætextu Literarum sensim sine sensu Ipsis suadere ut suam quam vocat Religionem, aliquando omnes facti viri Anglicam amplectentur fidem & sic fide & amicitiâ conjuncti, nullum amplius Inter eos exoriatur Bellum, &c.,* si ita dicunt silvestres Primo (ut opinor) Hæc iis dictabas. Nunquam Audivi silvestres Hoc modo loqui At Aliter Locuti sunt nonnulli eorum sed Quisquis ita dicit Tantum Id supponit et suppositio vel Imaginatio Absurda non probat Rem.

Dicis *Intelligo Te nescire argumentari in formâ.* Sed quomodo Hoc intelligis? Posteà dicis *Responsiones vestræ ad Argumenta Theologica sunt circum-*

locutiones &c. Sed Quomodo hoc cognoscis? nunquam vidisti (ut opinor) meas Responsiones ad ulla Argumenta Theologica non respondebam talibus Argumentis in Epistolâ Quam ad Te misi et Quia non respondebam Haec consequentia deducere videris, viz: non possum respondere alicui Argumento in formâ. At non Recte deducitur Haec consequentia.

Argumenta de Quibus Locutus sum in Præludio Prolixæ Epistolæ continentur ubi dicitur *Quinquaginta ab hinc Annis iverant nonnuli ex silvestribus Emptionis causa in urbem Quebec cum autem vidissent Templa eorumque ornatus nec non sacerdotes sacerdotalibus indutos sacra facientes tum alios magnifice indutos ipsis ministrantes tum ceremonias ab Illis actos &c. His ita moti sunt ut in admirationem raperentur &c. Apud vos autem non moverentur silvestres Templorum magnificentia ornatu aut decoratione, &c.*

Haec non sunt Argumenta Theologica, Tantum Argumenta ad homines. Et Profecto ea de Quibus Loqueris Pueris Placita sunt Potius quam viris. Et in Istis verbis non argumentaris in forma.

Magnopere gloriaris dicendo *In decursu autem Epistolæ multa sunt Argumenta spinosa, Pungentia &c. Dico, & sustineo Te neque ullum vestrum posse ea solvere.* Sed nonne scriptum est in Prov. 27.2 Laudet Te os extranei non autem Os Tuum, Alieni non autem Labia Tua & in 1 Reg: 20.11 ne Jactet se qui accingit se ut Qui discingit. Multi sunt nostrum Qui respondere possunt Tuis Argumentis in formâ & indicare ea inania & vacua esse. Sed intelligo Te repletum esse Iracundiâ. Quamvis dicis Te iracùnde Loqui non Reperiam Tamen Te Iracùnde Loqui & Excandescentia scribere reperi non tantum in Epistolis Quas mihi misisti: sed etiam in

Epistolâ Quam ad Gubernatorem nostrum scripsisti & dicitur in Prov: 22.24 ne colas Amicitiam cum Iracundo & in Prov: 29.20 vidisti virum Præcipitem verbis suis Expectatio est de stolido melior quam de Illo. Cum omnis Amaritudo & Excandescentia & Ira a Te sublata fuerit & cum Lenitate receperis Insitum Sermonem Qui possit servare Animas ad Tua Argumenta Respondebo.

Vale Domine
Tuus sum
J. Baxter.

INDEX.

Abagadasset Point, 318.
Abagahamak, 327.
Abnaki Language, studied by Rale, 36.
Abnaki Mission, Ralé at, 36, 37; Ralé in charge of, 38; mentioned, 17.
Abnakis, the, zealous converts, 141, 142; prefer to trade at Quebec, 142; tie which binds them to the English, 142–143; complained because hostages were held in Boston after paying for damages done, 158, 159, 160; the English refused to sell food and ammunition to, 160–161; Castine a commander-general of, 161; killed three ministers, 173; mentioned, 111, 112, 115, 116, 117, 118, 128, 135, 164, 165, 166, 168, 170, 175, 183, 184, 185, 203, 300, 307, 328, 334, 335, 341, 342, 345, 385.
Abomazen, 285, 322.

Abraham, 327.
Acadia, 29, 33, 64, 80, 126, 135, 136, 155, 156, 167, 215, 277, 278, 304, 335, 373, 387.
Acadia, see Taschereau.
Acadia, History of, see Tibierge.
Acts, Memoires, etc., Concernant La Paix d' Utrecht, cited, 155.
Adams, Rev. Hugh, cured Ralé of the gout and rheumatism, 66, 67, 118; became friendly towards the " Blackrobe," 67; predicted the overthrow of Ralé, 118, 119, *n*.; biographical notice of, 118.
Albany, to be attacked from Canada, 15, 17; expedition from, to Montreal, 22; mentioned, 124, 327, 328, 330, 331, 348, 350, 353, 375, 386.
Alexander, Ja., 356, 357, 358.
Algonquins, the, 97, 108, 183, 184.

Index

Algonquin Tongue, studied by Ralé, 38.
Allen, Ebenezer, 292.
Amalingans, the, 206, 207, 211, 212, 213, 214.
Andros, Sir Edmund, held a conference with the Indians at Pemaquid, 13; robbed Castine's trading house, 13–14; unsuccessful in conciliatory measures, 14; released Indian prisoners, 14, 19.
Andros Tracts, cited, 14.
Androscoggin, Indians from, at Casco conference, 44.
Androscoggin River, 242.
Anmoukangan River, 113.
Annales de la Propagation de la foi, Les, 267.
Annapolis Royal, 387.
Anne Queen, 366, 372.
Apparitions, believed in by Ralé, 89, 90.
Appleton, John, 58.
Appleton, Samuel, 58.
Argal, Samuel, broke up the mission at St. Saveur, 10; took Biard and Massé prisoners, 11.
Arrows, 198.
Arrowsic, Indians with French leaders appear at the conference at, 110; letter delivered at, 111–118; Adams at, 118; Indians failed to come to a conference appointed at, 159; conference at, 216; mentioned, 66, 68, 84, 96, 102, 128, 129, 279, 305, 307, 308, 320, 367, 368.
Ashley, Capt., 333.
Atwater, Mehitabel, 53.
Aubrey, Father, 95.
Avignon, 10.
Azcoytia, 7.

Bagaduce, 243.
Bancroft, George, History of the United States, cited, 44, 54.
Bane, Lewis, Deposition of, 279; mentioned, 281; Deposition of, cited, 91.
Bangor, formerly Kenduskeag, 10; mission to be established at, 10.
Baxter, Rev. Joseph, at Arrowsic conference, 69, 71, 80; a missionary among the Indians, 71; letter from Ralé to, 77, 85; replied to Ralé, 85–86; a temporary visitor to the Kennebec, 86; his

Index. 407

knowledge of Latin compared with Ralé's, 87; a man of a well-trained mind, 87; preached at Georgetown, 89; reported that Ralé predicted the speedy end of the world, 89–90; Ralé's sneer at, 103–104; letters to Ralé, 145–147, 147–153, 397, 399; mentioned, 218; biographical notice of, 71; Journal of, cited, 80, 89, 90.

Bayberry, wax obtained from the, 137, 138.

Bayeux, 31.

Bean, Joseph, 282, 292.

Bear, Indian legend concerning the, 190.

Beaudoin, Michael, king displeased with, 33; praised, 34.

Becancourians, the, 253.

Becancourt, 109, 111.

Begon, Michel, instructed by the king to prevent traffic between the English and Indians, 93; letter to Ralé, 294–297; mentioned, 65, 110, 121, 162, 275, 304, 369, 390; letter of, cited, 95, 105, 107, 113, 151.

Belcher, Andrew, 58, 69.

Belknap, Jeremy, History of New Hampshire, cited, 18.

Bell Isle, 307.

Bellamont, Richard Coote, Earl of, 42, 57, 366.

Berwick, 317.

Besancour, 295, 297.

Biard, Pierre, first of the Jesuits to visit this continent, 10–11; taken prisoner by Argal, 11; mentioned, 12; biographical notice of, 10.

Bibles, Wiwurna wants none of the English, 77.

Bigot, Brothers, the, influenced the Indians to attack the English, 16; had a mission on the Chaudière, 17; mentioned, 36.

Bigot, Père James, his mission joined in the descent upon York, 25; conspicuous in inciting the savages against the English, 28; a blind leader of the blind, 31; biographical notice of, 17.

Bigot, Vincent, biographical notice of, 17.

"Blackrobes," 7.

Bled de Turquie, 141, 180.
Board of Trade Papers, cited, 107.
Bollan, William, Importance and Advantage of Cape Breton, cited, 155.
Bomazeen, at Casco, conference, 44; reported that the French were trying to break the friendly relations between the Indians and English, 46; killed, 238, 262; mentioned, 68.
Bonnaventure, Sieur de, 29.
Bonnier, Carle, 392.
Boston, governor and garrison of Port Royal brought to, 22; expedition to Quebec sailed from, 22; plan formulated to capture, 40; Indian parties about, 41; envoy sent to, to declare peace, 54, 56; resolution to bring Ralé a prisoner to, 92; English families to be sent to Panaowamské from, 94; Ralé's letter read by the magistrates of, 104; Indians held as hostages in, 110, *n.*, 112, *n.*, 113, *n.*, 156, 157, *n.*, 158, 160, 319, 375, 376, 377; Indians that killed cattle retained at, 117–118; indignation at, concerning the Indians threatening letter, 119; Castine a prisoner at, 119, 165–166; Ralé's scalp exhibited in, 273; Indian captive died in, 321; mentioned, 55, 105, 116, 153, 222, 256, 263, 278, 331, 332, 333, 349, 378, 379, 381, 382.
Boudoin, Père Michael, refused absolution to murderers, 32, 33, *n.*; founded a mission among the Choctaws, 33.
Boundaries, undetermined, 44.
Boundary between the English and French possessions, 371, 372, 373, 374, 387.
Bourbourg, Brasseur de, Histoire du Canada, 267.
Bourdet, Nicholas, 392.
Bradstreet, Gov. Simon, 22.
Braintree, 118.
Brandy, trade of, in Canada, 101–102.
Brantry, 71, 72.

Brasaway, 321.
Brookfield, 317.
Brown's Farm, 319.
Brunswick, 90, 101, 128, 129.
Brunswick Historical Magazine, cited, 244.
Burnett, Gov. William, 347, 355, 356.
Busenbaum, Hern, copy of his Medulla Theologæ Moralis owned by Ralé, 246; described, 247; extracts from, 247–250.
Byfield, Nathaniel, 341.

Cabins of Indians, 175–176.
Cahnawagaw, 327.
Canada, Massé returned to, 11; an attack planned to invade the English colonies from, 15, 17; government in a disorganized condition, 16; expedition of 1690 against, unsuccessful, 23; prisoners from York taken to, 27; did not know in 1712 that peace had been concluded, 55; Indians at peace with the English could not live in, 96, 97; brandy trade in, 101–102; Indians of, to be sent to the proposed conference with the English, 109; Ralé fled to, 127; mentioned, 115, 116, 132, 134, 223, 237, 245, 319, 320.
Canada, L'Héroine Chrétienne du, see Faillon, E. M.
Canada River, 136.
Canibas, the, 24, 29.
Cape Cod, 118.
Cape Cod, History of, see Freeman Frederick.
Capon, Mr., 343, 372.
Capt. Job, 323.
Capt. John, 318, 322.
Capt. Joseph, 282, 287.
Capt. Nathaniel, 318, 330, 333.
Carp, Indian legend of the, 189.
Casco, people encouraged to settle by the treaty at, 13; conference appointed at, 44; conference held at, 45–46; Ralé present at, 47; Ralé's account of, 47–48; attacked by French and Indians, 1703, 50; Rolfe at, 53–54; savages went to, to sue for peace, 63; mentioned, 58, 285.

Casco Bay, 59, 60, 247, 283, 287, 291, 365, 396.
Castine, Jean Vincent, Baron de, Andros robbed his trading house, 13–14; his enmity aroused, 14; joined Portneuf, 19; friend of Thury, 31; to be a leader in capturing Boston, 1697, 40; went with the Indians to Arrowsic, 110; considered a conspirator with Ralé, 119.
Castine, Anselm de, considered a conspirator with Ralé, 119; arrested and taken to Boston, 119, 127, 161, 163–165; treated with consideration, 119–120; his mother an Abnaki, 161, 166; at an Indian conference, 161; commander-general of the Abnakis, 161, 166; examined and liberated, 166.
Castine, Anselm de, mentioned, 308, 383, 385.
Cerfeuil, 186.
Chalmers' Papers, cited, 22.
Chambly, 350, 375.
Champigny, Jean Bochart de, Memoire du Roi à cited, 23; letter of, cited, 28.
Champlain, Sieur Samuel de, Voyages of, cited, 11.
Chandler, Col., 348.
Charlevoix, Rev. P. F. X. de, falsely depicted the affair at Norridgewock, 3–4; an inspector to make memoirs, 3, 4; probably received his story from an Indian, 5; report of, concerning Ralé, 95; untrustworthy as a historian, 130, 162, 165, 167, 168, 250, 259, 266; account of a conference between Vaudreuil and the Indians, 164, 165; came to inspect the country, 304; mentioned, 42; Histoire Generale de la Nouvelle France, cited, 18; Memoire sur les limites de l'Acadia, cited, 95.
Charnizay, D'Aulnay, 277.
Chase, George Wingate, History of Haverhill, cited, 54.
Chasse, Rev. Peter de la, sentiment of 65, 65, *n.;* interested in the threatening letter of the Indians, 1721, 108.

Index. 411

Chasse, Rev. Peter de la, sent to Norridgewock, 109; gathered Indian recruits and went to Arrowsic, 109–110; wrote a letter in three languages for the Indians, 160; as a historian, 250, 259, 261, 262, 267; Ralé's unfinished letter to, 251; the single original French account of the attack on Norridgewock, the basis of many other accounts, 267; mentioned, 111, 113, 159, 161, 164, 165, 245, 271, 272, 295, 296, 301, 337, 351; Lettres Édifiantes et Curieuses, par quelques Missionaires de la Compaignie de Jesus, cited, 4–5, 38, 66, 174, 259.

Chaudière River, mission on the, 17.

Chaumont, Père, 183.

Chebeague, 69.

Chebuctou, 32.

Chierdau, Capt., 378.

Choctaws, the, 33.

Christian, a Mohawk, set Norridgewock on fire, 245.

Christianizing, doubtful if there was much genuineness in that of the savages, 88.

Clark, Lieut. Thaddeus, killed, 19.

Clergyman acting as a physician, 66, 67.

Coddington, Col. William, 364.

Coffin, Peter, 58.

Colden, Dr., 356, 357.

Collection of Manuscripts, cited, 115, 165, 265.

Conference at Arrowsic, *see* Treaty at Arrowsic.

Connecticut, 340, 347, 354, 359.

Corwin, Jonathan, 57.

Costebelle, 56.

Coton, Father, 10.

Council Records, cited, 168.

Coureurs de bois, Les, 24.

Courtemanche, Sieur de, leader of the war party into Maine, 18.

Cousin's Island, 69.

Cranston, Gov. Samuel, letter to, 339; mentioned, 276, 355.

Creation of the earth, Indians' account of the, 187, 188, 189, 190.

Cremation among the Indians, 187–189, 190.
Croisel, Mons., went with the Indians to Arrowsic, 110; mentioned, 295, 297, 307.
Currebooset, 291.
Cushing, Mr., 348.

Damaras-Cove, 309.
D'Aulnay, Charles D. M., Lord, 275, 277, 373.
David, 392, 393.
Davis, Capt. Sylvanus, surrendered Fort Loyal, 19; Declaration of, cited, 20.
De Croisel, see Croisel.
De Laune, Mons., 376, 378, 382.
De Monts, Pierre du Guast, 155.
De Pourtrincourt, 10.
De la Chasse, see Chasse de la.
Deautell, 325, 326, 328.
Deerfield, 317.
Delalande, Jean, 391, 392, 393.
Denonville, Jacques, René de Brisay, Marquis de, government at Quebec under him in a disorganized condition, 16; said the English considered the French missionaries as their enemies, 21, 21, *n.;* friend of the Jesuits, 35; desired more men for the mission of St. Francis, 35; mentioned, 16.
Deramsey, Gov., 325, 333.
Dickeson, 369.
Doane, John, 377.
Documentary History of Maine, cited, 15.
Documentary History of New York, see O'Callaghan, E. B.
Dover, 118.
Dracut, 317.
Dudley, Gov. Joseph, sought friendly relations with the Indians, 44; held conference at Casco, 45, 365; conversed with Ralé, 47; entered upon the war with zeal, 52; desired the French governors to stop the Indians from scalping, 53; letter from Capt. Moody to, 55; treaty with Indians at Portsmouth, 57–58; succeeded by Shute, 68; mentioned, 285, 365, 366, 367; letter of, cited, 52, 53.

Index. 413

Dudley, William, 58, 100, 353, 370, 374, 375, 388, 391.
Dummer, Rev. Shubael, killed, 26, 267, 270; Mather's lines on, 27; biographical notice of, 26, 267.
Dummer, Mrs. Shubael, followed her child into the Indian camp, 27, 267.
Dummer, Gov. William, letters of, to Vaudreuil, 267, 268-270, 337, 370; letter from Vaudreuil to, 341; letter of, to Gov. Wentworth, 354; letter of, to Gov. Cranston, 355; letter of, to Gov. Burnett, 355; letter of, to Gov. Talcot, 359; letter from Gov. Talcot to, 361; letters of, to the Lords Commissioners, 393, 396; mentioned, 264, 267, 281, 350, 356, 357; Papers of, cited, 1.
Dunstable, 369.
Dupy, Father, 257.
Dyer, John, 311.

Eaton, Moses, tortured by Indians, 128-129.
Edgar, Henry, 318.

Eliot, Benjamin, 84.
Eliot, John, 71.
Elizée, Père, taught the gospel of peace, not war, 33, *n.;* his character, 34.
Elliot, Robert, 58.
"End justifies the means, the," 250.
English, the, adopt the false story of Charlevoix, 5; not the aggressors, 6; hated everything French, 12; the Jesuits encouraged the Indians to repel, 12-13; considered rebels by the French, 14, 35, 38-39; plot to exterminate, 14-16, 17-18; the Jesuits instigate the Indians against, 1689, 16-17, 27-28, 31; atrocities inflicted upon them by the Indians, 18; the war against, became a religious crusade, 19-20; considered the French missionaries their enemies, 21; not to be easily rooted out of American soil, 22; Norridgewock imperilled the existence of, 23; Frontenac ordered to

53

persist in the warfare against, 23-24; Indians to be prevented from being at peace with, 26, 29-30; given no quarter by the Indians, 41; tortured by Indians, 41; character of the war waged against, 1697, 41-42; French opposed friendly relations between the Indians and, 42, 46; the enemy carefully studied the defences of the towns of, 42-43; irritated by the meddling of the French, 43; Ralé's deceitful talk concerning the war with, 47; Indians desired them to feel secure, 48; attempted treachery of the Indians toward, 48-49; accused of tricks and artifice, 51-52; Indians confirm the rights of, 57; to return to their ruined village, 60, 63, 64; the French continued to plot and excite the Indians against, 64, 65; a war with, is favorable to the French, 65, 66, *n.;* Ralé could have, but would not have their friendly feeling, 66; gave Ralé medical aid, 66, 67; prevented from settling on the Kennebec, 67-68; not to be disturbed by Indians, 74, 77-78; declared to be trespassers, 75-76; the Indians thankful they settle on their lands, but want no more, 76; confirmed by the Indians to the lands they held, 81; Ralé displeased because they had established a missionary at Arrowsic, 84-85; harassed by the Indian outbreaks, 90; the Indians desired to be friendly with, 90, 91; Ralé continually urged the Indians to attack, 91, 92, *n.*, 94; animosities of, awakened, 92; resolution to send men to Norridgewock abandoned, 92, 103; Indians dreaded war with, 92; Vaudreuil urged Ralé to prevent their settlement, 92; Indians hindered in the traffic with, 93; had as much right as the French to settle their frontiers, 94; settlers to be sent to River St. John, 94; build the church at Norridgewock, 95; the indignation of, aroused by Ralé's letter to Moody, 96–97; tell the Indians false news, 98; their interpreter speaks only gibberish, 99, 101; their manner of purchasing lands, 99–100; the Indians will force them to quit their lands, 100; Ketermogus a friend of, 101; Ralé said there is no justice among, 102; accused of causing the war, 103; Ralé on their treatment of the Indians, 104; the source of their peril revealed to them, 104; the Indians appeared determined to intimidate, 105; Indians reluctant to have another war with, 105–107; the French exaggerated the acts of, 106; Indians protest against the settlement on the Kennebec, 1721, 108; Indian conference to be held with, 108, 124; cattle of, killed by Indians, 111, *n.*, 163; believed Ralé and the Castines to be conspirators against, 119; sent Westbrook to apprehend Ralé, 120; astounded by Vaudreuil's duplicity, 123; their houses plundered and burned, 1722, 128, 170; Ralé's prejudice against, 130; their borders scenes of desolation and cruelty, 131, 132; Ralé desired to excite the rage of, 132, 133; determined to drive Ralé from the Kennebec or capture him, 134, 167, 168; not preferred by the Abnakis, 142; machinations of, to secure the Indians, 142–143, 153–154, 221; Acadia conveyed to, 155; the Indians no match for, in a fair fight, 158; held Indians as hostages till payment was received for depredations, 158–159; refused to sell ammunition and food to the Indians, 160–161; seized Castine,

161, 162–163; Ralé's reason for their hatred toward him, 165–166; not to be permitted on the Kennebec, 163; killed one of Ralé's captains, 206; tried to draw the trade of the savages, 215, 217; villages of, devastated, 220; offer a reward for killing Ralé, 221; to rebuild the church for the Indians, 224, 225; Mohawks friendly to, 237; expedition of 1724 against Norridgewock, 237–238; coolness of, at Norridgewock, 240; their duty to destroy the source from which spread ruin, desolation, and death, 241; their destruction of the village of Norridgewock the work of a few moments, 241; Indians induced to make slaves of the, 352, 353.
Envieux, L', 29.
Escutcheon of Loyola, 7.
Essex, 278.
Etat, Présent, cited, 32.

Faillon, Etienne Michel, L'Héroine Chrétienne du Canada, Villemarie, etc., cited, 21.
Falmouth, Portneuf and his party arrived at, 18–19; attacked, 19, 21; mentioned, 69, 247, 291, 396.
Fetter Lane, 1.
Fisk, Mary, 72.
Fisk, Rev. Moses, 71, 72.
Five Nations, the, 327, 328, 331, 353, 386.
Flynt, Henry, 67; Journal of, cited, 68.
Forsyth, Alexander, 292.
Fort Chambly, 330.
Fort Loyal, Indian prisoners released from, 14, 19; Indians act as guides against, 19; attack and surrender of, 19.
Fort Richelieu, Massé died at, 11.
Fort Richmond, 237, 259, 319.
Fort St. John, Thury at, 41.
Fort at Brunswick, 101.
Fort at New Casco, 45.
Fort at St. George, 255.

Index. 417

Fox Island, 383, 384.
France, James *II.*, fled to, 14; mentioned, 288.
Franche Comté, 34.
Freeman, Frederick, History of Cape Cod, cited, 119.
French, the, no doubt of their attempts to ruin the English colonies, 3; to embark in vessels against Boston, 40; after the treaty of Ryswick opposed the friendly relations between the Indians and English, 42, 46; carefully studied the defenses of the English towns, 43; Indians to stand by the, 48; prepared to kill the English at the Casco conference, 49; joined with the Indians in a descent upon the English, 49-50; gave premiums for scalps, 52-53; attacked Haverhill, 53; continued to plot and excite the Indians against the English, 64, 65, 386; war with the English favorable to the, 65, 66, *n.;* excited the Indians to prevent English settlements in Maine, 93-94; placed the acts of the English in the worst possible light to the Indians, 106; the agents of, active in making the savages dissatisfied, 107; secretly supplied the savages with arms, 131; conveyed Acadia to the English, and yet sought to rule the Indians of that country, 155; the Indians no match for, in a fair fight, 158; Indians pretend they expected no help from, 171; Indians firmly attached to, 216, 218; induced the Indians to go to war, 222-223; condemned the English because their traders sold fire water to the Indians, 265; ordered to assist Indians, 280, 295, 298, 302, 303; ordered the Indians to take captives, 319; mentioned, 1.
French Archives, 3.
French Wax, (a sachem) 378.
Freye, Thomas, 364.
"Friar Ralé's railing Letter," 96.

Frontenac, Louis de Buade, Count de, became governor of New France, 14; the diabolical plot committed to his execution, 15; sailed from Rochelle, 16, 34; reached Quebec, 16; organized the plot intrusted to him, 17; defeated Phips, 22–23; ordered by the king to continue the war, 23; excited the savages by promise of booty, 24; accompanied by Ralé, 34; letter from Tibierge to, 41; mentioned, 29; Instructions to, cited, 15; Memoire of the king to, cited, 23.

Gay, Père, leader of the Indians, 20; his address to incite the Indians, 20, *n*.
George *I.*, 70, 74, 78, 91, 98, 280, 308, 315, 326, 338, 343, 372, 377, 386.
George's Fort, 384.
Georgetown, Baxter preached at, 89; Indian council held at, 106; conference with Indians at, 281, 291; mentioned, 279.

Gerard, J. W., Peace of Utrecht, cited, 155.
Geste, Sieur de la, 336.
"Gibralter of America, the," 242–243.
Giles, Capt. John, spoke only gibberish, 99, 101, *n.;* advised the people where to settle, 100; mentioned, 70, 89, 90, 286.
Gold, David, 277.
Goold, Daniel, testimony of, 383.
Goold, William, Portland in the Past, cited, 56.
Goolde, Daniel, 371.
Great Britain, 1, 288.
Great Lake, the, 61.
Green, B., 84.
Gregory *XV.*, Pope, 8.
Grenoble, 10.
Groton, 369.
Guerchville, Marchioness, 10.
Gulf of St. Lawrence, 300.

Hamilton, Alexander, Journal of, 317; mentioned, 317, 318, 319, 320, 321, 322, 323, 324, 325, 326, 327, 328, 329, 330, 331, 332, 333, 334.
Hampshire, 278.

Handsord, William, 318, 323, 324, 325, 326.
Hardwicke Papers, cited, 155.
Hare, the Great, Indian legend concerning, 187–188.
Harison, Mr., 356, 357.
Harmon, Col. Johnson, attacked the Indians at Pleasant Point, 128–129, 171; unjustly criticised, 130–131; led the unsuccessful expedition of 1723, 173; head of an expedition against Norridgewock, 235–236; leader of expedition of 1724 against Norridgewock, 237, 242; killed two Indians and captured a third, 238; divided his forces, 239; joined Moulton, 245; reported the result of the expedition against Norridgewock at Boston, 263; received a Lieutenant Colonel's commission, 263; received a reward of £100, 264; mentioned, 242, 243, 247, 259, 267, 281, 291, 394; biographical notice of, 239.

Harmon, Mary, 242.
Harpswell, 242, 244.
Harris, Samuel, testimony of, 384.
Harris, Dr. Thaddeus Mason, cited, 244.
Harvard College, 22, 26, 53, 118, 121, 267, 268.
Hatfield, 369.
Haverhill, attacked, 53; Rolfe killed at, 53, *n.*; mentioned, 317.
Haverhill, History of, *see* Chase, G. W.
Heath, Joseph, sent with a message to Norridgewock, 91; letter of, cited, 91.
Hegen, Richard, 377.
Hegon, John, 282, 286, 290, 291, 292.
Hendrick, 332.
Hertel, François, led the war party into New Hampshire, 19; joined Portneuf, 19.
Hertel, Joseph, 391, 392.
Higginson, John, 58.
Hilton, Col., destroyed Norridgewock, 52.
Histoire et Description Generale de la Nouvelle France, 165.
Hobington, H., 358.

420   *Index.*

Hopegood, at Casco conference, 44.
Hosanoueskact, 343.
Hudson River, the line of the depredations which were planned from Canada, 15.
Hunkin, Mark, 58.
Hurons, the, 97, 108, 109, 111, 116, 127, 164, 182, 183, 184, 187, 253, 254, 257.
Hutchinson, Gov. Thomas, carefully gathered the material for his history, 3; sustained by the French archives, 3; gives a carefully compiled account of the affair at Norridgewock, 258, 267.

Illinois Indians, Ralé started to join them, 37; well received by them, 38; mentioned, 183, 184, 185, 187, 193, 194, 195, 197, 199, 201, 202, 203.
Indian Wheat, 180.
Indians } people misled
Savages } in regard to the complicity of the Jesuits with the, 1, 16; probably told the story of Ralé's death to Charlevoix, 5; notoriors falsefiers, 5, 259; encouraged by the Jesuits to repel the English, 12–13, 27–28, 31, 40; conference with Andros at Pemaquid, 13; espoused the cause of Castine, 14; retaliation not prevented by Andros conciliatory measures, 14, 19; their outbreaks of 1689 promoted by the Jesuits, 16, 17; atrocities inflicted upon the English, 18; acted as guides against Fort Loyal, 19; led by Père Gay, 20; Gay's address to incite them, 20, *n.;* the English would not permit the Jesuits among, 21; subjects of the king of France, 21, 29, 343, 344; outdone in savagery by the *coureurs de bois*, 24; not permitted to make peace, 24, 26, 29–30; exhorted and influenced by the clergy to continue the war, 24, 28–29; led against York by Thury, 25, 26, *n.;* massacre at York, 26; left

old women and children behind, 27, *n.;* carried their prisoners to Canada, 27, *n.;* their confidence in Thury, 28; Ralé played an important part in their wars with the English, 34; induced to leave Maine, 36; Ralé journeyed among, 36, 37, 38; Ralé established among, 40; led by St. Castine, 40; to assist in the capture of Boston, 40; parties of, near Boston, 41; burned their prisoners, 41; gave no quarter to the English, 41; French opposed friendly relations between the English and, 42, 43, 46; Massachusetts expelled the counselors of, 43–44; Dudley sought friendly relations with, 44; at Casco conference, 44–45; the action of reassuring, 46; attempted treachery of, at the conference, 48–49; join with the French in an attack upon the English, 49–50; their war inaugurated by a feast, 50; attended confession and received communion before starting on the war path, 50, 51; debauched and under the control of the Jesuits, 52; receive bounties for scalps, 53, 266; attacked Haverhill, 53; desire peace, 56, 63–64, 351, 352; agree to forbear all acts of hostility and confess they have broken their agreements, 56–57; agree to the treaty of Portsmouth, 57–58, 62; number of, at different villages, 59; what the English said to the, 59; go to Quebec for powder, 63; Ralé falsely reported they were not satisfied, 63; their jealousy continually excited by the French against the English, 64; their idea of territorial rights, 64–65, 76, 79; Vaudreuil supplied them with weapons to use against the English, 65; held no council without calling Ralé, 66, 96, 99, 102–103, 226–227; called to a conference with Shute, 68; at Arrowsic, 69, 110-124; Sewall the staunch friend of, 69; carried the English flag to the Arrowsic conference, 70; pleased with the appointment of Shute as governor, 74; disliked English forts, 79; departed leaving the English colors, 79-80; Ralé's attempt to influence them against the English, 80, 91, 92, *n.*, 94; they beg Shute to return, 80; asked for the English colors, 80-81; confirmed the rights of the English to their lands, 81; desire trading house and locksmith, 82; their deceptive character, 85, 92; why they were drawn to the Roman rather than the Protestant faith, 87-88; doubtful if there were many genuine conversions, 88-89; their evidence unreliable, 90; Ralé may have taken advantage of their superstitious minds, 90; desired to be friendly with the English, 90, 91; said Ralé lied when he wrote to Shute, 91, 92, *n.;* continually urged by Ralé to attack, 6, 91, 92, *n.*, 94, 371, 374, 395; the English alarmed by the threatening attitude of, 92; resolution to force them to make amends abandoned, 92; dreaded war with the English, 92; their reply when urged by Vaudreuil to prevent English settlements, 92-93, 103; hindered in traffic with the English, 93; not to pay for the cattle they destroy, 93, 97; those who cannot support themselves against the English, 94; Shute desired some to go to Europe, 96; Ralé threatened to excommunicate all such as went, 96; English aroused at Ralé's assumption in preventing the friendly relations with, 97; attend to their own affairs, 98; will force the English to quit their lands, 100; how they shall receive their rum, 101–102; Ralé describes their treatment by the English, 103–104; depredations of, on the Kennebec, 105; Shute's threat supposed to be to intimidate, 105; reluctant to have another war with the English, 105–107; held council at Norridgewock, 106; two parties, 106; elect a chief, 106; held council at Georgetown, 106, 281; French agents active among, 107; made to feel the displeasure of Vaudreuil, 107; sent a threatening protest to Shute, 108; objected to the settlements on the Kennebec, 1721, 108; the peace party of, aroused Ralé to action, 108–109; the war party strengthened, 109–110; kill Englishmen's cattle, 110, 163, 304, 310, 367; held as hostages in Boston, 110, 112, 113, *n.*, 156, 157, *n.*, 158, 159, 319, 375, 376, 377; letter presented by, 111, 294; complain that hostages are held after paying the debt, 112–113, 117–118; declare their deeds void, 117; warned Ralé of the approach of the English, 120, 168; considered Westbrook's expedition a warrant for further depredations, 127; to meet at Norridgewock, 128, 170; commenced their depredations, 1722, 128, 170; at first did not slaughter or hold all their captives, 128, 171; later began a wholesale slaughter, 128, 130 ; attacked by Harmon, 129; Ralé's distorted account of their depredations, 129, 130; Shute's proclamation concerning the peaceful, 131; Ralé accompanied them in their raids, 132; instructed in the Christian virtues, 135, 138; assist Ralé in performing mass, 136, 138; religious emulation among the women, 137; Ralé at their councils, 139–140; forbidden to interrupt Ralé when at his devotions, 140; build temporary chapels when hunting and fishing, 140–141; collect maple sugar, 141; machinations of the English to secure, 142, 153-154; minister sent from New England to convert them, 143; trading houses introduced among them before Ralé's time, 153; asked Vaudreuil about the treaty of Utrecht, 154-155; must have been deceived by the governor, 155, *n.;* the French sought to rule them, though they had no legal jurisdiction over the country, 155; Ralé's false story of some which are held as hostages, 156, 158; Ralé's account of their bravery, 157–158; no match for the civilized man, 158, *n.;* held as hostages till the cattle they had killed were paid for, 158-159; objected to the English holding them as hostages after they had paid a debt, 158-159, 160; not present at an appointed conference, 159, 368; English refuse to sell food and ammunition to, 160–161; their patience exhausted, 161; Castine an officer of, 161; conference with Vaudreuil, 162; chanted the war song, 170; their cabins, 175–176; clothing, 176; description, 177; occupation, 178, 180; canoes, 178; food, 179–180; language, 181–184; origin of the tribes, 187, 189, 190; cremation among, 188–189; burials and funerals among, 190–191, 196; religion among, 191, 192; deliberate upon important affairs at their festivals, 193-194; feast described, 194–195; costumes of, 195–196; position of women among, 196–197, the Illinois the richest, 197; hunters and fishers, 198; public esteem among, 198–199; his height of glory, 200; reviving the dead, 200; torture, 201; prefer polygamy to prayer, 201–202; drink an obstacle to Christianity, 202; as converted by Ralé, 205–206; the English try to obtain the trade of, 215–216, 217; war feast to be made, 218; Ralé exhorted them not to be cruel, 219–220; mode of warfare, 220; are used as an arm by the French, 223; the English to rebuild their church, 224, 225; despoiled the country of moose and deer, 225; subsist on vegetables and fish, 225–226; 227–228; venerate Ralé, 229; alarmed for his safety, 229–230; informed Ralé of the approach of the English, 230–231; conveying news by signs, 234; discovered the presence of Moulton near Norridgewock, 239; failed of true heroism when matched by civilized men, 240; fled from Norridgewock, 240, 261, 271; buried Ralé's body, 245; hastened to Canada for the protection of Vaudreuil, 245; Vaudreuil could craze them with brandy, 265; received bounties for English and French scalps, 266; assisted by the French, 280, 295, 298, 301, 312, 322, 393; totems of those at the conference at Georgetown, 292; declaration of Gov. Shute concerning, 314–315; act of Representatives of Massachusetts concerning, 315–317; capture Hamilton, 317; depredations of, 318, 338, 339, 368, 383–384, 384–385; to take captives in lieu of hostages held in Boston, 319; send reports of their depredations to Canada, 319; well received by Vaudreuil, 319–320, 321; supplied by the governor with stores, 320, 321, 327, 330; carry captives to Quebec, 321; headed by Jesuits at Arrowsic, 322; deliver Handsord to the governor, 324; conclude to bury the ax and send captives home, 325; stopped by Vaudreuil, 325–326; sent envoys to Albany, 327; bring to Quebec English scalps, 327; set out to avenge the loss of, at North Yarmouth, 327; return from Albany, 327; to visit New England with a large army, 330; their trade with Albany prohibited, 330; the old desire peace, the young desire war, 331; to make a peace at Boston, 331, 333; always true to France, 342; claimed as subjects of England, 342, 343; would be sad to see their priest taken from them, 345; the English the cause of the depredations, 345; the depredations of, to be reported to the government, 349; treaty of peace must be made in the presence of Vaudreuil, 351, 377, 387; induced by the French to make slaves of the English, 352, instigated by the French, 352, 369; 386; treaties of, broken, 365–370; claim that the English encroach upon their ground, 378; prevented from making peace by Jesuits, 379, 380, 381, 382–384; capture Daniel Goold, 383–384; capture Samuel Harris, 384–385; told what to say by Vaudreuil, 387; demands of, 387; claimed by the French as subjects, 390; mentioned, 1, 337.

Instructions to the Commissioners for Canada, 346.

Iripegouans, the, 193.

Iroquois, the, 41, 108, 115, 116, 182, 183, 201, 252, 266.

Isle of St. John, 300.

Jakis, the, 193.

James *II.*, exiled, 14; mentioned, 35.

Jaques, Benjamin, 244.

Jaques, Daniel, 242.

Jaques, Marianna, 244.

Jaques, Mary, 244.

Jaques, Mary Williams, 242.

Jaques, Lieut. Richard, son-in-law of Johnson

Harmon, 239, 243; frustrated the design of Moulton, 242; caught Ralé in the act of loading a gun, 243; demanded the priest to surrender, 243; shot the priest, 243, 260; his story doubted, and he reprimanded by Moulton, 244, 260, 261; went to his grave the self-acknowledged slayer of Ralé, 261; biographical notice of, 242.

Jeffries, John, 318.

Jesuit Catalogue, cited, 35.

Jesuites, Relations des, cited, 11.

Jesuits, people misled in regard to their complicity in the depredations of the Indians, 1, 16; the people of New England had no doubt of their attempt to ruin the English colonies, 2–3; their character a strange commingling of diverse elements, 8; society of, formed, 8; followed the track of the great voyagers, 9; achieved a measure of success, 9; the product of their age, 9; pioneers in the work of uplifting men, 9; preceded the Puritans, 12; in dangerous proximity to the English, 12; not indifferent to the encroachments of the English, 12; encouraged the Indians to repel the English, 12–13, 16, 27–28; influential in shaping the government's proposals for an Indian outbreak in 1689, 16, 17; missions extended into Maine, 17; considered by the English as their enemies, 21; abundant proof to show that they identified themselves with the savages, 29; those who taught peace and not war, 32, 33, *n.*–34, *n.;* their names should be held in grateful remembrance, 34; to oppose all communication between the Indians and English, 42, 43, expelled from Massachusetts, 43; priests driven from New York, 44; endeavored to break the friendly relations between the English and Indians, 46; had command of the Inland Indians, 52; received medical aid from the English, 66, 67; predicted the end of the world soon, 89; accused of lieing, 91–92; is no cipher, 96; is not a Baxter or a Boston minister, 104; influenced the Indians to make war upon the English, 111, 167; the authors of the threatening letter sent to Gov. Shute, 119; reward for capturing, 168; the war of 1722 traced to, 174; forbidden within English territory, 174, 308, 371; kept the Indians faithful to the French, 216, 221; a book of high authority among, 247; Martyrs de Canada Bibliogr, Les, cited, 267; instigate Indians, 167, 280, 288, 298, 352, 374; headed Indians at Arrowsic, 322, 323; desired a continuance of the war, 329; influenced Vaudreuil, 352, 353, 379; prevent the Indians from making peace, 379, 380, 381; would kill the peace commissioner, 381; mentioned, 276, 288, 319, 322, 323, 325, 329, 331, 332.

Job, Capt., 323.
John, Capt., 318.
Jordan, Capt., 277.
Jordan, Samuel, Indian interpreter, 70; desired by the Indians as locksmith, 82; mentioned, 70, 282, 292.
Jordan, Capt. Samuel, Declaration of, 375.
Joseph, Capt., 282, 287.
Journal of the Commissioners to Canada, 350.
Journal of the Expedition from Boston to Port Royal, cited, 22.

Kadesquit, mission to be established at, 10.
Katholisches Kuche in dem Vereinigten Staten, Die, 267.
Kenduskeag, mission to be established at, 10.
Kennebec Indians, 281.

Index.

Kennebec Mission, Indians from, at Casco conference, 44, mentioned, 41.
Kennebec River, English settlements on, prevented by Ralé, 67; mentioned, 25, 29, 79, 81, 86, 95, 105, 108, 113, 115, 128, 134, 156, 215, 237, 242, 291, 309.
Kennebec Savages, 91.
Ketermogus, desired to remain at peace with the English, 101; obnoxious to Ralé, 101, *n*.
Kettera, 292.
Ketterremuggus, 282, 291, 292.
King Philip's War, 36.
Kingnessanach, 186.
Kip, Rev. William Ingraham, 135.
Kirk, Sir David, 11.
Kounaouons, 253, 254.

La Longue, Mons., 333.
La Loureur, Jean, 392.
La Rond, Sieur, 336, 337
Lackwadawmeck, 291.
Lake Superior, 331.
Lalande, Jean de, 391, 392, 393.
Lalemant, Père, 10.

Lancaster, 317.
Languile, Gov., 325.
Lannerjat, letter of, to Ralé, 338; mentioned, 276.
Larrabee, Benjamin, statement of, in regard to Ralé's death, 261.
Laurels, 137, 138.
Laurone, Mons., 376, 378, 382.
Lauverjeat, encouraged the Indians to make war, 174.
Le Clerc, Nicholas, 135.
Le Ronde, Sieur, 336, 337.
Lefevre, 343.
Lettres Édifiantes et Curieuses, par quelques Missionaires, *see* Chasse, Rev. Peter de la.
Locksmith, wanted by Indians, 82.
Longuile, Charles de Moyne, 386.
Lorette, 109, 111, 127, 164, 170, 320, 321, 327.
Lorette Indians, 323, 327.
Louisbourg, 242, 243.
Louisiana, 33.
Love, Robert, 318.
Loverjat, Father, 255.
Loyard, Father, 257.
Loyola, Don Iñigo Lopez de Recalde, de, founder

of the Jesuits, 7; biographical notice of, 7.
Lynde, Benjamin, 58, 384, 385.
Lynde, Samuel, 279, 281.
Lyons, 10.
Lyons, Province of, 35.

Machova, 190.
Mackinac, Ralé at, 37.
Macuas, the, 350.
Madelaine, Jean, 392, 393.
Magerlaine Island, 300.
Maine, Jesuit missions extended into, 17; war party to set out against, 18; leaders of the war party, 18; Jesuits active in inciting the Indians of, 27–28; Indians induced to leave, 36; Indians of, debauched by the Jesuits, 52; the English again took root in, 64; the Indians excited by the French to prevent settlements in, 93–94.
Maine, Indians of, sent a protest to Shute, 108; mentioned, 317.
Maine, History of, *see* Williamson, William D.
Maine Historical Quarterly, cited, 91, 108.
Maine Historical Society, 2, 123.
Maine Historical Society Archives, 90.
Maine Historical Society Collections, cited, 32, 84.
Maize, 141.
Malaowins, the, 300.
Manitou, 191, 192.
Manuscrits, Collections de, cited, 17, 21, 22, 23, 25, 26, 28, 31, 32, 34, 41, 42, 63, 66, 94, 95.
Maple Sugar, 141.
Maquas, the, 350, 353, 355.
Marblehead, 383, 384.
Martin, Père, Les Jesuit Martyrs de Canada, cited, 35.
Maruelet, 391.
Mary, the, 383.
Maskoutings, the, 193.
Massachusetts, Jesuits expelled from, 43; mentioned, 13, 57, 315, 346, 350, 356, 357, 364, 365, 368, 385, 386.
Massachusetts Archives, cited, 168, 263, 264.
Massachusetts General Court, resolved to arrest Ralé, 92, 119, 167, 168.

Massachusetts Historical Society Collections, cited, 20, 56, 91, 96, 118, 244.
Massé, Enemond, first of the Jesuits to visit the continent, 10–11; taken prisoner by Argal, 11, *n.*; mentioned, 12; biographical notice of, 10.
Mather, Cotton, Magnalia Christi Americana, cited, 18, 20, 22, 27, 42; mentioned, 270, 271.
Matsidouanoussis River, 113.
Maurice, Claude, 392, 393.
Medfield, 71, 89.
Medocteh, 112, 164, 165.
Memoire sur l'enterprise de Baston à Versailles, cited, 41.
Menaskeh, 117.
Menaskous, 112, 165, 222.
Meneval, Robineau de, commander at Port Royal, 21; taken prisoner by Phips, 21–22; Lettre de, cited, 22.
Merriconeag Neck, 239. 242.
Merrymeeting Bay, Indians desire people removed from, 282, 284, 287, 291; mentioned, 318.

Mesambomett, at Casco conference, 44.
Miamis, the, 183.
Michabou, 187.
Michibichi, 192.
Micmacs, the, 59, 108, 116, 257.
Middlesex, 278.
Minot, Mr., asked to manage the trading house, 82.
Minot, John, sent with a message to Norridgewock, 91; deposition of, 279, 280–281; mentioned, 281; deposition of, cited, 91.
Missilimakinak, Ralé at, 187, 193.
Missionaries, whose names should be held in grateful remembrance, 34.
Missionaries, French, *see* Jesuits.
Missions de l'Amerique, Le, 267.
Mississippi River, discovered by the French, 52.
Mississippi Valley, 304.
Mitchell,——, held a prisoner by Ralé, 241, 243; tortured by Ralé, 243–244, 244, *n.*

Mitchell, William, killed at Scarborough, 241–242; his son held a prisoner by Ralé, 241.

Mogg, firing from his cabin at Norridgewock, 241; killed a Mohawk, 241–242; killed with his wife and children by the Mohawk's brother, 242; mentioned, 282, 283, 292.

Mohawks, the, 97, 237, 320, 323, 327, 328, 331, 332.

Montreal, expedition from Albany to, unsuccessful 22–23; mentioned, 323, 324, 325, 326, 330, 337, 350, 351, 353, 375, 376, 377, 382, 391, 392.

Montserrat, 8.

Moodey, Major Joshua, 247.

Moody, Capt., 54, 68, 96; letter of, cited, 55.

Moody, Capt. Samuel, 275, 281, 291, 294.

Moose, 177.

Moses, Capt., 282, 320.

Moulton, Capt. Jeremiah, led expedition against Norridgewock, 236, 237; found the village deserted, 236–237; forbade his men doing any injury to the buildings, 237; his magnanimity called cowardice by Ralé, 237; killed two Indians and captured a third, 238, 262, *n.*; divided their forces, 239; approached the village, 239; allowed the Indians to fire first, 240; gave orders to spare Ralé, 242, 266; his orders disobeyed, 242; doubted the story of, and reprimanded Jaques for killing Ralé, 244, 260, 261; left the village unharmed, 245; found Ralé's *vade mecum* and an unfinished letter to De la Chasse, 245–246, 251; mentioned, 239, 247, 259, 261, 267; biographical notice of, 236; his character, 236, 237, 240, 244, 245, 271.

Moulton, Mary, 239.

Mount Agamenticus, 25.

Mount Desert, Biard and Massé at, 10; called St. Saveur, 10; mission established at, 10; mission destroyed by Argal, 10–11.

Index.   433

Moxus, at Casco conference, 44; mentioned, 68, 72, 320.
Munjoy Hill, 19.

Namepick, 189.
Nanrantsouak, 55, 93, 94, 95, 111, 112, 116, 136, 174, 215, 279, 28c.
Nanrantsouak, see Norridgewock.
Nanrantsouaks, the, 93, 342, 343, 344.
Nathaniel, Capt., 318, 330, 333.
New Casco, see Casco.
New England, Puritans settled in, 12; French machinations against, 13; diabolical plot against, 15, 17–18; imperilled by Norridgewock, 23; a Jesuit who became most famous in, 23; enabled to cultivate the arts of peace a short season after 1697, 42; greatly troubled by the Jesuits, 52; in a serious condition, 53–54; most honorable men of, agree to the Portsmouth treaty, 63; mentioned, 1, 126, 135, 136, 143, 167, 215.

New England, History of the Wars of, see Penhallow, Samuel.
New France, the southern borders of, in close proximity to the English, 12; Jesuits gained an ascendency in, 12; Frontenac became governor of, 14; the rulers of, continued to plot against the English, 64, 65.
New France, see also Nouvelle France.
New Hampshire, war party sent into, 18, 19; mentioned, 58, 347, 349, 354, 360, 366, 385
New Hampshire Historical Society Collections, cited, 118.
New York, to be attacked from Canada, 15; the king haggled over the cost of the expedition into, 23; priests expelled from, 44; mentioned, 278, 353, 354, 355, 356, 357, 360, 386, 396.
New York, history of, see Smith, William.
New York Colonial Documents, see O'Callaghan, E. B.
Newbury, 53, 242.

Newman, Thomas, 292.
Niagara, 265.
Nismes, College at, Ralé an instructor in the, 35.
Nordon, Nathaniel, 384.
Norridgewock, Ralé slain at, 1; the battle at, depicted in a false light, 3; the hotbed of an influence imperilling the English, 23; Ralé in charge of Abnaki mission at, 38; chapel built at, 39–40; the Indians at, in favor with Ralé, 40; Indians from, at Casco conference, 44; expedition planned against, 1705, 52; destroyed by Hilton, 52; number of people at, 59; apparitions at, 89; Minot and Heath sent with message to, 91; resolution to send an armed force to, 92, 119; the English allowed to settle half way to, 93; the savages of, excited by Ralé not to permit the English to extend their settlements, 94; church built by the English with funds furnished by the French, 95; Ralé's letter from, 135, 174; chiefs sent from, to Vaudreuil, 105, 164; Indian council held at, 106; De la Chasse sent to, 109; Westbrook sent to capture Ralé at, 120; appointed as a place for the warriors to assemble, 128, 170; Ralé, remained at, 134, 171–172; Ralé describes the churches at, 136, 137; Vaudreuil held a conference. with the Indians at, 162; Indians met at, 165; expedition planned against, 1723, 173; Moulton in command of an expedition against, 236; deserted when the English arrived, 237; Moulton's magnanimity, 237; expedition of 1724 against, 237, 238; to be captured by surprise, 238; Moulton's force discovered by a savage who gave the war cry, 239; the savages wildly discharged their guns, 240; contained the source from which spread ruin, desolation, and death, 241; the firing came from two cab-

ins, 241; occupied by the English, 245; left unharmed by Moulton, 245; set on fire by Christian, 245; the French account of the battle a tissue of errors, 258-266; Hutchinson gives a carefully compiled account of, 258, 267; Harmon's report of the affair at, 261; under the government of Great Britain, 308; soldiers sent to, 1722, 309, 311; Hamilton and other captives carried to, 318, 319; paper taken from the church door, 334; mentioned, 123, 127, 276, 289, 307, 308, 322, 323, 370, 387, 394, 395.

Norridgewock, *see* Nanrantsouak.

Norridgewocks, the, 108, 254, 261, 291, 307, 320, 372.

North Yarmouth, 327.

Northfield, 317, 369.

Nouvelle France, Histoire et Description Generale de la, cited, 11, 17, 20; Manuscripts relating to, cited, 15, 17.

Nouvelle France, *see also* New France.

Nouvelles des Missions, Les, 267.

Nova Scotia, 1, 2, 126, 373.

Noyes, Thomas, 58.

Obomawhawk, 282, 290, 291, 292.

O'Callaghan, E. B., Documentary History of New York, cited, 20; New York Colonial Documents cited, 20.

Omikoues, the, 193.

Onondaga River, 353, 386.

Orleans, Duke of, 95, 161.

"O Salutaris," translation of, 184.

Ouaourene, praised by Ralé, 106; flattered by the governor, 107; mentioned, 97, 113.

Ouarinakiens, the, 253, 254.

Oussakita, 191.

Outagamis, the, 193.

Outaouacks, the, 187, 189, 190, 193.

Owreno, 300.

Pannaouanskeians, the, 253.

Panouamské, 112.

Panouamsque Indians, the, 342, 343.
Parker, John, 292.
Parkman, Francis, error of, concerning Jaques, 244.
Paul III, Pope, 8.
Pauscawen, 258.
Pegonakki River, 116.
Peguncourt, M., 378, 379.
Pehonuret, 113.
Pejepscot proprietors, 242.
Pemaquid, Andros' conference with Indians at, 13; mentioned, 60, 78.
Pemkuit, 40.
Pemondaki Indians, 164, 165.
Pemster, 115.
Penhallow, Samuel, at the Casco conference, 48; signed the Portsmouth treaty, 58; mentioned, 69, 113; Indian Wars of New England, cited, 46, 48, 50, 54, 58, 129, 262, 267.
Penobscot, 289, 371, 383, 384, 385.
Penobscot Mission, Indians from, at Casco conference, 44; number of savages at, 59; savages leave, for Quebec, 63.

Penobscot River, Thury established a mission on, 17; mentioned, 25, 40, 109, 126, 127.
Penobscots, the, 91, 164, 372.
Penondaky, 112.
Pentagoet River, 28.
Pentagouet, 29, 31, 40, 41, 156.
Perubres, M., 376.
Peskadoe, 117.
Petit, Mathurin le., refused absolution to murderers, 32, 33; became superior of the Jesuits of Louisiana, 33; the king displeased with, 33.
Phips, Spencer, 58.
Phips, Sir William, maxim adopted by, 21; captured Port Royal, 21; commanded expedition against Quebec, 22; not successful, 22-23; mentioned, 24, 57, 365, 366, 372.
Pickering, John, published Ralé's dictionary, 121.
Pigwacket, 49, 289.
Pike, Rev. John, Journal of, cited, 28.
Piscataqua, 98, 285.
Piscataqua Indians, 165

Index. 437

Piscataqua River, 110
Plaisance, 60, 62, 222, 223.
Plaisted, Ichabod, 58.
Plaisted, John, 58.
Pleasant Point, 128, 171.
Plot to exterminate the English, 14–16.
Point Claire, 392
Ponaowamské, 94
Ponchartrain, Count Louis P. de, Letter of, 33.
Port Royal, captured by Phips, 21; mentioned, 10, 24, 60, 62, 215, 222, 223, 257.
Portneuf, Sieur de, leader of the war party into Maine, 18; joined by Castine and Hertel, 19; mentioned, 21.
Portsmouth, 349, 366.
Potherie, Bacqueville De La, Histoire de l'Amerique, cited, 18.
Prayer, wheel of, in continual motion, 22.
Prise du Port Royal par les Anglois de Baston, pièce anonyme, cited, 22.
Protestants, why they did not succeed in converting the savages as well as the Romanists, 87–88.

Provincial Council, 236.
Puants, Bay of the, 193.
Public Records Office, London, 44, 53, 56, 108, 123, 127, 251, 299.
Puddlestone Island, 69.
Puritans, erected their altars in New England, 12.

Quebec, Frontenac arrived at, 16; government disorganized, 16; war party set out to Maine from, 18; the center of French power in America, 22; naval expedition sent against, 22; Rahlé arrived at, 36; Ralé journeyed from to the Illinois, 37: Ralé returned to, 38, 185; to remain to the French, 60, 62; savages go to, for powder, 63; sample of Ralé's wax sent to, 138; the Abnakis prefer to trade at, 142; provisions sent from, to Ralé, 169; Indians desired Ralé to return to, 171; mentioned, 37, 38, 54, 55, 60, 62, 153, 175, 202, 219, 221, 224, 268, 270, 320, 321, 322, 324, 327,

328, 329, 337, 371, 384, 385.
Quebec, the Bishop of, 28, 30,
Quebec Seminary, 31.
Quentin, Père, 10.
Querebemit, 81, 82.
Quincey, Major John, 311.
Quincy, Edmund, 58, 69.
Quinibequi River, 156.
Quinibiquy Mission, 41.

Raimbault, Joseph, 392, 393.
Ralé Père Sebastian, an array of papers against, 1; best known of the Jesuits in New England, 1; his true story not told by Charlevoix, 3, 4; falsehood continued by Chasse, 4–5; calls the Indians dishonest, 5, 259; incited the Indians, 6, 65, 91, 92, 94, 167, 174, 279, 281, 288, 303, 374, 387, 395; stories unjust to his memory not given, 6; birth of, 34; entered the society of the Jesuits, 35; instructor at Nismes, 35; arrived at Quebec, 35–36, 175; learned the Abnaki tongue, 36, 175, 180–181; his missionary apprenticeship, 36–37; journeyed to the Illinois Mission, 37, 185, 193; joined the Mackinac Mission, 37; spent the winter in study, 38; spent two years among the Illinois, 38, 203; returned to Quebec, 38, 185, 203; sent to take charge of the Abnakis at Norridgewock, 38, 175; to aid in preventing the English from sowing heretical seeds, 39; set to work to build a chapel, 39–40; met Gov. Dudley at the Casco conference, 47; did not intend to be seen, 47; said his presence prevented Dudley from saying all he wished, 47; the governor's remarks to, 47; his account of the conference, 47–48; administered the communion and heard the confession of the Indian warriors, 50–51; hypocritically admonished them, 50–51; accused the

English of tricks and artifice, 51-52; his chapel destroyed, 52; heard of the negotiations of peace, 54; letter to Capt. Moody, 55; must have known that peace was declared, 56; sent a false report of the Portsmouth treaty to the Governor-General, 59-62, 63-64; compelled to let the savages act, 62; gave his aid to stimulate war with the English, 65; the savages held no council without calling him, 66, 66, *n.*, 96, 99, 102, 103, 226-227; could have had the esteem of the English, 66, received medical aid from Adams, 66, 67, 118; opposed the English settling on the Kennebec, 67, 68, 110, *n.;* a speech which contradicted his position, 75-76; his hand shown in Wiwurna's speech, 77; artful act of, at the conference at Arrowsic, 80; letter to Shute, 80, 91; his animosity aroused by the establishment of a Protestant missionary at Arrowsic, 84-85; sent a letter to Baxter, 85, 144; his opinion and remarks upon Baxter's answer, 86; waited two years before he wrote again, 86; *lied* when he said he overcame Baxter in a discussion, 87, 144; his knowledge of Latin compared to Baxter's, 87, *n.;* a believer in omens and visions, 89; predicted the end of the world soon, 89; may have taken advantage of the savages' superstition, 90; his letter to Shute shown to the savages, 91; the savages said he lied, 91, 92, *n.;* continually urged the Indians to attack the English, 91, 91, *n.*, 92, *n.*, 94; the English resolved to arrest him, 92; the resolution abandoned, 92, 103; urged by Vaudreuil to prevent English settlement, 92, 103; prevented the Indians from paying for the cattle they destroyed, 93, 97; the king gratified by his attempts to excite the savages, 94, 103, 163; feared to exert all his authority, 95; roused the indignation of the English by his letter to Moody, 97; letter in full, 96–104; threatened to excommunicate the Indians, 96; assumed that the end of the conference was null, 97, 99; knew of everything that passed in Europe, 98; sneered at the governor and interpreter, 98–99; his manner of purchasing lands, 100; why he disliked Ketermogus and Giles, 101, 101, *n.;* says the Indians shall kill if rum is refused him, 102; can use his own will for or against war, 102; threatens war, 102; says the English cause the troubles, 103; composing a book to be presented to the king, 103; sneer at Baxter, 103–104; his letter revealed the source of the Englishmen's peril, 104; opinion of the Boston people of his letter, 104–105; sent word to the Governor concerning the savages and the threat of Shute, 105; unsuccessful in arousing the savages against the English, 106; wrote in chagrin to Vaudreuil, 107; sent savages to the Governor, 107; the public indignation aroused against, 108; supposed to have written the protest to Shute, 108; the peace party among the Indians aroused him to action, 108–109; packed the conference at Arrowsic, 109, 110–112; assisted by Vaudreuil and de la Chasse, 109; sent message to Vaudreuil, 110–113; his overthrow predicted, 118, 119, *n.;* the General Court proposed to demand his surrender, 119; the Castines his allies, 119; Westbrook sent to capture him, 120; informed of the approach of the English, 120, 168; swallowed the consecrated host and fled, 120, 127, 168–169; his papers captured, 121; his dictionary found and published, 121, 121, *n.*; the notice on his church door, 122, 334; copies of his papers sent to England, 123; his box owned by the Maine Historical Society, 123; the great incendiary, 127, 134; tells of the Indians preparing for war, 127–128; his distorted accounts of the depredations of the Indians, 129–130; accompanied the savages in their raids, 132; desired to excite the rage of the English, 132; 133, his account of the attack upon the English, 132–133; regarded by the English as the chief cause of the war, 134; to be driven from the Kennebec, or captured, 134, 167, 168; letter to his nephew, 135; said he instructed the savages in the Christian virtues, 135, 138; in 1722 occupied the third church erected by him, 136; made his candles, 137–138; assisted at the Indian councils, 139–140; too busy to perform his devotions, 140, 206; accompanied the Indians on their hunting expeditions, 140–141, 227–228; his only food, 141; belittled a brother missionary, 143; lied concerning Baxter, 144–145, 153; his hypocrisy disclosed, 145, 147; letters of Baxter to, 145–147, 147–153, 397, 399; his Latin criticised, 147, 148, 149; false story concerning Indians held as hostages, 156–159; records a boastful Indian story, 157–158; inferred that the English were cowards, 158, *n.*; misstatement concerning appointed conference at Arrowsic, 159; his method of writing history, 161, *n.*, 171, *n.*; satisfied the king, 163; packed the Indian conference, 163, 165; his reason for the hatred of the English toward him,

166–167; his account of his escape from capture in 1722, 167–169; received provisions from Quebec, 169; said the Indians chanted the war song, 170; the spirit exhibited in religious works compensates his assumption of superiority, 172; his lack of charity, 173; he took up the sword by which he was to perish, 173; letter to his brother, 174; embarked from Rochelle, 34, 175; how he crossed the river of ice, 178; his translation of "O Salutaris," 183–184; describes his journey in a canoe, 185–187; at Missilimakinak, 187; given a feast by the Indians, 193; converts and shrives an Indian girl, 203–204; hardly finds sin among his converts, 205; entered into the Indian's temporal affairs, 205–206; feared the approach of the Amalingans, 206; address to the Amalingans, 207–210; visited and converted the Amalingans, 212–214; at Arrowsic conference, 214; intended to keep hidden, 216–217; salutations with the governor, 217; conference with the governor, 218; exhorted the Indians not to exercise cruelty, 219–220; reward offered for his head, 221; the cause of the Indian outbreaks, 221; decorated the new church, 225; goes with the Indians on their excursions, 227–228; carries the the church decorations on hunting excursions, 228; venerated and protected by the Indians, 229; Indians alarmed for his safety, 229–230; informed of the approach of the English; 230; fled with the Indians, 231; privations and hardships of the retreat, 231–233; fled at the approach of Moulton, 236; called Moulton's magnanimity cowardice, 237, 238; refused to withdraw to

Index. 443

Canada, 237; his neophytes have no heroism when matched with civilized man, 240; firing from his cabin, 241, 260, 261, 266; held as a prisoner and abused a fourteen-year-old boy, 241, 243, 244; Moulton designed to take him prisoner to Boston, 242; caught in the act of filling his gun, 243; refused to surrender, and met his deserved death from the gun of Jaques, 243, 260, 261; Indians returned and buried his body, 245; his *vade mecum* and an unfinished letter to De la Chasse found, 245–246, 251, 339; Larrabee's evidence in regard to the death of, 261; his body mutilated, 262; his scalp carried to Boston, 263, 273; advised the Indians that war was just, 264–265; must be regarded as an agent of the French, 265; not a martyr, 266, 270–271, 273; much sentimental writing upon his death, 266–267; his death due to his meddling with affairs outside of his professed duty, 268, 370–371; pronunciation and spelling of his name, 269; displayed himself to anger his enemies, 270; letter from Begon to, 294–297; letter from Vaudreuil to, 299; letter from Lannerjat to, 338; house plundered, 344; Vaudreuil on the cruelty of the English towards, 346; his papers prove he instigated the Indians, 387, 390–391; French intend to complain of his being killed, 394; death of, 370, 394; burial of, 271–272, 272, *n.;* character of, 35, 86, 250, 273; mentioned, 275, 276, 299, 302, 303, 308, 341, 344, 379, 390; letter of, cited, 51, 63.

Ramesay, Claude de, 378.

Relation de la Prise du Port Royal par les Anglois pièce anonyme, cited, 22.

Report of the Conference at Arrowsic, printed, 84.

Rhode Island, 339, 340, 347, 354, 360, 364.
Rishworth Edward, 26.
River of Canada, 136.
River of the Illinois, 193.
River St. John, number of savages at, 59; trading place to be established at, 60; mentioned, 94.
Rochelle, 16, 34, 55, 175.
Rock tripe, 186, 232.
Rolfe, Rev. Benjamin, killed, 53, 267; mentioned, 270; biographical notice of, 53, 268.
Rolfe, Mrs. Benjamin, killed, 54.
Roman Catholics, to be exempt from pillage and death, 15; why they succeeded in their attempts at missionary work better than the Protestants, 87–88.
Roxbury, 26.
Rum, how Ralé proposed the Indians should obtain it, 102.
Rutland, 168, 268, 269, 317, 369, 371.

Saco River, 351.
Sagadahoc, 93, 215.
Sagsarrab, 339.
St. Castine, *see* Castine.
St. Francis, a call for more men at, 35; mentioned, 295, 297, 322, 325, 326, 330, 376.
St. Francis Indians, 109, 111, 125, 164.
St. Georges, fort at, 255.
St. Georges River, 317, 342, 351, 371, 372.
St. Pierre, Count de, 300.
Saltonstall, Col., 363.
Samuel, Capt., at Casco conference, 44; reported that the French were trying to break the friendly relations between the English and French, 46.
Sankderank, 215.
Saussaye, Sieur de, 10.
Savage, Habijah, 279, 281.
Savages, *see* Indians.
Scalps, price paid for, 328.
Scatacooks, the, 350.
Schuyler, Col. John, 323, 333.
Schuyler, Col. Peter, the savages gave way before, 20; Report cited, 18.
Schuyler, Philip, 323, 324, 331, 332, 333.
Sea-flower, the, 384.
Senecas, the, 386.

Index. 445

Sewall, Samuel, 57, 69, 70, 96, 119, 278; Papers cited, 96.

Shea, John G., his Charlevoix, cited, 168, 259, 260, 264.

Shute, Gov. Samuel, heard Ralé boast of his influence over the savages, 66; became governor, 68; took measures to have a conference with the Indians, 68; held conference at Arrowsic, 69-84; Ralé sent letter to, 80, 91; sent Minot and Heath with a message to Norridgewock, 91; letter from Heath and Minot to, 91-92; desired some Indians to go to England, 96; Ralé assumed that his Arrowsic conference was null, 97; threatened to send men to protect the settlers on the Kennebec, 105; received a letter from the savages, 108; sent Vrudreuil's letters to the home government, 123, 125; sent a letter to Vaudreuil, 123-127; proclamation of, relative to peaceful Indians, 131; letters of, to Vaudreuil, 159, 298-299, 305-309; letters of, to Lords Commissioners, 301-302, 302-304, 312; declaration of, 313-315; mentioned, 3, 297, 366, 393, 395.

Simon, Père, taught the savages the gospel of peace and not war, 33, *n.;* his character, 34, *n.;*

Skamgar, 180.

Smith, Rev. Thomas, 247.

Smith, William, History of New York, cited, 44.

Snow-shoes, 176.

Society of Jesus effected, 8.

Society of Jesus, *see* Jesuits.

Soldiers, number of, fit for duty, 1722, 316-317.

Soulé, Pierre, 269.

South Carolina, 118.

Southerland, 173.

Stevens, Joseph, 173.

Stoddard, Col. John, 359, 363.

Stoughton, Gov. William, 43, 278; letter of, cited, 44.

Subercase, Daniel d'Auger de, asked to prohibit scalping, 53.

Suffolk, 278.
Sunderland, 317.
Swan Island House, 319.

Talcot, Gov. Joseph, letter of, to Gov. Dummer, 361; mentioned, 276, 347.
Tallard, Mons., 55.
Taschereau, Rev. E. A., Memoir sur l'Acadie, cited, 22.
Taxous, died, 106, mentioned, 297.
Taylor, Isaac, 292.
Temple, Robert, 292.
Temple, Capt. Robert, 318.
Terreamuggus, 288, 290.
Thaxter, Samuel, 353, 375, 388, 391.
Thet, Gilbert du, at Mount Desert, 10; killed, 11.
Three Rivers, 324, 378, 381.
Thurber, Col. Samuel, 374.
Thury, Père Peter, established a mission on the Penobscot, 17; exhorted the Indians to continue the war, 24; led in 1692 the expedition against York, 25, 26; joined by Indians from Bigot's mission, 25; conspicuous in inciting the savages against the English, 28, 31, 40; thanked and rewarded by the government, 28–29, 30; a blind leader of the blind, 31, 39; harangued to excite the Indians, 31, 32; to lead in the capture of Boston, 1697, 40, 41; at Fort St. John, 41; biographical notice of, 31; letter to, cited, 30, 31.
Tibierge, Memoire sur l'Acadie, cited, 28; letter of, cited, 33, 41.
Ticonic Falls, 238, 245.
Tomahawks, 199.
Totems of Indians at Georgetown Conference, 292.
Townsend, Penn, 58, 316, 368.
Trading Houses, three to be established, 60.
Trading houses and provisions desired by the Indians, 82; early introduced among the Indians, 153.
Travels of Learned Missionaries, cited, 32.

Treaty at Arrowsic, 66, 68–84, 96, 97, 99, 101; of Casco, 1678, 13, 78; of 1703, 45; of Portsmouth, 56, 57–58, *n*., 62, 64, 70, 82, 83; of Ryswick, 42; of Utrecht, 56, 63, 125, 155, 326, 335, 337, 338, 345, 349, 360, 373, 386, 390.
Trescott, Zachariah, 318, 325, 326.
Tripes de roches, 186, 232.
Trois Rivieres, 324, 378, 381.
Truck houses, early introduced among the Indians, 153.
Tuddebawhunjerit, 282.
Tuddebawhunsewit, 292.
Turkey wheat, 141, 180.
Turner, Col., 311.
Turner, John, 385.

Vanhorn, Abrah, 356, 357.
Varones, Cassani, Patrignani Menologie, cited, 267.
Vaudreuil, Phillippe de Rigaud, Marquis de, Dudley asked him to prohibit scalping, 53; character of, 65; attached the interest of the Indians to the French, 65; did not cede the lands of the Indians to the English, 80; advised Ralé to prevent English settlements, 92; instructed by the king to hinder traffic between the Indians and English, 93, 103; Ralé sent information to, 105, 164; his odious character revealed, 107, 123; to assist Ralé in hindering the peace conference of the English and Indians, 109; sent De la Chasse to Norridgewock, 109; his letters to Ralé captured, 121; copies of his letters sent to the government, 123, 125; the English astounded by his duplicity, 123; letters from Gov. Shute to, 123–127, 159, 298–299, 305–309; Indians asked him about the treaty of Utrecht, 154; must have lied to the Indians, 155, *n*.; did not strive to prevent war, 161, *n*., 162, 382; instigated the Indians

against the English, 162, *n.*, 164, 165, 386; gave protection to the Indians, 245; could craze the savages with brandy, 265; his epitaph, 265; accused the English of murder in Ralé's death, 267; Dummer's reply to, 267, 268–270; letter of, to Ralé, 299–301; cheerfully received the Indians after they had depredated the English, 320, 321, 323; supplied the Indians with stores, 320, 321, 393; permitted the enslaving of Hamilton, 321; released and entertained Hamilton, 322; would not permit Hamilton and Handsord to leave Canada, 324; did not trust the English in exchanging prisoners, 325; displeased because Deautell interceded for the release of prisoners, 326; refused to allow Hamilton to depart, 328; abused the English for extravagance in the reward for scalps, 328; sent Deautell to the Goal, 328–329; accompanied by Hamilton goes to Quebec, 329; double dealing with Hamilton, 333, notice to the Governor of Boston, 334; letter from Gov. Dummer to, 337; letter from, to Gov. Dummer, 341; commissioners sent to demand captives taken by the Indians and make treaty of peace, 347, 348, 354, 357, 359, 360, 362, 388–391; commissioners meet, 350–351; desired to have peace, 351, 378; honorable when separated from the Jesuits, 352, 379; angry with the Governor of New York, 253, 386; commissioners sent to, 375, 376, 385–388; met the commissioners, 386; present at the treaty, 387; denied having encouraged Indian outbreaks, 387; mentioned, 5, 102, 110, 111, 271, 272, 275, 276, 294, 295,

Index. 449

296, 297, 301, 303, 312, 379; letters of, cited, 66, 94, 95, 105, 107, 113, 151.
Vaughn, William, 58.
Versailles, 16, 30, 31, 33, 40, 41, 42.
Villebon, Robineau, Chevalier de, 30, 31, 33, 42; Lettre du Roy, au, cited, 25; letter to the minister, cited, 26.
Villemarie, 391, 392.
Virginia, 52.
Voyage de l'Acadie, cited, 32.

Wainwright, Mr, 348.
Wainwright, Capt. John, 281, 291.
Waldron, Richard, 58.
Waller, Capt., 356, 357.
Wallis, Capt. Joseph, 384.
Walton, Shadrach, 58, 275, 281, 291, 294, 367.
Wanadugunbuent at Casco conference, 44.
Warraeensitt, 59.
Warrawenset, 282.
Watanummon, his treachery in delaying coming to the conference, 49.
Watt's House, Arrowsic, 69.

Wax, from bayberries, 137-138.
Weare, Nathaniel, 58.
Wells, attacked by French and Indians, 1703, 50; mentioned, 317.
Wells, Mr., 68.
Welsteed, William, 247.
Wendell, Jacob, 332.
Wentworth, Gov. John, letter from Dummer to, 354; mentioned, 58, 69.
Wesememis, 323.
Westaminut, 322.
Westbrook, Col. Thomas, sent to apprehend Ralé, 120; at Norridgewock, 120-121; captured Ralé's papers, 121; his expedition considered a warrant by the savages to extend their depredations, 127; mentioned, 90, 91, 246, 263, 264, 317.
Westfield, 333.
Wewarena, 318, 322.
Wewenack, 322.
Wexar at Casco conference, 44.
Wharton Deed, 79.
Wheelwright, John, 58.
Willard, Rev. Joseph, killed, 173, 267, 269, 369, 371; his scalp taken

to Quebec, 371; mentioned, 271; biographical notice of, 173, *n.*, 268.
Willard, Josiah, 58, 123, 258, 278, 294, 297, 301, 309, 310, 315, 334, 338, 340, 346, 347, 348, 349, 353, 354, 355, 358, 361, 364, 370, 375, 383, 392, 393.
Williamson, Joseph, manuscripts cited, 90.
Williamson, William D., History of Maine, cited, 28, 236.
Willis, William, 247.
Winslow, 238, 276.
Winthrop, Gov. Fitz-John, in command of expedition against Montreal, 23; failure of his expedition, 23.
Winthrop, John, 12.
Wessememet, champion of peace, 106; elected chief, 106; nicknamed by Ralé, 106; made to feel the governor's displeasure, 107.
Wiwurna, 72, 73, 74, 75, 76, 77, 79, 81, 97, 282.
Woman, Indian legend concerning, 189; position of, 196–197.
Wood Creek, 350.
World, the speedy end of, predicted by Ralé, 89.
Wowurnapa, 292. (Wiwurna)
Wyllys, Her: 364.

Yale College, 173, 268.
York, descent of Thury upon, 25; massacre at, 26; Shubael Dummer the first minister at, 26, *n.;* mentioned, 236, 239, 279, 280, 315, 317.
Yorkshire, 236.

www.ingramcontent.com/pod-product-compliance
Lightning Source LLC
Chambersburg PA
CBHW031955300426
44117CB00008B/772